WORKING
THE
SHADOW
SIDE

GERARD EGAN

WORKING
THE
SHADOW
SIDE

A GUIDE TO POSITIVE
BEHIND-THE-SCENES
MANAGEMENT

Jossey-Bass Publishers • San Francisco

Substantial discounts on bulk quantities of Jossey-Bass books are available to corporations, professional associations, and other organizations. For details and discount information, contact the special sales department at Jossey-Bass Inc., Publishers. (415) 433-1740; Fax (415) 433-0499.

For sales outside the United States, please contact your local Paramount Publishing International office.

Manufactured in the United States of America. Nearly all Jossey-Bass books and jackets are printed on recycled paper that contains at least 50 percent recycled waste, including 10 percent postconsumer waste. Many of our materials are also printed with vegetable-based inks; during the printing process these inks emit fewer volatile organic compounds (VOCs) than petroleum-based inks. VOCs contribute to the formation of smog.

Library of Congress Cataloging-in-Publication Data

Egan, Gerard.
    Working the shadow side : a guide to positive behind-the-scenes management / Gerard Egan.
      p.   cm.—(The Jossey-Bass management series)
    Includes bibliographical references and index.
    ISBN 0-7879-0011-7
    1. Management.   2. Organizational behavior.   3. Corporate culture.
I. Title. II. Series.
HD31.E454   1994
658.4—dc20   94-26576
                                                              CIP

FIRST EDITION
HB Printing   10 9 8 7 6 5 4 3 2 1   *Code 9489*

THE JOSSEY-BASS
MANAGEMENT SERIES

CONTENTS

PREFACE

G IVEN TODAY'S PACE of business and institutional life, and
given all the uncertainties of the business environment,
managers are increasingly being forced into the role of
managing chaos and change. While the technology of such change
is comparatively straightforward and easy, the politics of change
can prove impossible. Thus, the best managers are always looking
for ways to become more adept at dealing with the *shadow side*
of the organization—the unspoken, unacknowledged, behind-the-
scenes stuff that stands in the way of getting things done efficiently,
or even getting things done at all.

In today's organizational and business climate, becoming
skilled at behind-the-scenes management is not an amenity but a
necessity. Failure to deal with the shadow side of change can lead
to the failure of the business itself.

Purpose of the Book

Working the Shadow Side shows managers how they can develop
a set of skills and strategies for both supporting a preferred culture
and challenging and changing a dysfunctional one; for dealing sen-
sitively and constructively with the idiosyncrasies of people, with
a view to helping them give their best; for understanding and

mining value from the vagaries of the company's social system; for developing a "positive politics" culture at the service of driving out the politics of self-interest; and for understanding and leveraging the arrangements of the *hidden organization*—the organization behind the organization.

It takes competence and guts to deal with shadow-side realities creatively. No one book could possibly deal with all of its ins and outs. This book, then, should be seen as a kind of starter kit. The framework, categories, methods, and skills I present are meant to help managers see what they are already doing to manage such realities and to further develop their own understanding and resources.

Background and Overview

In 1993 I published a book, *Adding Value*, that outlined a comprehensive business-based management system based on three open-systems frameworks: Model A, Model B, and Model C. Model A deals with the master tasks of management: strategy, operations, structure, human resource management systems, management and supervision, and leadership. Model B presents a framework for initiating and managing innovation and change. Model C focuses on the shadow-side activities and arrangements that permeate the processes and tasks of Models A and B. This book, *Working the Shadow Side*, develops Model C; it provides a framework for understanding shadow-side realities and offers methods for exposing and constructively dealing with them in the service of the business.

It would be a mistake, then, to view the shadow-side framework as a stand-alone model. Shadow-side arrangements and activities, for weal or woe, permeate all the master tasks of Model A. Shadow-side realities can also stymie the change efforts outlined in Model B.

Pros and Cons of Working the Shadow Side

I have often said to managers in seminars and workshops after describing the three models, "We have time to work with only one. Which do you choose?" They inevitably choose the shadow-side framework. There are some good and some questionable reasons for this.

First, the good reasons. As soon as I use the phrase "shadow side of the organization," they immediately know what it means. They are familiar with it and yet frustrated by it. They want to know how to get rid of it, cope with it, or creatively manage it.

Second, savvy managers also instinctively realize that shadow-side issues can be quite costly and challenging. How much time and energy are consumed in dealing with a difficult employee? How much more energy is needed to manage a group that is guarding its turf to the detriment of the business? What is a manager to do about a covert organizational arrangement that is limiting the effectiveness of the business? Or, conversely, what is a manager to do about a covert organizational arrangement that violates some of the company's rules but adds value to the business? What if the covert assumptions, beliefs, values, and norms of the prevailing culture do not support the new strategy?

When managers are given an opportunity to name and discuss shadow-side realities, the floodgates open. They say that in times of crisis over 80 percent of their time and energy is consumed with the arationalities of the system. Even in so-called normal times, many managers claim that over half of their energy is taken up by these concerns.

But percentages are not important; adding value by managing the shadow side is. Many of the costs associated with the shadow side are lost-opportunity costs. If energy had not been spent in shadow-side activities, other things could have been accomplished.

Third, the best and brightest managers realize that dealing with the shadow side also constitutes opportunity and competitive advantage. And they know that not everything that occurs in the shadows is bad or costly. Bending rules to serve the business, for example, is a time-honored shadow-side activity that, in moderation, adds value. Those who understand and constructively deal with these off-stage activities and arrangements, good or bad, can be of great benefit to the company or institution.

A questionable reason for focusing on the shadow side is that it is exciting—it has a catchy quality to it typical of a fad subject. *Working the Shadow Side* would be a failure were it to do nothing more than start another fad. Fads such as total quality management and process reengineering are, at best, rediscoveries of value-added but underutilized managerial practices. At their worst, they are expensive distractions, rather than solutions for business problems. Increased skill in managing the shadow side, then, can add great value to the business, but it is not a panacea; it is an important part of an overall managerial system.

I'd like to thank editors Bill Hicks and Cedric Crocker for the give-and-take that finally led to the present book. And special thanks to Harris Wilkinson for his invaluable help in the sprint to the finish line.

Chicago, Illinois   GERARD EGAN
July 1994

THE AUTHOR

GERARD EGAN is professor of organization development and psychology in the Center for Organization Development of Loyola University of Chicago.

Egan consults to a variety of companies and institutions worldwide. Clients he has worked with extensively include Amoco Corporation, British Airways, the International Rice Research Institute in the Philippines, the National Health Service in the United Kingdom, Montgomery Ward, universities in the People's Republic of China, Washington National Insurance Company, the World Bank, and YMCA-USA. He specializes in long-term work with chief executives and senior managers on strategy, business and organization effectiveness, management development, leadership, the design and management of change, and organization culture. He also provides workshops in these subjects both in the United States and abroad.

Egan has written more than a dozen books, including *The Skilled Helper* (1994, fifth edition), *People in Systems* (1979, with M. A. Cowan), *Change Agent Skills in Helping and Human Service Settings* (1985), *Change Agent Skills A: Designing and Assessing Excellence* (1988), and *Change Agent Skills B: Managing Innovation and Change* (1988). *Adding Value: A Systematic Guide to Business-Based Management and Leadership* was published in 1993.

WORKING
THE
SHADOW
SIDE

WHAT
GOES ON
IN THE
SHADOWS

1

WHAT IS THE SHADOW SIDE? THE COVERT, UNDISCUSSED, AND UNDISCUSSABLE THINGS THAT DRIVE YOUR ORGANIZATION

MANAGERS AND WORKERS ALIKE know that a wide range of activities and arrangements take place "behind the scenes" in most organizations. Deals are cut, reputations are ruined, money disappears, rules in the company's manuals are not enforced while unwritten rules are, innocent people are blamed, the guilty are promoted. Such occurrences are costly, yet few figure up the costs. Welcome to the shadow side of organizational life.

One of the findings of a recent study of European managers (Bloom, Calori, and de Woot, 1994) was that the managers believed it was better to be "shrewd and cunning" than merely rational. I would rather say that managers need to be more than just intelligent and technically competent. They need to be wise. Understanding and managing the shadow side of a business is a key part of the pragmatic wisdom required to face the bewildering changes that are occurring in the workplace.

As we shall soon see, not all aspects of the shadow side are bad or costly. Some shadow-side activities and arrangements are beneficial. Those who understand these off-stage activities, good or bad, and deal with them positively can add great value to the company or institution. But it takes competence and courage to deal with the shadow side creatively and effectively.

3

The Covert, Undiscussed, and Undiscussable

What is the shadow side? Since many believe that the term refers only to the dark side of human nature, it needs more precise definition in a business and organizational setting. While the darker side of human nature is certainly included, the shadow side has a much broader meaning in organizational settings. Essentially, the shadow side consists of all the important activities and arrangements that do not get identified, discussed, and managed in decision-making forums that can make a difference. The shadow side deals with the covert, the undiscussed, the undiscussable, and the unmentionable. It includes arrangements not found in organizational manuals and company documents or on organizational charts.

Consider the following case. In a midsize company that supplied parts to the automotive industry, bad blood between the director of manufacturing and a plant manager led to costly delays in getting product to customers and caused unrest among plant workers. But the relationship between these two gentlemen and its negative impact on both productivity and the quality of work life were never discussed in any formal way. A covert assumption of the company culture was that "relationships are people's private business." Therefore, since personal relationships, whether they enhanced or limited the business, were not discussed in decision-making sessions, they remained outside ordinary managerial control.

However, all this was soon to change. When a new CEO arrived, he quickly learned about the stormy relationship and brought it up in a management committee meeting. By his action he let people know that relationships, to the degree that they interfered with the business, were now discussable. At the meeting, the members of the committee, including the director of manufacturing, squirmed. Afterward, the CEO called a private meeting with the director of manufacturing and the plant manager. He told them that they had to work out their differences for the sake of the company. When he met with the director of manufacturing in their first performance review session, the CEO told the director to "take the lead in straightening this thing out." But dealing with relationships rather than plant scheduling was a new world for the director of manufacturing. By the end of the following year he was gone. After his departure, productivity at the plant increased some 15 percent.

The covert assumption that "relationships are people's private business" was handled in the following way. A task force was set up to plan and implement a company renewal process. Since task force members were drawn from many different parts of the organization, there was broad support for the renewal effort. During this exercise, it became clear to task force members that the stormy relationship between the director of manufacturing and the plant manager had been a sign of a deeper, "what's in it for me?" culture. Instead of surfacing and indicting the assumptions and norms of this dimension of the company's culture, the task force took a much more positive approach, making teamwork one of the foundations of the renewal effort. The espoused and promoted norm of the new team-based culture, "Good relationships make all the difference," was almost the opposite of the traditional, covert, "what's in it for me?" norm. The plan was not to decry the old norm but to drive it out by explaining the advantages of teamwork and rewarding it. This upbeat approach paid off.

Note that the relationship between the director of marketing and the plant manager was not some dark secret. It was freely discussed in informal settings. But it was a shadow-side issue because it was not discussed in a setting where something could be done about it. Such shadow-side issues as company-limiting personal styles, political maneuverings, and dysfunctional cultural norms are often freely discussed in corridors, cafeterias, rest rooms, bull sessions, on the shop floor, and in other informal settings. But little can be done to manage them in such sessions.

A more formal description of the shadow side of a business has the following three dimensions:

1. The shadow side refers to significant activities and arrangements that remain unidentified or, for whatever reasons, undiscussed in some decision-making setting of the company or institution.
2. Since shadow-side factors are not formally discussed, they fall outside the reach of ordinary managerial intervention.

3. Shadow-side activities and arrangements often substantially affect both productivity and the quality of work life in the company or institution.

Decision-making settings include management committee meetings, one-to-one performance-management sessions, team discussions, cross-functional planning groups, the discussions that take place in task forces and corrective-action teams, and the like.

Let's start with a dark-side example of shadow activity: a salesman's kickback deals with customers are hidden and therefore remain undiscussed in formal company settings, fall outside the reach of ordinary managerial control, and affect company productivity. This example involves simple venality.

Another company-limiting example: In one manufacturing firm, the engineering department repeatedly failed to hire the right kind of people for its projects without anyone saying, "Hey, what's going on here?" The head of the engineering department, the one responsible for hiring, was the nephew of a senior manager. While he had some substantial engineering skills, he was a poor judge of people. The members of the engineering unit were simply afraid to challenge a relative of this senior manager, a man known for his explosive temper. The cost? Tens of thousands of dollars were being wasted annually. Hiring mistakes in themselves are not shadow-side phenomena; they are merely indications of managerial incompetence. But if repeated mistakes go undiscussed because of someone's power and personal style, then we are dealing with the shadow side: important matters that do not get identified and discussed in forums that can make a difference.

Understanding shadow-side realities more fully and developing the ability to manage them constructively will ultimately benefit both you and your institution. The following basic questions about the shadow side are addressed in this chapter: What do upbeat or positive shadow-side activities and arrangements look like? What are the major shadow-side forms or categories? In addition, this chapter and the next will include definitions of terms and concepts essential to the exploration of the shadow side.

Finally, since shadow-side realities affect everyone, not just managers, the ability to deal with the shadow side is not just a managerial prerogative. Anyone with the understanding and competencies outlined in this book can play a part in getting the shadow side to add value rather than cost.

Value in the Shadows

Aren't all shadow-side activities bad by definition? No. Many shadow-side activities and arrangements are ethical and add value to the company in themselves. In an accounting firm, Reg, a young consultant, had a boss who had little time for him. The only time he heard from his boss was when he made a mistake. The young man felt that he was not developing personally and adding value to the company the way he could. He was befriended by Larry, another manager in the same department, who appreciated his potential. Informally, Larry became Reg's mentor and even his shadow-side manager. Since Larry was highly respected in the firm, he found tactful, behind-the-scenes ways of keeping Reg's boss off the young man's back. For political reasons, however, he could not change the arrangement and become Reg's formal manager. But the informal arrangement added a great deal of value to the company.

Here is a different kind of shadow-side arrangement, one that is a little trickier: In an office products company, Ken, the star salesman, unobtrusively but consistently broke some of the rules in the company manual. For instance, he went home early when he had important domestic tasks to do, he routinely booked hotel rooms that were a bit more expensive than allowed, and he occasionally moonlighted as a sales consultant to a non-competing business. But Ken was a very good salesman—so good, in fact, that other companies had tried to hire him away.

Ken's immediate boss and two senior managers of the firm knew of these indiscretions, but they never brought them up, not even among themselves. In itself, this undiscussed arrangement was not costly, even though there was some downside risk. The boss and the two senior managers realized that a couple of Ken's colleagues knew about some of his little games and envied his ability to get away with them. But in the eyes of management a bit of isolated colleague grousing was, on balance, less important than sales results. Moreover, these two colleagues knew in their hearts that they would be allowed greater flexibility were they as productive. So they never brought the issue up in any formal setting nor discussed it with other colleagues. The arrangement went on for years, was never discussed with Ken, and was never brought up in any formal meeting. This is not to say that it was an ideal to be copied by others. But there it was, and it added value. Ken loved the freedom he had and never thought twice about offers from other companies.

The essential point once more is this: When you hear the term *shadow side,* do not immediately wince and think "bad." There is a lot of value in the shadows. Learning to distinguish between company-enhancing and company-limiting shadow-side arrangements and activities is a key part of managerial wisdom.

Five Shadow-Side Categories

When people first enter an organization, they initially see only what is taking place on the surface, somewhat like a two-dimensional movie. After a while, they begin to see beneath the surface activities—that is, they begin to see the company as multidimensional. Identifying and managing the shadow side—a side that profoundly affects both productivity and the quality of work life—means understanding five categories of shadow-side activity: (1) organizational culture, (2) the personal styles and behaviors of individuals, (3) organizational social systems, (4) organizational politics, and (5) the hidden organization.

These shadow-side categories are not depicted in organizational charts or discussed in company manuals. Rather they undergird or permeate and affect every aspect of the business—strategy, operations, structure, human resource management systems, management itself, supervision, and leadership. At the heart of the shadow side are the covert, the undiscussed, and the undiscussable—the issues that don't get the hearing they need in forums where something can be done about them. A shared understanding of these five shadow-side dimensions, like other shared managerial frameworks, models, and systems, helps decision makers talk to one another more clearly, pointedly, and pragmatically. Common managerial understanding leads to focused managerial action.

Organizational Culture: The Controlling Factor

An organization's culture takes two forms. First of all, there are the published and espoused beliefs, values, and norms that are supposed to drive organizational behavior but may or may not do so. A common published belief in many companies is that "people are our most important asset." Some companies both espouse this belief and put it into action. Second, there is also a set of unpublished or covert assumptions, beliefs, values, and norms that drive organizational behavior. This latter set sometimes contravenes the published set, causing both confusion and cynicism.

Consider the "people are our most important asset" belief. I brought a company manual with me to a meeting with a group of workers and read this belief out to them. They laughed. "If you believe that, then you are more naive than we are," one worker asserted. "Well then," I said, "what are some of the real beliefs, values, and norms regarding people around here?" Their list differed dramatically from what was in the manual. "People are expendable." "You're only as good as yesterday's results." "If there's a drop in sales, hide, because you, not managers, are going to be blamed." "Find out what's in your boss's mind and do it." "Keep innovative ideas to yourself." The list went on. Even if some exaggeration is factored in, it is clear that there was a serious gap between the espoused beliefs in the manual and the norms that were practiced every day.

Culture is the largest and most controlling of the shadow-side categories, because it sets the standards for "the way we do things here." It affects not only overt business and organizational behavior but also the behavior in all the other shadow-side categories. For instance, it dictates how informal or individualistic people in the workplace are permitted to be. My best bet is that the culture of IBM, a company currently wrestling with massive business problems, is still less tolerant of diverse personal styles and individualistic behavior than the culture of, say, some start-up computer firm making IBM clones.

Culture also lays down norms for the way the social systems operate in the workplace. In one manufacturing concern it was required that an employee be an engineer in order to rise to a senior management position. Engineers in that company constituted an elite, a higher social class. There was no published rule about this, of course—it was just the way things were. In a Midwest bank an employee could never be made an officer of the company if he or she wore polyester clothes. Culture tells us what kinds of politics are allowed and just how members of an organization are allowed to play the political game. In one large British company, self-interest agendas were not only allowed but even encouraged. The unspoken question was, If this does not help me and my career, why should I do it? It goes without saying that this culture of self-interest added enormous costs.

The principle is simple: the culture should serve the business. However, while everyone talks about culture, there are very few companies that have shared working models of culture. Chapter Five provides such a framework. Still fewer companies train managers to work with, promote, challenge, and change the culture in order to align it with the business. Chapter Six provides methods and skills for challenging and changing a dysfunctional culture.

Personal Styles

What is the cost of employee theft? We think we know. The cost of such undiscussables as the arrogance and/or incompetence of some managers? We're finding out. Much of the literature on organizations ignores the vagaries of the human condition. Human beings are both glorious and bottomless pits of shadow-side activity. There are company-enhancing and company-limiting personal styles and behaviors. Many are double-edged swords that add value only if managed carefully. The problem is that the upside and the downside of personal styles do not usually get discussed in decision-making forums. The CEO of an international retailer recently resigned because of a difference of opinion with board members on "investment policy decisions." This was strange, since capital expenditures in general were above expectations. Insiders knew, however, that this explanation was code for something else. It was not just a disagreement. It was a question of the CEO doing things his way and only his way. "I know best" was part of his style. When the company hired him, they should have realized that his ego, aggressiveness, and arrogance could add either great value or cost to the company. Indeed, the board members should have discussed this with the candidate. But personal style is often one of the un-discussables. The costs of hiring the CEO, dealing with his arro-gance, coming to the agreement to part ways, coming up with a suitable separation package, remaining rudderless for months, and finding a suitable replacement may well have outweighed the value he added while he was there.

People develop workplace styles. Some add value, some cost. Take the quality of entrepreneurial flair, called "intrapreneurial" (Pinchot, 1985) in some larger organizations. While often prized, it is seldom a part of an employee's job description, perhaps because it can have both a bright side and a dark side. Consider the case of British Airways, well documented in the daily press. In the early 1990s it was discovered that some of the airline's employees were using unethical, if not illegal, methods to filch passengers from a competitor, Virgin Airlines. If these "dirty tricks," as they were called in the press, were not condoned by higher authorities—the dynamics of that might well be hidden forever—then some rogue operators within the company apparently decided to take compet-itive matters into their own hands. The economic impact of such idiosyncratic shadow-side behavior has been quite negative for "the world's favourite airline." It was not just a case of money, the fine paid. The image of the airline was tarnished, at least for a while, and a cloud of suspicion drifted over its senior managers.

Contrast this with the intrapreneurial behavior of a local Federal Express manager. A bad snowstorm knocked down tele-phone lines atop a local mountain and made it impossible for the small-package shipping company to serve its customers. The tele-phone company said that service would be out for a couple of days. Unable to make it up to the top of the mountain in his four-wheel vehicle, he doubled back, drove into the local airport, hired a he-licopter, got dropped into a snowbank on top of the mountain, and restored telephone service—all without getting approval from either his boss or the phone company. Where many companies would have fired him for exceeding his spending authority, Federal Ex-press gave him a bonus.

It may well be that the intrapreneurial flair of the Federal

Express employee might have gone unnoticed but for this incident.
This leads to a very serious question: How much worker talent,
wisdom, wit, and determination go unnoticed in our institutions,
remaining undiscussed in decision-making forums? So-called empowerment programs are just beginning to find out. I witnessed the
following drama on the shop floor of a manufacturing concern. A
manager from headquarters was talking to a group of workers about
empowerment. At one point he asked, "Right now, what ideas do
you have that might help make this business better?" One of the
workers described a different approach to maintaining the plant's
rather complex machinery. The HQ representative was wide-eyed.
"Why," he stammered, "if we were to do that, we could save thousands of dollars per month." The worker replied, "I first mentioned
this idea to a foreman six years ago."

What can be done to identify and deal with both the upside
and downside of personal styles? The answer is positive: much more
than is currently being done. For instance, managers can use the
insights of psychology without having to become professional psychologists. Chapter Eight deals with managing the shadow side of
individuals, including their undiscussed and therefore untapped
creativity.

Organizational Social Systems

Organizations do not just have divisions, functions, departments,
units, and teams. They also have in-groups, out-groups, cliques,
tribes, and warring factions. That is, each organization and each
unit within a larger organization is a social system with all the
vagaries of social relationships. For the most part, the social systems
of companies and institutions go undiscussed. This can prove to be
costly. Workers meet many of their social needs through interactions with suppliers, colleagues, and customers. *How* they do so can
add value or cost. A purchasing agent for a computer manufacturer
who had developed superb personal relationships with the sales
agents of a key supplier saved the day when his company received
a huge unexpected order from one of its best customers. One of the
supplier's agents delayed his vacation to make sure the order was
filled. Another even got permission to have part of the order filled

by one of the supplier's competitors. Personal relationships, then, can be assets. They can also be serious debits.

The emotions that swirl around ethnic and racial issues—the "diversity" aspect of workplace social systems—can call for extraordinary social tact and ingenuity, managerial qualities that are not listed in job descriptions. Consider the following example. I was talking to a glum-looking manager of an international development institution. When asked what was wrong, he replied that he was having trouble with J.B., one of his direct reports. When I heard the story—the manager's version, of course—I asked, "Why don't you fire her?" "I can't," was his reply. Taking a rational approach, I pointed out to him that current institutional rules, regulations, and policies certainly allowed him to fire her, with some room to spare. "You don't understand," he said.

"Let me tell you why I can't fire her," he continued. "She's a member of the X Social Club," X referring to a particular nationality. Since over a hundred different nationalities were represented in the institution, he could have mentioned any of the other national social clubs. She happened to belong to the X Social Club. "What makes the X Social Club so sacred?" I asked. He went on to say that X was no more powerful or sacred than the A, B, or C social clubs, but that he had to do a lot of work with a director who was also a member of the X social club. "If I were to fire her, this could well sour my relationship with him, though he would never admit it. I need him as an ally over the next year or so to make sure that two projects move forward. I can't afford to take the risk." It is not uncommon for the members of a subsociety to protect their own. The fact that these social clubs were subsocieties within a large institution did not change that social rule. He ended by saying, "I'll have to find ways of walling her off so that she does not cause any harm. It's not my biggest problem. I'm just very annoyed with her today." He was managing the shadow side at the service of the institution. He adopted a short-term solution that kept a key business relationship intact, that avoided psychological and social pain that could well have led to a lawsuit, and that freed him up to engage in higher-priority business-related behaviors that added value to the institution. Chapter Nine focuses on the shadow side of social systems.

Organizational Politics

The organization is political if any of the following conditions exist: there are players who enjoy the use of power, both individuals and organizational units vie for scarce resources, stakeholders protect their turf, and players with different ideologies and values want theirs to prevail. Since these conditions prevail in all institutions, the issue is not whether the organization is political but how virulent internal politics are and whether they enhance or limit the institution's productivity.

There are two kinds of politics: the politics of self-interest and positive, institution-enhancing politics. The former can be quite costly, while the latter can add great value. We all know what the politics of self-interest are. John wants Jessica in his department and will pull whatever strings he has to get what he wants, even if the common good of the company suffers. The notion of positive politics is newer. The starting point for positive politics is what a sponsor sees as an institution-enhancing agenda that is open to debate. In one large computer manufacturer, one department head proposed entering a partnership in one product line with a rival company. The debate that ensued set off a struggle between competing departments and shed light on a number of problems—including outmoded products, poor customer service, and poor cross-functional planning—that had remained in the shadows for years. In the end the senior management team agreed to pursue the partnership over the howls of those whose empires would be diminished. United States auto manufacturers, in the face of Japanese competition, belatedly realized that they simply could not afford the politics of turf protection. In the blink of an eye, as it were, cross-functional teams swept away empires that had lasted years. This hardly eliminated the politics of self-interest, but it did reset the political game.

Creative contention is at the center of positive politics. When open debate on key issues is bypassed, then covert, self-serving deals are struck, critical problems are avoided, opportunities are missed, and the company, together with its shareholders, takes an economic hit. While the politics of self-interest will never be eliminated, they can be managed. Chapter Ten deals with the economic ups and downs of internal politics, and Chapter Eleven provides a framework for engaging in positive politics.

The Hidden Organization

The term *organization* here includes such things as structure, including the overall structure found on organizational charts and job structure within individual organizational units; communication processes, including information technology systems; interunit coordinating mechanisms; decision-making processes; and control mechanisms. Sometimes managers put in place ad hoc organizational structures and processes that parallel and overlap those already in place to help make the latter work more efficiently. For instance, one company put together a vertical-slice task force during a restructuring effort. The job of this temporary "parallel organization" or task force was to make sure that fresh new solutions were found to existing organizational problems. Overt efforts like this are not part of the shadow side.

The hidden organization is one that grows up informally alongside or, perhaps more accurately, within the overt organization to provide services and benefits not provided by the overt organization. The phrase "informal organizational arrangements" aptly describes how the hidden organization evolves. These arrangements can parallel, complement, or even replace formal organizational structures and processes. Let us focus on organizational control mechanisms for a moment. Formal control processes include publicly endorsed rules, regulations, standards, and auditing procedures. But inevitably, covert arrangements arise without official endorsement that augment, reset, complement, clarify, take precedence over, or even contravene formal rules, regulations, and policies. These hidden arrangements can either enhance or limit the productivity of the system.

Many managers contravene rules, not for personal benefit, but to get their work done more effectively and efficiently. I asked managers in one institution what their favorite hidden-organization activities were. The winning categories were getting around the outmoded recruitment system and fudging the budget to accomplish departmental goals. One manager fudged the budget a bit to hire a work-design consultant. Since hiring consultants was not allowed, it was called something else in the books. In hiring the consultant, he assumed that she would be worth much more than she was going to be paid, and his calculations corroborated his assumption. The whole process added value—the redesigned work processes shaved some 10 percent off operational costs—even though it was "illegal." On the other hand, some managers fudge the budget to conceal their incompetence or even to steal. In both cases, this parallel arrangement—the covert versus the official budget—remains undiscussed. Chapter Twelve discusses some of the forms the hidden organization takes, how they add either cost or value, and how they can be managed.

Each of the five shadow-side categories—culture, personal styles, social systems, politics, and the hidden organization—is discussed in a separate chapter. But before then, three questions need to be asked: What can be done to get broader discussion of shadow-side issues? What is the economic impact of the shadow side? What generic processes can be used to manage shadow-side issues? These questions are addressed in the next three chapters.

2

GETTING ATTUNED
TO THE SHADOWS

EALING WITH THE SHADOW SIDE effectively means getting attuned to the way it works—being able to identify important shadow-side issues and bring them out into the open. As we shall see later, not every shadow-side arrangement, once identified, should be brought into a public forum. On the other hand, critical shadow-side issues that should be discussed in some decision-making forum often stay buried. This happens because (1) shadow-side activities and arrangements are simply not known, or (2) they are known, but for a number of reasons—mostly related to defensiveness—they are avoided. Bringing issues out of the shadows—that is, surfacing the *unknown* and therefore undiscussed issues—is the first topic of this chapter. Moving beyond defensiveness—that is, removing obstacles to the discussion of *known* issues—is the second topic. Questions and suggestions to help you and others name and surface key shadow-side issues are scattered throughout the discussion.

But a caution is in order here. Developing the attitudes and skills needed to surface and deal with critical shadow-side issues—that is, both those that limit the business and those that, if discussed, could be translated into increased opportunities for the business—is in no way the same as establishing a culture of tattling, informing, and squealing. Such gross immaturity has no place in

17

organizations of integrity. What is said here is meant to promote a culture of the kind of open communication that serves the business and those who are committed to promoting the business.

Bring Issues Out of the Shadows

Managing the shadow side begins with identifying and surfacing that which is unknown and thus undiscussed. If one doesn't even know what's in the shadows, one can hardly discuss or deal with it. There are a number of reasons why people don't know what's going on in the shadows: shadow-side activities and arrangements are intentionally hidden from others; shadow-side realities are embedded in the culture and habits of the institution and therefore go unnoticed; institutional and personal blind spots abound; some managers are naive; and some managers simply don't want to know what's in the shadows.

Hidden Arrangement and Activities

Some issues remain unknown—and undiscussed—because they are intentionally hidden from other players in the institution and especially from people with authority. For instance, individuals try to hide their darker sides, defects, and shortcomings. In some cases they spend a lot of emotional energy keeping a facade intact, not knowing that others would accept them as they are. Of course, people also hide their unacceptable behavior. Embezzlement depends on the ability of the embezzler to hide the siphoning of funds. Some people love sharing gossip, even when it is destructive, but they certainly don't want to be known as gossips.

People also hide institution-enhancing activities if revealing them will thwart their value-adding goals. For instance, many managers fudge the rules to get their work done. It is not uncommon for instructors in universities to quietly bend the rules in order to prevent the school bureaucracy from standing in the way of education and learning. They get deserving students into courses even though they technically don't qualify. They eliminate or lessen required but useless hurdles. It goes without saying that in some cases workers fudge the rules for personal gain. One manager did not turn in appraisal reports on his direct reports for over two years. No one seemed to notice that the reports were missing. At least no one said anything. He hated doing the reports and was using this ploy to test his power within the institution. None of this was ever discussed.

Bear in mind the following do's and don'ts when ferreting out and handling hidden or unknown shadow-side activities and arrangements:

- *Do not become a cop, detective, or spy.* Do not go around snooping into the affairs of others as a matter of course. You will become an object of suspicion and defeat your purpose. We all dislike managers who give the impression that workers are guilty until proved innocent.

- *Be alert and inquisitive rather than suspicious.* Spot clues that indicate that something is going on in the shadows. Explore situations that don't feel right. If a worker is disappearing at odd times, this might deserve a bit of investigation. In one factory a manager found out that a disappearing worker had a side job of selling drugs. In another case the worker was slipping home to help a spouse who had fallen into a deep depression. The manager helped the worker find assistance for her. In one classic case a dean discovered that a prized teacher was not on campus very much because he had taken a second full-time job at another university.

- *When you need to act, act decisively.* Do not hesitate to deal with activities or arrangements that violate the values of the business. If you look the other way, you legitimize the institution-limiting behavior or may fail to prevent problems down the road. The manager of the drug peddler called in the police. The worker and one of his suppliers were arrested.

- *Exercise prudence in condoning so-called minor infractions and institution-enhancing shadow-side arrangements.* Carefully review activities and arrangements that seem to add value to the institution even though they contravene existing rules. Hopefully, they do indeed add value. One professor who was spending more time than allowed on paid consulting projects was turning this work into excellent research studies that were published. Another case did not turn out as well. One manager who suspected minor drug use on the part of one of his employees said nothing.

But when the worker had an accident, tests showed that drugs might have been a contributing factor. If you do look the other way, know why you're doing so. Not wanting to cause waves is usually not a good excuse.

• *Do not immediately try to formalize covert institution-enhancing arrangements.* Some may ask, if an undiscussed activity or arrangement benefits the institution, why not name it, formalize it, and celebrate it? Sometimes this may be the way to go. Revel in it. Make it part of the overt culture. One human resources manager did a quiet study of the appraisal system. She discovered that more than 50 percent of the appraisal forms were late or missing. The ones on file were almost never used. She brought the results of her study to the management committee. They suspended the use of the review system until they could design one that worked. However, publicly naming some institution-enhancing shadow-side arrangement or activity might destroy it. If the shadow-side behaviors of the star salesman mentioned in the last chapter had been named and discussed, let us say, in the management committee, that might have spelled the end of this arrangement, and the star might have left the company. It would be naive to think that the company could establish a policy saying, in effect, "If you are really good we will grant you exceptions to rules that lesser mortals must still obey."

Embedded Arrangements and Unwritten Rules

Some activities and arrangements, together with their economic consequences, remain undiscussed because they are in some way buried in the institution. Many of the company's cultural assumptions, beliefs, values, and norms fall into this category. It is not that they are deliberately hidden from view. Rather they have become so much a part of the fabric of the institution that they have disappeared from sight. They have become institutional habit, part of the daily way of doing things.

Buried norms become the unwritten and undiscussed rules of the organization. An unwritten rule in one insurance company was, "Don't question your boss's behavior." A complementary rule was, "Don't question the behavior of veteran employees." These two rules had soaked into the wood paneling of the company's offices.

When a new CEO was brought in to turn the place around, he hired a new senior team and a cadre of managers at the next level to lead the charge. They soon discovered that these two unwritten rules had played a critical role in bringing the company to the brink of financial disaster. Few managers seemed to know how fat, lazy, sloppy, and unaccountable the company had become.

Unwritten rules can, of course, add value. One company had a chief executive who was an absolute tyrant. But there was an unwritten rule that stated, "Protect the innocent from the boss's wrath." No one ever named the rule, but as part of the company's unconsciousness, so to speak, it drove behavior. Savvy managers routinely made excuses for the behavior of subordinates that needed no excuse. They went so far as to hide certain employees when the boss visited their areas. There was, in sum, an unspoken, company-enhancing conspiracy to both humor the boss and protect precious human assets.

Here are some suggestions for dealing with embedded arrangements and unwritten rules:

- *In decision-making forums, find probes that get at dysfunctional norms.* For instance, ask such questions as, What is it beyond a lack of business acumen and making business mistakes that keeps this company from moving ahead?

- *Explore attics and closets.* Try to find out what institution-limiting issues are locked up in the attic. Discover what keeps people from opening the attic and exploring the closet. One new manager found out why sales personnel never wanted to talk about their compensation program. They were being paid way beyond the industry standard, and the compensation and benefits person in the human resources department had many close friends among them.

- *Become sensitive to the idea of unwritten rules.* Name some of the unwritten rules of your company. Every company has some. In one large institution one covert rule was, "It is all right to come late to meetings." Meetings started from fifteen minutes to a half hour late. People laughed about it informally, but it had never been brought out in the open. One consultant calculated the cost per year in wasted managerial time and lost opportunities at some $2 million.

• *Determine which unwritten rules add value.* A covert rule
in one company was, "Seek permission only when you add significant risk to the company, the unit, or the project." The rule was
never named or discussed. It even contravened some policies on the
books. But, in the long run, it added far more value than cost.

• *Determine which covert rules add cost rather than value
and challenge them.* In one university a new dean realized that the
covert rule "Avoid committee work; let the drones do it" contributed significantly to the mediocrity of the place. Creative ideas from
faculty went into teaching and research but contributed nothing to
the growth of the institution itself.

• *Always explore possible consequences.* Before challenging covert rules that seem to limit the institution, review the consequences of disclosure first. In one company there was a norm that
stated, "Don't challenge a superior in public." At first glance it
seemed that openly surfacing and challenging the rule was the way
to go. Further reflection suggested that the strategy might backfire.
Since the overall goals were open communication and the promotion of innovative ideas, a new norm was developed: "Help superiors challenge themselves." Trusted peers and subordinates took it
upon themselves to prepare managers for greater candor. The process worked. In one dramatic session, the CEO reviewed the company's rather mediocre results and then asked the senior managers
assembled, "Should I resign?" This led to one of the most creative
discussions the managers of this company had ever had.

Blind Spots

Both individuals and companies have shadow-side blind spots.
Blind spots are unexamined and undiscussed facts, assumptions,
prejudices, and the like that keep a problem or issues from being
seen clearly. For instance, some companies have blind spots about
the capabilities and productivity of older workers. It is often assumed that older workers are less flexible, more constricted in their
thinking, less productive, and more expensive than younger workers. Research shows that the opposite is true. Therefore, companies
that routinely dismiss older workers are hurting themselves economically. Savvy companies enter into win-win arrangements with

older workers. The company protects this important talent base and draws its own benefits.

Business blind spots can keep a company mired down in mediocrity. One hotel chain tried all sorts of ways to increase profitability, including firing a series of chief executives. No significant change took place, however, until someone finally named a key blind spot. "We are good at managing hotels," he said, "but we are not good at dealing with bricks and mortar." The company sold most of its hotels and took back lucrative management contracts. Its profitability increased dramatically. The opposite of blind spots are new perspectives that add value to the business.

Here are suggestions for handling blind spots:

• *Legitimatize the search for and the naming of blind spots.* Give workers permission, as it were, to name and discuss key issues they believe are being overlooked.

• *Ask the questions behind the questions.* For instance, first ask, What's going on here? Follow up by asking, What's *really* going on here? When things are not going right, and the immediately apparent mistakes have been examined, try to determine what is being overlooked or what biases, assumptions, or other facts might be behind the problem.

• *Welcome new perspectives from others.* Some poet once said, "Oh, to see ourselves as others see us." Individuals benefit greatly from feedback that helps them break through blind spots in their personal styles. The friend of one manager said, "You see yourself as humorous; others see you as sarcastic." The value of consultants often lies in their ability to ask the "naive" question that helps a company break through a blind spot.

Naiveté

Some managers don't know what's going on in the shadows because they are simply naive. They cannot imagine that someone would steal, make self-serving political deals, or go back on promises. One smart but politically naive manager volunteered to start a controversial business development unit. His work was brilliant, but he never noticed the wolves circling in the distance. He thought he was receiving the cooperation he needed from the new-product development group when all he was getting was lip service. Some friends slipped him a few warnings, but they were too subtle for him. In the end the new venture collapsed, the company suffered, people were laid off, and the manager in question had a black mark on his record. After it was all over, he still did not know what had happened. He was in agony, but he did not know why. In these complex days, companies cannot afford naive managers. Here are starting points for addressing the issue of naiveté:

• *Think about ways you might be "in the dark."* Get feedback from others you trust on your naiveté quotient. There is a big difference between being able to rise above company politics and not even knowing they exist.

• *Explore the ways you have been surprised by behavior or events over the past year.* When you are surprised when things go awry—the business-limiting antics of individual co-workers, the viciousness of company gossip, or the virulence of internal politics—it might be time to ask yourself, "How am I blindsiding myself?"

• *Don't become a busybody.* Remember there is a huge difference between an astute observer of the social, political, and cultural scene and a busybody. Taking steps to overcome naiveté is a far cry from becoming a meddler.

Desire Not to Know

Finally, some managers don't know what's going on in the shadows, not because they are particularly naive, but because they don't want to know. Their principle, usually unspoken even to themselves, is: "If I know, I will have to act." Therefore, they send unspoken messages like, "Don't tell me," "Don't burden me," "Take care of it yourself," "Leave well enough alone," and so forth. They want all the dirt swept under the rug so they can get on with the business. This refusal to see the world as it really is means that they are almost inevitably less effective than they might be: "None are so blind as those who refuse to see." Just as companies cannot afford naive managers, neither can they afford managers who choose to wear blinders. An attempt to handle this issue begins with the following steps:

• *Ask yourself what you would rather not know.* If you

don't want to know the company gossip, that's probably quite healthy. If you consistently ignore messages that come through the company grapevine, then you may be ignoring information that could help the business.

• *Find out why you don't want to know certain shadow-side activities.* This is not an exercise in psychoanalysis, but a pragmatic shadow-side audit. If you prefer being left alone to get your work done, it may represent a failure to see yourself as part of the team. If you don't want to review the political implications of a project you are proposing because you feel you're "above all that," it may be that you lack some basic political skills. Once more, discussing your reluctance to pay attention to shadow-side issues with a trusted colleague may help you move from smart to wise.

Move Beyond Defensiveness

In many cases, people are aware of issues that are at work in the shadows. But, for a number of reasons, they want to avoid surfacing them, and they have developed tactics for keeping them at bay. Individual, group, and institutional *defensiveness*—self-protection against undesirable consequences—is at the root of such avoidance. Those who would manage the shadow side must find tactful but robust strategies for helping organizational players move beyond their defensiveness and start dealing with key shadow-side issues, arrangements, and activities. Understanding the workings of such avoidance—the rationales, defensive routines, fears, and discomforts that form the wall of protection—is the place to start.

Many shadow-side realities never make it to a public forum because they are deemed, in one way or another, undiscussable. It is one thing if issues are in the shadows simply because they have not been identified and discussed or because they are known but have not been put on the table for discussion. It is quite another thing if issues are seen as undiscussable for personal reasons, because the boss doesn't want them discussed, or the culture limits or forbids their discussion.

Consider this example. In one large East Coast trucking firm, working long hours had become part of the culture, a sign of commitment and loyalty. Even though many managers talked among themselves about how this practice did psychological and economic damage to the company—good managers would finally get sick of the hours and quit—it was never brought up at any formal meeting. Those who quit were seen as "lacking fiber." The long-hours norm was one of the company's undiscussables. What makes issues undiscussable? Such factors as fear of consequences, discomfort with shadow-side issues themselves, self-interest, and unmentionability.

Some see shadow-side issues as undiscussable because they fear the consequences of surfacing and discussing them, thinking, "If I discuss it, I will get hurt, my friends will get hurt, my unit will get hurt, or the company will suffer." For some, confronting shadow-side issues, especially those dealing with the darker side of human nature, is like opening Pandora's box. Things will escape that cannot be controlled. In a word, some managers tend to *catastrophize* about the impact of shadow-side revelations. They overemphasize the negative impact that dealing with these issues head-on will have.

This is not to say that some of the feared consequences are not real. One middle manager told me a horror story about a case of sexual harassment she had to deal with. At the end she said, "Whistle-blowers are hated here—hated by management, hated by co-workers. Usually, I cope and look the other way." In another company, a young accountant who had been with the firm for about a year talked about some of his manager's actions that bordered on the unethical. Then he said, "If she gets a hint that I think this way, then my career will be in jeopardy. If I told anyone else, it would get back to her. That's the way this place is. So I'm working very hard for a promotion so I can get away from her." The range of possible feared consequences includes discomfort, embarrassment, and threats to one's self-interest.

Here are some general suggestions for moving undiscussables into open forums:

• *Identify the consequences of not discussing the issue.* Leaving an issue undiscussed may affect the company's future and therefore the future of those who work there. Not reporting instances of sexual harassment, for example, may put others in jeopardy.

• *Use a confidant to discuss fears about downside consequences.* If you see an issue as undiscussable, so do others. Sharing your concerns with a confidant is the first step toward company- and employee-enhancing openness.

• *Determine what can be done to minimize possible negative consequences.* Even if there are some negative consequences from surfacing and discussing an undiscussable, the benefits often outweigh the cost. This is especially true if strategies are devised to minimize possible negative consequences. One worker did this by discussing what she saw as instances of sexual harassment with a superior known for his integrity. He was also a friend of the perpetrator. He took the initiative to get the issue into the proper decision-making forum.

Suggestions for moving toward the kind of open communication needed to manage the shadow side are outlined here. Some of these strategies relate to individuals, while others must be carried out by the organization itself.

Deal with Rather Than Avoid Discomfort

Some players are reluctant to discuss issues that make them feel uncomfortable: "I just don't like to talk about those things." Some people are uncomfortable with human folly. Shadow-side issues involving such things as revenge, lust, greed, hatred, ambition, pride, dishonesty, and stupidity are just too sensitive, too laden with emotion. Some managers would like to think that human folly and the emotions associated with them are left behind at the workplace door. An irate employee in one company was haranguing her boss: "Why didn't John get fired? He screwed up royally. If any of the rest of us had screwed up like that, we would have been fired. I've seen it." He answered, somewhat weakly, "Well, actually John has a lot of talent, he has a lot to offer this company." For obvious reasons he could not bring himself to say, "The real reason why John did not get fired is that he is the blue-eyed boy of the vice president of marketing."

Here are suggestions for overcoming discomfort with issues that may need discussion:

• *Identify issues that you are reluctant to discuss.* Sometimes merely naming them to yourself is enough to summon up the

courage to address some key issue that has up to now seemed undiscussable to you.

• *Identify issues that others are reluctant to discuss.* If you
are reluctant to discuss certain issues, so are others. In meetings,
watch how some heads droop when certain sensitive topics are
brought up. In one company, no one dared to challenge some of the
actions that were being taken in the name of "diversity." People had
become captives of a kind of political correctness that discouraged
discussion of its negative aspects. Naming such issues to yourself is
the first step in beginning to address them.

• *Search for strategies to discuss issues that are considered
off-limits in the company.* Some companies use E-mail bulletin
boards to get undiscussable issues on the table. One manager used
the social system. His wife was a good friend of a department head.
She discussed an issue with her friend, who discussed it with her
husband. Obviously, such strategies can backfire. Use your imagination to find strategies that are robust but that do not threaten the
climate of trust needed for open communication.

Challenge Laziness, Indifference, and Cynicism

Even among managers who recognize the importance of shadow-
side issues, shadow-side laziness is all too common, and it leads to
avoidance: "It will take too much time and effort." It does take time
and effort, but the trade-offs make it worthwhile. "I can't waste my
time on all that soft-side stuff. I'm an engineer, not a psychologist,"
one manager said. He overlooked the fact that one of his engineers
had lost three technicians within a six-month period because of her
acerbic interpersonal style. In this case the time and effort would
have been well worthwhile.

Shadow-side indifference is also common enough: "It's none
of my business, so why should I bother?" One manager realized that
one of his subordinates who was gay was being given a hard time.
He chose to ignore it. "It goes with the territory," he said to himself.
Two costly things happened. The subordinate quit in the middle
of an important project in which he played a key role. Second, he
invoked the city's anti-discrimination law and sued the company.
Another manager handled a similar situation by introducing a

managing-diversity program that challenged a wide range of prejudices among the work force. The gay worker was not singled out. This positive approach prevented unnecessary personal misery, social disruption, and financial cost.

If naiveté is at one end of the continuum, then cynicism is at the other. The cynic is a person who has given up but not shut up. Cynics have an uncanny ability to sniff out the downside of things and exaggerate them. But this is not done in a way and in forums that can make a positive contribution. The smart alecky—and sometimes amazingly insightful—remark is an end in itself. This is a counterfeit of openness. Moreover, cynics, emphasizing and even exaggerating the negative, want others to feel stupid for caring, believing, working hard, trusting, and sacrificing for the common good. A top-notch cynic could well make hay of not only the contents of this chapter but also the thesis of the entire book. It provides fodder for their smugness. The main point here, though, is that cynics make it very difficult for others to speak up. Everything—except their own cynicism—is open to ridicule.

There is a bit of the cynic in most of us. It is our flawed defense against naiveté. But, in the end, cynicism is both cheap and unproductive. As one poet put it, a vein of cynicism much indulged in coarsens everything within us. Naiveté and cynicism are different sides of the same coin. They are both inappropriate responses to what lies in the shadows. We need a different coin, and enlightened realism is that coin. In a world in which reengineering, downsizing, and cost containment are the order of the day, it is time to reengineer the shadow-side realities of the business. It's worth it.

Here are suggestions for challenging laziness, indifference, and cynicism:

• *Develop a culture and a management system that do not tolerate laziness, indifference, and cynicism.* Since the lazy, indifferent, and cynical are not self-managing, the system itself must find ways of managing them. This means emphasizing a manager's responsibility and accountability for company-limiting shadow-side activities from the start of that manager's career. If politics are standing in the way of moving a key project forward, then the manager should intervene. Intervening in the shadow side needs to be part of the job description.

• *Develop work teams that monitor member behavior.* The new focus on teams is an antidote to the kinds of laziness, indifference, and cynicism that prevent the identification and discussion of key shadow-side issues. Colleagues are often less forgiving than superiors of this kind of behavior.

Develop the Courage to Push Beyond the MUM Effect

Unfortunately, quite often it is impossible to surface a shadow-side issue without challenging yourself, others, or the company itself. Challenging creatively takes both courage and skill. Neither the skill of effective challenging nor the courage to use it is widely distributed among the general population, including managers. Research shows that even when managers know that their challenges will be well received, they are still reluctant to challenge. This is called the MUM Effect (Rosen and Tesser, 1970; Tesser, Rosen, and Tesser, 1971).

Self-defense is at the root of the reluctance to challenge. First, even though managers say that they are reluctant to challenge others because they don't want others to feel bad, in truth, challenging makes *them* feel uncomfortable. It is a form of direct human contact with an edge to it that they would rather avoid. Second, since they don't know how to do it well, they refrain because they don't want to fall on their face. Too many managers have seen their own bosses do it poorly. In one West Coast company the director of planning decided to challenge the senior team. The company pretended to have a strategy when in fact it had none. Senior managers pretended to be strategists even though they were not. So he called their bluff. Unfortunately, he had the courage but not the tact or the skill. He did it publicly and ineptly. He might well have put an ad in the paper saying, "Our emperors have no strategic clothes." His days were numbered.

Start to address the problem of the MUM Effect by taking the following steps:

• *Think about how prevalent the MUM Effect is in both yourself and your company.* There are probably few who know how to deal creatively with the communication of bad news.

• *Think through the potential responses to reasonable*

challenge. Before challenging others by surfacing some shadow-side issue, put yourself in the shoes of those hearing the bad news. Understanding any lack of receptiveness can help you find better ways of communicating the issue.

• *Improve your own willingness both to challenge skill-fully and to respond nondefensively to reasonable challenge.* There are communication skills programs that can help you do precisely this (Egan, 1994). More is said about such communication skills in Chapter Seven.

Turn Embarrassment and Disruption into Learning

At the root of much shadow-side avoidance is the fear of causing or experiencing embarrassment or disruption as a consequence of confronting tough issues. While it is hardly laudable to set out to cause others to be embarrassed or upset, these responses are a part of life. If they are unintended consequences of surfacing key undiscussed issues, so be it. No one has ever died of them. A cultural norm of some organizations is, "Never cause embarrassment or disruption." If this is the case, the culture itself has to be challenged. Sometimes embarrassment and disruption act as stimuli for improvement. When an embarrassed manager says, "I'm never going to let that happen to me again," the embarrassment might well have paid off. Of course, he could mean, "I'll become more effective at hiding my mistakes." This can be warded off by developing a learning-from-mistakes culture.

The following suggestions are departure points for handling fear of embarrassment and disruption as an impediment to surfacing tough issues:

• *Think about the extent to which the "avoid embarrassment and disruption" norm is part of the culture.* If it is, then surfacing shadow-side issues that cause disruption is going to demand more courage or more ingenuity on your part.

• *Discover what you can do to deal more creatively with both your own and others' embarrassment.* It is helpful to begin discussions with such statements as, "My intent in talking about this is not to cause embarrassment, but . . . " or "I find this embarrassing to say, but the issue is more important than my discomfort."

• *Turn embarrassment and disruption into learning opportunities for yourself and others.* Embarrassment and disruption add drama to interactions. The interactions become more salient in the minds of the players and in the corporate memory. This drama or saliency can be turned into a stimulus for learning. One manager in a meeting said, "We are all embarrassed by this revelation, so let's leverage the messiness. Let's use it to learn something." Take stock of the disruptive or embarrassing events and take steps to change the conditions that precipitated them.

Monitor Self-Interest

Some issues are undiscussable because they affect the player's self-interest. It is as if one could hear him or her saying, "I'm sorry, but the current shadow-side arrangement benefits me and my unit—in that order—so you won't be hearing from me." A common shadow-side reality is the refusal on the part of some managers to view issues in terms of their overall impact on the company or institution. It is too often a question of *my* career or *my* unit. Blatant self-interest is, by definition, undiscussable. Over a two-year period I watched a manager deep into self-interest. He was clever. He had a way of disguising self-interest as company interest or loyalty to the people in his unit. At first, then, the extent of his self-interest was hidden. But gradually, both superiors and co-workers began to notice his game. Still no one said anything. For instance, his boss never addressed this player's me-first style in his performance reviews. The MUM Effect was in full force. Then, out of the blue, his boss invoked the employment-at-will agreement and fired him. Failure to manage the shadow side in this case meant that everyone lost.

Here are suggestions for minimizing problems that stem from individual self-interest:

• *When people make proposals, try to determine their motivation.* This is not a guilty-till-proven-innocent approach but rather a valid effort to determine a proposal's ramifications. Who benefits from the proposal? Don't hesitate to ask directly how the proposal will benefit the company and at what cost.

• *Discuss the possible downside of proposals that seem to come from self-interest.* One manager said to the sponsor of the proposal: "If we carry out this project, your unit will have to remain fully staffed, while others will be downsizing, some of them drastically. Let's review the implications of this."

Recognize Rationalizations for What They Are

Managers and workers alike present a million good reasons for not discussing shadow-side issues: "I don't want to get my people in trouble." "The company's image will suffer." "The issue in question is inconsequential." "That's not my territory." "I don't want anyone to think I'm a snitch." In a word, rationalizing—the ability to give excuses that are not good enough—is alive and well in the workplace. It is true that surfacing some shadow-side activities and arrangements in the wrong forum can cause more harm than good. But this is not the usual case.

A recent TV exposé illustrated how deeply rooted rationalizing about the shadow side is. Investigative reporters discovered that a number of workers in a large postal facility routinely drank heavily during working hours. Hidden cameras caught groups of them drinking in mid-morning. Many of the co-workers of the offenders knew what was going on and talked freely about it among themselves and eventually with reporters. But they did not want to "rat" on their colleagues. Paradoxically, they were very angry with their colleagues because they had to make up the work the drinkers were not doing. A few feared for the reputation of the postal service: "Everyone thinks we're awful. Why make things worse?" Still others said that the whole incident was inconsequential: "You have lousy workers in every company. We're no different from others. And, anyway, the mail gets through." Many of the workers said simply: "That's why we've got supervisors. Why should we do their work?"

Frontline supervisors of the facility predictably expressed ignorance of the situation. When reporters said that it was their job to know, they replied, "Our job is to get the mail delivered, not to be nursemaids to a few slobs." The superiors of these frontline supervisors, expressing amazement and horror, promised to clean up the mess. Three or four people were fired. Some were suspended. But all in all, one was left with the feeling the roots of the real malaise had not been touched. One manager I know forbids excuse making. His justification: "I already know the valid excuses for business mistakes and failures, and I have no stomach for the lame ones."

Here is a contrasting example with a message. A few years ago the head of an important agency of the federal government came under fire because the agency had showed favoritism in hiring the sons and daughters of the well-connected in Washington. Instead of engaging in the usual excuse-making game, the director admitted what had happened, said that it was wrong, and outlined how it would be corrected. The issue dropped out of the press almost instantly.

A healthy corporate culture is one in which excuse making is discouraged. Here are guidelines for moving in that direction:

• *Determine the kinds of excuse making and rationalizing that are part of your company's organizational culture.* Savvy managers automatically ask themselves such questions as "Is this a *reason* or an *excuse?*" or "Is this person trying to explain the facts or save face?" Understanding the business in depth helps them see the difference. A consultant at the yearly management meeting of one company listened while manager after manager gave his or her set of excuses for why some one million pounds of product had to be dumped because of poor quality. When this bit of theater came to an end, he said simply, "Now let's have a conversation about the reasons behind all those reasons. What's really going on here." It was a tense and difficult but ultimately very productive conversation.

• *Develop a "you-should-have-known-about-it" culture.* More and more ignorance of what is happening in the shadows is no longer an acceptable excuse. If something untoward happens on your watch, you're responsible. The trick, once more, is staying vigilant without becoming paranoid.

• *Find ways of helping people save face, but don't reward rationalizing.* There is no reason for pushing people's noses in it once the truth comes out. A compassionate but hard-nosed realism is called for. A climate of learning from mistakes helps. But people have to know that excuse making in general is the refuge of the weak manager. If people rationalize and get away with it, they will keep on rationalizing.

Find Ways to Minimize Defensive Routines

What Argyris (1985, 1986) has called "defensive routines" are more difficult to handle because they are used by otherwise very bright organizational players to keep *themselves* in the dark. Defensive routines are ways of thinking or acting designed to avoid surprise, embarrassment, or threat—that is, any outcome that is uncomfortable or ego-challenging. Through defensive routines, managers misuse their substantial communication skills to avoid conflict and disturbance in the workplace and, in so doing, send mixed messages to those with whom they work. Furthermore, since defensive routines are time consuming, managers who use them often fail to make timely business decisions.

One brilliant and personable technician who headed up a project that was running late and over budget was asked to meet with the senior management team to discuss the project. In retrospect, his unconscious aim for the meeting was to avoid personal embarrassment and discomfort as he faced committee members. In effect he, not the members of the team, ran the meeting. He set the context of the discussion so that the questions they asked could be easily answered. No really hard-hitting questions were asked. Fears were calmed. Everybody got back to business. Two months later, three key financial backers pulled out of the project. It had to be put on hold, and the company lost millions of dollars. When questioned by a consultant, he talked about how the senior management team had failed to pose the right questions and how they had not consulted with him early enough in the design of the project. Defensive routines had become second-nature to this person—and costly for the company.

It is a strange, company-limiting problem. According to Argyris, managers addicted to defensive routines do not always say what they really mean, though they skillfully deny this when challenged. They pretend to engage in open communication, but in tight situations they are not open at all. Worst of all, smart as they are, they do not even realize what they are doing. "The ability to get along with others is always an asset, right? Wrong. By adeptly avoiding conflict with coworkers, some executives eventually wreak organizational havoc. And it's their very adeptness that is the problem. The explanation lies in what I call skilled incompetence, whereby managers use practiced routine behavior (skill) to produce what they do not intend (incompetence). We can see this happen when managers talk to each other in ways that are seemingly candid and straightforward" (Argyris, 1986, p. 74).

These routines are not just part of the communication style of individual managers; they become part of the organization's covert culture. How they limit the system's effectiveness is usually not seen until some disaster occurs. To cite Argyris once more: "Defensive routines exist. They are undiscussable. They proliferate and grow underground. And the social pollution is hard to identify until something occurs that blows things open. Often that something is a glaring error whose results cannot be hidden. The . . . space shuttle disaster is an example. The disaster made it legitimate for outsiders to require insiders to discuss the undiscussable" (p. 77). Given the intelligence of the users, defensive routines, at first glance, look like straightforward conversation. They are not.

Here are some suggestions for identifying and countering defensive routines:

• *Find out the degree to which you use communication to hide things.* To do so, you will have to ask others who interact with you a lot. Ask them to give you feedback on what your communication is like in times of crisis.

• *When others talk, especially about difficult issues, try not to be blinded by their skill in communicating.* One manager I knew was good at this. He would say things like, "Put that in simpler language for me," "Boil what you just said down to three key issues," "Now just tell me how this is going to turn out and what you base your judgment on," and "Okay, I've heard you, and now I want to hear the downside."

• *Provide the kind of secure atmosphere where people can say what they mean.* If defensive routines are used in order to avoid uncomfortable situations, then minimizing strain and discomfort can lead to straighter talk. A manager might say, "This is not a 'who's right and who's wrong' situation. We just need to get more facts on the table." Or, "This is not a witch hunt. I hate witch hunts, but I do like to know what's going on."

Deal Tactfully with the Unmentionables

Some shadow-side realities may be so undiscussable that even their undiscussability is undiscussable. These are the *unmentionables*. This is not as crazy or as uncommon as it sounds. Sometimes in a marriage some issue such as childlessness or infidelity may become so sensitive that the norm "We never bring this up" cuts off any mention of the subject. Here is a situation that ultimately became public. The vice president of human resources met with a consultant off-site. He said that the meeting was completely off the record. He then shared his serious concerns about the integrity of the chief executive. He needed a sounding board. Since the chief executive would be moving on in a year's time, was it worth the effort to challenge what he was doing? Would such a course of action blow up in his face and in the end do even more harm to the company? He was struggling with the economics of managing the shadow side. At the end of the meeting he reiterated its off-the-record nature. "We never had this meeting, and we did not talk about these issues," he said. "If you ever mention it, I will deny it, and you will never do any more work for this company or its subsidiaries." In his mind, not only was this issue undiscussable but its undiscussability was undiscussable. The whole sordid affair eventually became public anyway. So there are not only the undiscussables, there are also the unmentionables. Some guidelines for dealing with them are as follows:

- *Identify unmentionables in your company. Identify your own.* Ask yourself what these especially sensitive issues are. In one company it was the way that managers all the way down the line mimicked the top boss's style, including the worst parts of that style. Since his name was sacred, criticism of anything about him—including cheap, company-limiting imitations of his style down the line—was not permitted.

- *Determine what makes these issues so sensitive.* One ambitious manager in a very conservative company lived in mortal fear that it would be discovered that he was gay. He suspected any line of inquiry that had a personal twist to it. But he had no idea how much this had affected his entire communication style. Even those who respected his intellect began to be confused by what one termed his "fuzzy communications."

• *Find ways of desensitizing the issues.* A good question is, If this issue is surfaced and faced, what is the worst thing that can happen? Very often the worst is not that bad. The manager above said, "Well, I wouldn't be fired. I don't even think my career would be put on hold, but I do know that it would be much slower. Anyway, given my qualifications and my accomplishments, I could get a good job in a less stuffy company. But, you know, I'm stuffy and I find the stuffiness here comfortable."

Some companies have taken a more radical approach to dealing with unmentionables and undiscussables by developing radically open cultures. Years ago a failing manufacturing firm in Brazil took the unheard-of step of opening up its books completely to all employees. This included the salaries of senior managers. When the new CEO was told that one manager objected, he replied, "Of course he would object. It will now be clear to everyone, and not just to himself, that he does little to earn that much money." SRC, a Missouri-based rebuilder of engines, has taken the same approach (O'Brien, 1993). Like the Brazilian company, its open-management style has been key to its continuing growth and profitability.

Use a Checklist of Attitudes and Skills

The following checklist can serve as a summary of the main points of this chapter and as a way of challenging yourself to develop the attitudes and skills needed to uncover shadow-side issues and explore them creatively in forums in which they can be managed. It can also be used in teams as a form of group challenge. Rate yourself on a scale from 1 to 7, with 1 low and 7 high. Since this is not a statistically standardized survey, you or the group must devise ways of finding meaning in the scores.

1. I continue to improve my ability to spot clues indicating shadow-side activities and arrangements needing attention.
2. Without becoming hypersensitive or cynical, I am becoming more sensitive to hidden agendas.

3. I am becoming better at spotting my own, my unit's, and my company's blind spots.

4. I am working at ridding myself of my shadow-side naiveté.

5. When I see indications that a shadow-side issue is something I would rather not know about, I work even harder to ferret it out.

6. I know which shadow-side issues to surface and which to leave alone.

7. I can clearly see when others move into rationalization mode.

8. I don't make excuses for my own mistakes.

9. While I understand the dynamics of rationalization, I find ways of helping people move beyond it.

10. When some shadow-side issue I should have known about becomes public, I accept responsibility for not knowing and find ways of being more vigilant.

11. I'm becoming better at overcoming both laziness and indifference in reading the shadow side of the institution.

12. I have developed the courage to break through the MUM Effect regarding shadow-side issues.

13. I am beginning to understand and come to grips with my own defensive routines.

14. I no longer let exaggerated fear of consequences keep me from naming and discussing critical shadow-side issues.

15. I have learned how to deal with the embarrassment caused by surfacing the undiscussables.

16. I have tempered my impulse to look the other way when negative shadow-side issues serve my self-interest.

17. I can now tactfully bring up issues that once could not even be named, that is, the unmentionables.

How well did you score? What work do you need to do to develop these shadow-side competencies?

MINING VALUE FROM THE SHADOW SIDE

3

UNCOVERING THE ECONOMICS
OF THE SHADOW SIDE

THE QUESTION ASKED in this chapter is: Why bother to deal with the shadow side at all? The answer is simple: there are significant economic benefits to doing so.

If day-to-day managerial activities and decisions are not given sufficient economic scrutiny, then shadow-side issues get even less. Better managers, of course, instinctively do cost-benefit analyses in setting priorities and making decisions in the course of day-to-day business. But when it comes to the economics of the shadow side, it is often a different story. Shadow-side issues, unfortunately, are often treated in the same way that the news covers crime. Most newspaper and magazine articles on crime focus on the personal misery, social disruption, and moral decay involved. A cover story in *Business Week* ("Economics of Crime," 1993), moving beyond this shortsightedness, estimated that the economic cost of crime in the United States was some $425 billion per year. In a similar way, negative shadow-side realities are often discussed in terms of personal misery ("the politics around here are killing me") and social disruption ("my boss keeps upsetting my staff by having them churn out reports that make him look good but that really have no value"). Nothing is said about the monetary costs involved; managers do not routinely analyze the economics of shadow-side activities and arrangements.

Because shadow-side realities are off-camera, little is done to determine their costs, on the one hand, or the economic value of dealing with them more proactively, on the other. In fact, managing the economics of the shadow side requires a balanced approach, recognizing three kinds of costs and benefits: psychological, social, and financial. In the upcoming discussion, it will become clear that psychological and social costs usually have financial implications, however hidden they might be.

The following example illustrates this kind of business-enhancing microeconomic skill or mentality. After the first day of a three-day seminar on coaching and counseling skills at the World Bank, one of the managers came up to me and said something like this: "I have done an economic analysis of what you are offering here these three days. If the managers of the bank were to adopt the methods you have outlined, I figure that this would increase the productivity of the bank by at least 5 percent." He then translated that increase into dollars and cents. I was struck by his overall economic approach. He saw the seminar not as a cost but as an investment, and a sound one at that. Of course, he was an economist by profession and looked at the world, at least partially, through the lens of cost-benefit analyses. But the upbeat economic mentality he was displaying should become part of the business style of all managers, especially when dealing with shadow-side issues.

Costs of the Shadow Side

The shadow side affects both productivity and the quality of work life. It adds value or cost. When it comes to the economic impact of negative shadow-side activities and arrangements, there are often three kinds of costs: psychological, social, and financial. Financial costs affect the bottom line directly. Psychological and social costs, as we shall see, affect the quality of work life directly and the bottom line indirectly.

Psychological Costs

Psychological costs refer to the various kinds of misery shadow-side activities can inflict on individuals. In one company a fast-track computer engineer who had been fired took his own life. Only later did it surface that he had been blamed for a big blunder his boss had made. Psychological costs run the gamut from passing annoyances to life-wrenching depression. Behind psychological costs are the financial costs associated with distraction from the business, decreased productivity, and lost opportunities. And yet psychological costs are seldom linked to financial costs. One financial manager, distracted by an affair he was having with the wife of one of his colleagues, made a blunder that cost the firm over $1 million. An ensuing investigation revealed that some of his colleagues knew of the affair, and a few had some idea of how it was affecting his work. But since the personal lives of employees were considered undiscussable in this company, the affair was never discussed in any decision-making forum. The psychological costs were devastating—as were the social and financial costs.

Social Costs

Social costs refer to the disruption of relationships and the turmoil caused in teams and groups by negative shadow-side activities and arrangements. Many events, both overt and covert, can cause social unrest in companies and institutions. A downturn in an industry (an overt phenomenon) makes people nervous about their jobs or concerned about the diminishing opportunities for advancement. But the social toll of negative shadow-side activities and arrangements is often ignored, as is the financial toll of social disruption. That fact is seen clearly in the following case.

A consultant friend of mine, unhappy with his work with a client named Tom, told me the following story. The main actors were Tom, who was a middle manager in an R&D department and supervised a number of R&D projects; his boss Hugo, the head of the department; Rosalind, a project director who reported to Tom; and members of a project team led by Rosalind. Tom complained to the consultant about Rosalind: "Rosalind made an end run and brought some ideas about the new project directly to Hugo, my boss. And he let her get away with it! Everybody in the department knows she's grandstanding, letting him think that our ideas are really hers. Afterward, Hugo came along and said how much he

liked Rosalind's ideas and even commended me for the way I've
been developing her. Well, I didn't teach her how to be slick, I can
tell you that. She arrived here with that talent. The project team
members don't even know yet whether the ideas she presented to
Hugo are viable. But once he makes up his mind, there's no changing it. Now I'm in the middle. If I get on Rosalind's case, it'll get
back to my boss, and there'll be hell to pay. If the project fails, we'll
all get blamed."

The undiscussables here were Rosalind's ambition and slick-
ness, Hugo's poor management practices, and the conspiratorial
arrangement between Hugo and Rosalind. And, in the end, Tom
was much more worried about his career than the failure of the
project. This, too, was undiscussable. The project team members
were angry with Rosalind for taking all the credit, with Hugo for
being gullible, and with Tom for doing nothing about it. Their
anger translated into a silent conspiracy to see to it that the project
failed. Ultimately, both Tom and Rosalind left the firm. And nobody learned. The cost of social disruption inevitably led to financial loss. The project failure cost thousands of dollars. Tom and
Rosalind had to be replaced. And the silent enmity of team members
toward Hugo was likely to cause further financial losses. My consultant friend was depressed because of the lost-opportunity costs.
He said that he had been afraid to bring the shadow-side issues
forward lest he lose the job. In the end, he lost his contact, Tom,
and the job.

Financial Costs

Financial costs refer to both the direct and indirect losses that stem
from shadow-side arrangements and activities. Many of the activities and arrangements in the shadows cost a lot of money, yet the
costs are not identified, or they are assigned to some rational ac-
countancy category. Dumping shadow-side costs into rational accounting categories keeps the shadow side covert.

What is the cost of an incompetent and oppressive manager?
There are plenty of these people, but company after company fails
to give them feedback and leaves them in place. What is the cost of

a self-serving deal secretly cut by the heads of two different departments? ("If we both say we need more time, they'll take the pressure off us.") What is the cost of a performance management and appraisal system that everyone tries to avoid or work around? Most of them are like that. No one analyzes the economics of this management system, balancing identifiable benefits against actual costs. What is the cost of a covert, business-limiting cultural norm? Ask IBM. In a number of ways their initial culture of service turned, in the eyes of many, into a culture of arrogance: "We know best." The company made business mistakes. They took their eyes off the marketplace. But mistakes are not in and of themselves shadow-side phenomena. Behind the business mistakes, in the shadows, was a growing bureaucratic culture. The financial cost of all this? It is documented almost daily in the business press.

In addition to making mistakes, individuals and companies often fail to learn from these mistakes and then make them again. This is what I call the *repeated-mistakes phenomenon,* and it can be costly. The way meetings are run is a good example. Companies and their managers devote a great deal of time to meetings, making them of paramount economic importance. Although managers worth their salt should know how to conduct them efficiently, meetings that are unproductive and poorly run are still common. Every once in a while someone complains and suggests doing something about the problem. The issue is addressed, everybody agrees to the solution, and the next couple of meetings go well—adding value to the enterprise. But then, in the rush of everyday business, meetings get sloppy and unfocused again.

Organizations make mistakes. They identify them. They establish a plan to do something about them. And then they make the same mistakes all over again. Very often the mistake itself gets discussed. Mistakes in and of themselves are not shadow-side phenomena. However, the dynamics underlying repeated mistakes do not get discussed. This is the shadow-side issue. The repeated-mistakes phenomenon is not only common but costly. Billions of dollars are wasted every year. And this is only one of the ways the shadow side can lead to financial losses.

Competencies Required for
Managing Shadow-Side Economics

The economics of the shadow side are much like the economics of quality. Managers began to adopt total quality management approaches once they were convinced of their overall financial benefits. Once they saw that wasteful, shoddy work added intolerable cost and that the pursuit of quality was, therefore, "free," they embraced the quality movement. In an analogous way, the costs of shadow-side activities and arrangements are hidden. Therefore, since the benefits in many cases outweigh the costs, managing the shadow side, like quality, is "free."

In order to become effective microeconomists in dealing with shadow-side issues, managers need to acquire the skill to do the following: (1) take an adding-value approach to managing, (2) identify the financial costs of shadow-side activities and arrangements, (3) translate psychological and social costs into financial costs, and (4) think in terms of lost-opportunity costs.

Take an Adding-Value Approach to Managing

One of the functions of a for-profit company is to create financial wealth. General Electric and Intel, for instance, strive to create financial wealth in which key stakeholders like employees and stockholders share. One of the functions of a not-for-profit human services institution is to create human capital. Hospitals create human capital when their patients leave the institution better able to live their day-to-day lives. Effective managers play a key role in this wealth-creation process by taking an adding-value approach to management (Egan, 1993). They are good at finding ways to add value instead of just accomplishing the next task that comes along.

Adding value requires an overall ability to integrate a cost-benefit analysis into daily activities. This basic microeconomic mentality and competency is the foundation of taking an economic approach to shadow-side issues. Since, as both research and experience show, the day-to-day lives of managers are somewhat chaotic, often with dozens of people and scores of issues vying for their attention, those managers cannot add value without doing quick-

and-dirty cost-benefit analyses in order to set priorities. ("Should I get back to my boss with the project report she wants or should I visit the customer who's upset about the proposed terms of a new contract?") Time management is really priority management—being able to quickly compare the costs and benefits of multiple issues. Managers who are good at this kind of ongoing cost-benefit analysis, basing it on a broad understanding of the business issues and stakeholders involved, tend to use their time more effectively and add more value. The microeconomics of priority setting is second nature to them.

This competency is also essential for managing shadow-side issues. A manager might ask herself, "Should I visit a key customer this afternoon or attend the meeting at which new human resource policies are being discussed?" She knows that visiting the customer will add value, but she also knows that the policy discussions will be highly political. Let us say that she is a manager of the utmost integrity and wants to balance the needs of customers, shareholders, and employees as equitably as possible. She might well say to herself, "The policy meeting will be filled with politics and competing agendas. I'll reschedule my meeting with the customer and fight for what I think is right at the policy meeting. Overall, I believe I'll add more value there." The politics of the policy formation exercise will not be discussed, but they will be in play. She wants to see the political ebb and flow herself so that she can help the company by proposing outcomes that move beyond individual self-interest. In sum, savvy managers take an adding-value approach to all managerial tasks, including the task of dealing with shadow-side issues.

Identify the Financial Costs of Shadow-Side Activities and Arrangements

In these days of cost cutting, downsizing, lean manufacturing, and the like, the ability to understand the costs and financial implications of one's managerial activities and decisions is becoming an essential skill. And once shadow-side issues are identified in terms of activities and arrangements, they must be assigned costs just as would other organizational activities and arrangements. The ability to do so is an important management competency. Activities take time and involve cost. Indeed, activity-based accounting has become more and more important. Shadow-side activities also have economic implications. Consider the following case. I once said to a client, "You have a very expensive culture." "What do you mean?" he asked, obviously intrigued. "Well," I said, "let me give you a few examples. Your company is very good at analysis. However, if something needs to be analyzed two different ways, you do it three ways and are looking for the fourth. There is a culture of perfectionism around here that is costly and does not add value. You have more analysts than you need, and the analysts you do have do more analysis than they need to. It is easy to figure out how much money you are wasting on analysis that adds little incremental value." A hint of a frown spread across his face.

"Another culture-driven set of behaviors," I continued, "is found in the way you go about approving projects. Projects start somewhere in the bowels of the organization and gradually make their way to the top. At each level there is at least one formal presentation. At the top a number of your vice presidents are involved in lengthy preparations for the final presentation to the management committee. One told me that his group had done eight dry runs for one presentation, and more were scheduled. They had developed forty-five slides for the presentation but had over two hundred in reserve so that every possible question could be answered. This is a very expensive process that adds little value. Moreover, informal presentations and approvals could easily replace the very formal process now in place without any loss of control. The costs of all the steps in the formal process now in place are easily determined."

Covert cultural norms driving these costly behaviors included "Beware of committing career-interrupting mistakes" and "Find out what is in your boss's mind in order to tailor your choice of projects and their presentation." "What you should do," I continued, "is let me help an internal team of your own choice explore the culture, put dollar amounts on culture-generated waste, suggest ways of reducing the waste, and implement cost-saving strategies. We'll call this reengineering the culture. The company would pay me a small percentage of actual savings. I'd say that 5 percent would make both of us very happy." "I'll think about it," he replied, and,

unfortunately, that's the last discussion we had about culture. Today the same company is searching for every possible way it can to
drive out costs, including challenging its culture.

Translate Psychological and Social
Costs into Financial Costs

While some managers get good at ferreting out the hidden financial
costs of, say, company politics, they are not as good at translating
psychological misery and social disruption in the workplace into
dollars and cents. With a little practice, they can acquire this valuable skill.

   It starts with being able to recognize that there are financial
implications to given arrangements. Let's say an inept manager is
kept in place because he is a crony of the boss. This arrangement
is considered undiscussable, and therefore the activities and impact
of the crony are also deemed undiscussable. Since his style alienates
the people in his unit, it most likely reduces their enthusiasm and
productivity. And since he does not listen to their ideas and does
little to develop them or allow them to develop themselves, all sorts
of opportunities are lost. Both reduced productivity and failure to
seize opportunities have financial costs associated with them.

   The next step is to actually calculate the financial costs. In
one company a manager with this skill spent two weeks doing an
audit of a small subsidiary company. In his report to the president
he estimated the lost-opportunity cost of the havoc caused by intran-
sigent managers and cliques at close to $1 million. (A new politi-
cally and socially savvy management team was later installed, and
productivity soared.)

   Translating psychological and social costs into financial
costs is not as difficult as it sounds. It starts with a key principle:
Personal misery and social disruption almost always detract from
productivity. Employees' minds are not fully on the business. They
are more prone to make mistakes. Deadlines are missed. Customers'
calls are not returned promptly. Decisions are delayed. Workers
spend time talking to one another about their misery instead of
getting their work done. Good workers leave. Poorer workers stay
and complain.

In one company, the director of human resources sat down with a couple of people from the financial department in an off-the-record meeting to figure up the costs of a reorganization that was being more or less forced on the company by the board. What the board should have done was fire the president, but they didn't have enough courage. Firing him was undiscussable. Instead, they forced him into a cost-cutting reorganization effort. Morale plummeted because many workers thought that they were being blamed for the president's failures. Here are some of the figures the group came up with during the meeting:

- The departure of three capable people, one in marketing and two in product development, because they were fed up with what was going on; the projected cost was $3 million over a four-year period because of an expected failure in quickly getting the right products to market.
- An expectation that about 30 percent of the work force would be working at three-quarter speed for at least six months because of the morale problem; the expected cost was about $1 million for the decreased productivity.
- The cost of the unneeded reorganization itself was some $500,000.
- The possible loss of one or two key accounts because of the social disruption caused by the reorganization; the projected loss of revenues was $400,000 to $800,000 per year until accounts are replaced.

In sum, the president's ineptness and the board's lack of courage were causing psychological and social turmoil with significant, negative financial implications.

I once tried to order some books from a publisher that was being taken over by a larger company. I was told that the books were not in stock. When I checked elsewhere I was told they were in stock. I placed an order. The order was lost. I replaced the order when they discovered that they did have the books. The books did not arrive. When I finally talked to a customer representative to cancel the order, she said, "There is so much uncertainty around here right now, I'm surprised that anything is getting done."

When it comes to figuring out the financial costs of social disruption, prevention is better than cure. In talking to a manager who was about to change a human resource policy that would save the company about $100,000 over a year's time, I asked him to pause a bit, outline the kinds of psychological misery and social disruption the change might cause, and try to figure up the associated shadow-side costs. Given the size of the company, they came to about $250,000 for the first year. And this was a conservative estimate. Yet, since these costs are usually hidden, they can easily be overlooked.

To analyze the economics of psychological misery and social disruption, managers have to move beyond the myths surrounding so-called soft-side issues and skills. Some managers see the shadow side generally as a soft-side issue, easily dismissed. Notions of psychological costs and social costs are even easier to dismiss. At least covertly, the term *soft side* is used to mean or at least connote "unimportant" or "irrelevant." That's nonsense. In discussing the future of his business, the CEO of an international $6 billion firm said to me, "The soft side is the hard side for us in two ways. First, since we have an engineering mentality, it is hard for us to think about much less manage so-called soft realities, especially the issues that deal with people. Second, I am convinced that hard results will come from managing the soft-side stuff like culture well." The issue is not whether something is "soft" or "hard" but relevant or irrelevant to productivity, performance, and economic outcomes. It is insane to call engineering "hard" and managing people "soft." Managing people well—that is, helping them optimize performance—is both hard to do and contributes to hard results.

Think in Terms of Lost-Opportunity Costs

Since highly effective managers think in terms of adding value, they think in terms of, and are sensitive to, lost-opportunity costs. If your money is locked into long-term investments with low yields, then you will suffer lost-opportunity costs as deals with higher yields come along. Negative shadow-side activities and arrangements have ways of restricting individual potential and stifling institutional opportunities. The shadows are filled with lost opportunities. For example, if there is an unwritten rule that your boss takes credit for all creative ideas in the unit, then fewer creative ideas will be generated. The potential of unit members remains locked up. The beliefs, values, and norms of the covert culture constitute an unseen drag on the company. One university, saddled with a very conservative culture masquerading for years under the guise of "good academic and business sense," looked on in disbelief as one of its competitors, thriving because of a risk-taking culture that had been dubbed "flaky," increased enrollments at a time when most universities were scrambling for students. These lost-opportunity costs can easily be translated into dollars.

Once more, this is the kind of skill that is based on a key idea: Important issues that remain unidentified, undiscussed, and undiscussable sap the company's potential. Effective managers develop a mind-set based on lost-opportunity cost. They not only can see the costs of time spent managing, say, a difficult employee but also have a sense of the opportunities that go by the board because this person is soaking up so much time. Time taken to contain the damage of a difficult employee is stolen from the time that could be given to helping others develop their potential. One manager said to me, "If only Jane's boss had noticed how unhappy she was, we could have done something about it, but now she's with a competitor and is both getting new customers and taking some of our best customers away." Jane's dissatisfaction never got discussed in any meaningful forum. Her leaving translated into lost opportunities with visible bottom-line impact.

4

BECOMING AN EFFECTIVE BEHIND-THE-SCENES MANAGER

T HE QUESTION ASKED in this chapter is: What do we need to do to manage the shadow side? Or, in economic terms, how can we mine value from it? A generic orientation for managing shadow-side issues is presented here. The spirit of this chapter permeates the approaches to managing each of the five shadow-side dimensions outlined in Chapter One and discussed in greater detail in Chapters Five through Twelve.

A student who worked in city hall once said to me, "Now that I have lost my shadow-side innocence, what do I do about it?" What indeed? If managers can't do anything about the shadow-side realities they uncover, then the second state is worse than the first. It is essential, therefore, to translate what we know about shadow-side issues into a process for managing them. The following set of guidelines can be used to prevent, contain, deal with, and even leverage or exploit shadow-side problems:

- Use the frameworks provided in this book to identify significant shadow-side issues.
- Use a cost-benefit analysis to determine which issues should be tackled and which should be left alone.
- Choose the appropriate decision-making forum for dealing with each critical issue.

- Initiate discussion of shadow-side issues assertively and tactfully.
- Use shared problem-solving methodology to find solutions.
- Use a double-loop learning approach to redefining the problem or issue.
- Emphasize prevention to avoid recurrences.

In subsequent chapters this process will be reflected in specific strategies relating to the particular shadow-side category being explored.

As with other step-by-step management models, it is not necessary to follow this process slavishly. Managerial common sense takes precedence over all models. Rather, this process outlines the kinds of things that need to be done to address shadow-side issues directly and professionally. The ideal is that these steps become second nature and integrated into day-to-day management. Since the shadow side permeates all business, organizational, managerial, and leadership categories, a more practical approach for managers is to deal with the shadow side in conjunction with the managerial issue at hand. "Let's stop and address the shadow side" cannot be the ordinary way of dealing with it. A more seamless approach is needed.

Consider, for example, the process of appointing a manager to a new position. Discussions with the prospective manager about the new role and its challenges should be a matter of course. But during these discussions, the new manager's boss might say something like this: "There are probably a couple of people in the unit who will resent your coming, since they believe that they should have gotten the job. And I know that there is one person in there that just doesn't like you. Let's talk about these issues and how to handle them." In this case, addressing shadow-side issues is simply part of the broader process of socializing a manager into his new job. An astute prospect for a managerial position asked her interviewer, "What things will I be expected to do that are not in the current job description?" She knew that she would have to deal with issues in the shadows and wanted to put them right on the table.

Identify Shadow-Side Issues

As discussed in Chapter Two, identifying shadow-side issues is the first step toward bringing them under managerial control. Of course, for many managers, identifying them is not the issue; they are awash with them. They want to know how to manage them. However, the ability to recognize vague clues is important. Recently a bank collapsed in Spain. In retrospect it was easy to spot all sorts of clues indicating that shadow-side activities and arrangements were putting the bank in jeopardy. But no one identified them, pulled them together into a pattern, and demanded that they be discussed.

Good counselors and psychotherapists are said to have a "third ear"—that is, they hear not only what clients are saying directly but also what they are only half saying and even things that they are trying to conceal from themselves. Good managers have a third ear and a third eye. In observing and listening to the workplace, they see the below-the-surface dynamics of their companies and departments. The kind of awareness needed is active rather than passive. On the one hand, managers and supervisors need not go out looking for trouble, but on the other they cannot afford to be surprised or blindsided either.

Once each of the five shadow-side dimensions are clearly understood, it will be easy to see what this third ear and third eye should be doing. For instance, once you know that a proposed project will mean the redistribution of scarce resources, you know that the discussions of it will be political. The third eye and the third ear of the shadow-side-sensitive manager will be scanning the remarks and the nonverbal language of the discussants for indications of political maneuvering.

Shadow-side awareness is also relevant to issues that are external, macro, and global in scope. In the early 1990s, eight oil companies—BP, Amoco, and Pennzoil among them—paid some $70 million in pre-signature bonuses leading up to a formal contract with Azerbaijan to exploit the oil buried under the Caspian Sea. One day later a new acting government decided to nullify the deal, although a spokesman asserted that the bonuses "were to be returned." The new government said that they were concerned about "rebels." The head of the Azeri state oil company resigned. Everything was up in the air, and sound intelligence was at a premium. Not knowing what was going on in the tumultuous shadows within the Commonwealth of Independent States, including macro-political maneuvering and the micro-politics of self-interest, had proved extremely costly for some companies.

These days many companies are, for strategic reasons, entering into alliances and partnerships with other companies, even competitors. Some companies have dozens of these arrangements. While it is important to carry out due diligence in the usual financial sense in choosing business partners, in many cases some shadow-side intelligence is also needed. A proactive approach to probing the shadow side of one's prospective partners without alienating them seems essential. How ethical is this company? Does it have a history of failed dealings with its stakeholders, including its employees? How does it use its political muscle? What is its culture like? What fit is there between our culture and theirs? What are the personal styles of key players with whom we will be interacting? Shadow-side due diligence complements financial due diligence. This intelligence can be gathered from the public record, by interviewing the target company's other partners, employees, and suppliers, and through discussions with key organizational players.

This might sound like dirty work, but in reality it is prudent work. Novell, the computer software manufacturer, has a set of more than two thousand questions it asks a potential merger candidate or partner (Anfuso, 1994). Many of these questions refer to human resource policies, issues, and practices, including performance evaluations, pay practices, and employee relations issues. The culture of the target company is analyzed by interviewing and observing people work within the company. The analysis includes such things as management styles. A process this thorough, no matter how above-board it seems, cannot help but surface shadow-side issues. The information gleaned is passed on to financial experts who figure out the costs of liabilities, including cultural liabilities. This information is then fed to the negotiators, who adjust the price offered accordingly.

Use a Cost-Benefit Analysis

Once shadow-side issues are identified, a choice has to be made about which ones to tackle. The best way to choose is to use some kind of cost-benefit analysis. This may be the simple, everyday process any good manager uses to make sense of competing demands on his or her attention, energy, and time. Consider the following case. Kingsley, a middle manager in an insurance company, was working long hours on a new customer service strategy. Her boss had set an almost impossible deadline. He was always doing things like that, but she felt that she could not yet discuss his management style with him. In the midst of all this a colleague told her that there was a rumor that one of the managers in her department was thinking of leaving because of the "lousy atmosphere around here." He had said nothing to her, so she did not know what was going on. She also learned from another colleague that some co-workers in another department were using the reorganization the company was going through to steal a couple of the best workers in her department. They were good because she had spent time developing them. But development was ignored by most managers because neither the culture nor the reward system supported it. That was a company-wide shadow-side issue. In all, the manager was looking at five problems that demanded her attention.

After juggling these issues in her mind for a while, she came up with the following strategy. First, she decided to ignore the complaining manager for the moment. Her best bet was that he would not quit. Even if he did, it would be an inconvenience, but no real loss. Second, she called her boss and asked for a half-hour of his time the next day to give him a status report on the customer service strategy. A half hour was enough because she knew that this was not the time or the forum to discuss his management style or the issue of the lack of strategy or culture of development in the company. That evening she pulled together a brief report on the customer service strategy and included the names of a few people who would be essential to its execution. Included were the names of the two workers who were in danger of being stolen from her. The meeting went well. Her boss was relieved when he saw the progress she had made and, since the success of the customer service strategy was important to him, he took note of the names she provided.

In this case the cost-benefit analysis was not some elaborate step-by-step process but an exercise in common sense. A more elaborate process can be used when the issues are even more substantive and the outcomes less clear. In a more formal shadow-side cost-benefit analysis, four questions can be asked.

• *Is this issue worth the time and effort in the first place?* Some issues are not worth addressing. A manager who realized that some department heads were fudging their budgets in innocuous ways looked the other way. He saw no malice in what they were doing—he had done it himself when he was a department head—and the economic impact was practically nil. In fact, most of them were just trying to do a good job. Making an issue of it would have been a waste of resources. Savvy managers see lots of things that are not right, but they focus on issues of substance.

• *What is the likelihood of getting this substantive shadow-side issue discussed or debated in some decision-making forum?* It was clear to some managers in an international institution that the institution did not have a viable strategy to provide clear-cut focus and direction for its five thousand employees and the clients they served. It was also clear to them that the current culture did not serve the original mandate of the institution. But the need to reformulate the strategy was undiscussable. Both the chief executive, who was near the end of his tenure, and the senior managers would say things like, "There are problems, of course. All institutions have problems, but we are certainly headed in the right direction." Middle managers who claimed that this was not true soon discovered that their careers were going nowhere. In this case, then, trying to force the discussion of a substantive shadow-side issue was futile. Since the issue remained undiscussable, few managers were willing to risk their careers by continuing to push for open debate.

• *Even if the issue can be brought into some decision-making forum for discussion and debate, what is the likelihood of a positive outcome?* In this same institution, when a new president arrived, he ordered a study and reorganization of the institution's structure. The possibility that the institution's strategy was flawed still remained undiscussable, but a few hardy managers thought that they could use the reorganization as an opportunity to audit and study the culture. The idea of a culture audit was opposed by the chief executive. After a great deal of pressure was put on him by the vice president in charge of the reorganization, he reluctantly changed his mind. However, he insisted that the culture audit be considered an "informal" process. Informal or not, an elaborate and expensive culture audit was mounted. A great deal of effort was spent getting at the covert beliefs, values, and norms that were "really running the place." Even though the audit caused a great stir in the institution, it was destined from the beginning to add little value. The audit itself produced a great deal of personal pain and social disruption. As interim reports leaked out, workers, both individually and in groups, began to see the enormous gap between the institution's espoused culture and the one that actually drove behavior. Whole units were distracted from their work, and productivity plummeted. In the end, since the audit was not official, practically nothing was done to act on any of its conclusions. Everyone's nose was rubbed in the downside of the culture, but all the money, personal agony, and social disruption went for naught. These were not the outcomes envisioned by the promoters of the audit. An understanding of the audit's chances for success would have pointed to a decision not to carry it out, or at least to delay it until a time when the outlook appeared more promising.

   • *Even if the outcome is positive, what is the likelihood that it can be sustained?* In another company a culture audit seemed to lead to much more positive outcomes. Covert, business-limiting norms were identified and named. A new set of values was formulated and adopted. There were some early wins. A few more managers began to take risks—risk taking was a value of the new culture—but they received little support from their superiors. And when they made mistakes, they were punished. Two years later, the old business-limiting norms were back, and little was said any more about the "new" culture. One manager said, "It would have been better if we had done nothing. We might just as well admit that we are cultural recidivists. We don't own our culture. It owns us."

   While all of this might sound negative, there are some useful messages. The shadow side is often a formidable adversary. Doing a cost-benefit analysis before tackling some part of it will help you formulate more substantial strategies than those tried in the examples above. Indeed, the purpose of Chapters Five through Twelve is to help you understand the power of your adversary and to learn how to develop effective coping strategies. The international institution mentioned above finally began discussing and coming to grips with its flawed strategy only after being pummeled by years of international outcry. That is, the power for change lay not inside but outside the institution. Had the managers who wanted a more enlightened strategy and a culture that better served the institution's mandate realized that change was not going to come from getting shadow-side issues debated inside the institution, they might have begun marshalling international public opinion right from the start.

Choose a Decision-Making Forum

The term *decision-making forum* may conjure up a formal group that looks something like the Supreme Court in session. This is not the case. Shadow-side issues of substance should be dealt with in whatever forum will yield desired results. It may be a formal group such as a management committee or task force or it may be a single manager with the authority and resources to deal with the issue. Here are some questions that can guide the choice of forum:

• *How important is the shadow-side issue?* An arrogant manager can be dealt with in a one-to-one meeting. However, if the CEO is embroiled in some kind of malfeasance of office, then the board and the senior management committee might well be appropriate forums.

• *How wide is its impact in terms of people, the business, the company, or the bottom line?* If petty political issues are disturbing one team, the forum may well be the team itself. But if the shadow-side issue involves, let us say, the integrity of the firm itself, then a range of forums might be called for. Recently, charges of fraud and deceitful practices have hit securities and insurance firms. The images of these firms have suffered greatly. The culture that allowed this to take place needs to be addressed not only at the very top but in every management forum down the line.

• *Which forum will be most efficient?* In these days of flatter organizations, increased delegation, and empowerment, the forum closest to the shadow-side issue may well be the forum of choice. If a line worker is caught in some misdemeanor, then his or her immediate supervisor is probably the forum of choice.

Forum overkill should be avoided. In one case, a highly

skilled and productive employee was found violating a number of different rules. Ultimately, his immediate supervisor felt incapable of dealing with him yet did not want to fire him because of his contributions. And so she brought in her boss. In another case, a manager heard from a couple of different sources that one of his subordinates was engaging in activity that might possibly be construed as sexual harassment. He took a preventive approach. He was chatting with the subordinate in question at the beginning of the Christmas party. They talked about the usual for a while, but before moving on, the manager, making sure that no one could overhear, said, "By the way, something off the record. There have been a few rumblings or grumblings from a couple of women about you. Nothing very specific. Nothing official. Just thought that you should know and handle it yourself." That ended the problem. There was no need to bring the issue into a formal one-on-one meeting.

Initiate Discussion Assertively and Tactfully

Savvy managers, understanding the roots of shadow-side defensiveness, find constructive ways to begin addressing shadow-side issues in appropriate forums. The two key competencies needed to do this are *assertiveness* and *tact*.

   Many managers are not as assertive as they might be in dealing with business and organizational problems and opportunities. This lack of assertiveness is even more pronounced in the case of shadow-side issues. Too many managers will allow a difficult person to remain difficult and disruptive of the work of others. Too many managers allow decisions based on the politics of self-interest to pass. Too many allow system-limiting informal arrangements to stay in place. For instance, currently members of boards of directors are under fire for failure to deal with the CEO when they see the company getting out of kilter. While it is not their job to intrude into day-to-day management, it is their job to confront and even remove him or her when he or she is placing the business in jeopardy. Many need to become more assertive for business and not just legal reasons. They often know what's in the shadows but choose to stay silent.

Assertiveness on shadow-side issues is needed in nonprofit as well as in for-profit institutions. Consider the following case. A member of the clinical psychology faculty of a university in the Northeast decided that it was time to buck the departmental culture. There was a long history of sweeping sensitive issues under the rug. In a faculty meeting toward the end of the school year he reported not only that two of his students were doing poorly in his course but also that he had some doubts about their overall ability to function as clinical psychologists. He was especially worried because these two students would be graduating soon. Gradually, one faculty member after another recounted negative experiences they had had with these same students. But up to that point no one had said anything in a decision-making forum. Their lack of assertiveness in bringing questions about these students' professionalism to a proper forum was an indictment of their own professionalism. The chairman of the department convened a committee, and the two cases were investigated. The students were warned, but went on to graduate. Later on, one of these gentlemen found himself in trouble with the law.

The way in which shadow-side issues are brought forward is often just as important as surfacing them assertively in the first place. The assertive manager, of course, is not to be confused with the aggressive manager. The latter tends to put people on the defensive and create resistance. There are plenty of managers who are ready to tell people what to do. Too many. Tact keeps assertiveness from becoming aggression. Since many shadow-side issues are politically, socially, and psychologically sensitive, a certain delicacy in dealing with them is called for. The manager who has to deal with someone engaging in self-serving politics does not have an easy task. Effective managers know what to bring into the light and what to leave in the shadows. Since, as we have seen, some covert arrangements add value to the business while others add cost, managers might well look the other way in the case of the former and deal with the latter case by case through a cost-benefit analysis. Should Pandora's box be opened or not? Sometimes it is better to leave things alone, but for the right reasons. There are economic benefits to right-minded tact.

In one company, a senior manager whose business had become lackluster and who had become a thorn in the side of both his own group and senior management was accused, though not publicly, of sexual harassment. In the quiet negotiations that ensued, he agreed to a severance package—a package much lower than the one he would have received had he stayed for two more years and retired at the normal time. Those who accused him of harassment were pleased that the company had moved so quickly. While a number of people suspected something, nothing surfaced that publicly tarnished the reputation of the individual or the image of the company. In a way, everybody won. The shadow-side issues were identified, managers moved quickly but not aggressively, the whole matter was handled with consummate tact, those who alleged they had been harassed were listened to carefully, the manager was challenged, and negotiation brought the whole process to a successful conclusion.

Use Shared Problem-Solving Methodology

Shared frameworks, models, and methods are powerful managerial tools. Recently, one large company claimed that one of the principal sources of its managerial strength lay in the fact that the firm had a shared model of problem solving that everyone learned and used on every problem that arose. The shared process together with its shared language allowed managers to attack problems with a focus and an intensity that would have been the envy of its competitors had they known of it. Many companies are only beginning to awaken to the value of such shared processes.

Shared problem-solving methodology, whether applied to shadow-side issues or to other managerial challenges, involves the judicious use of the following set of guidelines:

- Gather the organizational players who should be involved in the process.
- Identify problems, issues, concerns, difficulties, unused potential, or unexploited opportunities.
- Choose issues that have leverage potential—that is, problems or unexploited opportunities that, if managed, will make a substantive contribution to the institution.

- After exploring an issue and its causes, get a clear idea of the preferred scenario or end state. That is, answer the question, What will be in place when the problem is solved or managed that is not in place now?
- Determine which key stakeholders will be affected by the preferred scenario and get them involved.
- Devise value-adding action strategies or pathways to the solution or resolution of the problem or the development of the unexploited opportunity.
- Bring these strategies together in a lean, pragmatic, and viable plan of action.
- Name the key factors that will lead to the successful implementation of the plan.
- Execute the plan in such a way that it produces results that are sustainable.

This process is spelled out in greater detail elsewhere (Egan, 1993). Not all of these steps are necessary for every problem. Nor is the order in which the steps are presented here necessarily the order in which they are used in managing actual problems. Rather the steps are guidelines, and it may be necessary to move back and forth among them.

The spirit of the above process was used to manage the following case. A company, faced with an unexpected cash-flow problem, discovered that its chief financial officer had taken his eye off the ball. Difficulties in his private life had resulted in his giving less than half his time and energy to the business. Worse, the decisions he was making were clouded and flawed. All this had been well hidden under a number of smokescreens. It was a messy shadow-side crisis. A senior corrective-action team, using the methodology outlined above, put the CFO on leave and got him some help, quickly assessed the nature and extent of the damage, quietly obtained the collaboration of banks and suppliers as key stakeholders, drew up an outline of the immediate damage control package, cut through bureaucratic processes to put the package in place, and stemmed the hemorrhaging. Finally, they went on to do what the very best problem solvers do: they turned the crisis into an opportunity to realign the role, structure, and processes of the financial operations department. The second state, a year down the road, was better than the pre-crisis state. This is an excellent example of not just containing but leveraging a problem situation. The point here is this: the fact that they all worked from the same problem management process helped them move quickly and efficiently to a successful conclusion.

Some problems, of course, are more difficult to handle than others. What makes them so difficult are the kinds of blind spots and avoidance tactics discussed in Chapter Two, along with other shadow-side factors. In such cases, double-loop learning can help immensely.

Use Double-Loop Learning

What Chris Argyris (1982) called "double-loop" learning or problem solving complements the problem management process outlined above, making it a powerful tool for dealing with covert, undiscussed, and undiscussable issues. A *single-loop problem* is one that is clear and straightforward. An example is a business mistake that is evident and that organizational players really want to clear up. Such problems are amenable to straightforward problem management. An illustration: "We miscalculated the strength of our main competitor when we formulated our strategy. But now that we see our mistake, we can reset our strategy."

On the other hand, a *double-loop problem* is one that is murky rather than clear. Its murkiness comes from such things as false assumptions about the problem itself, political maneuverings among the players, and norms from the covert culture—in short, from the shadow side. An example: "When it comes to implementation of human resource initiatives around here, we frequently do not do what we say we're going to do. It's happening right now with the pay-for-performance initiative. Everyone wants it, but it's going nowhere." In the case of double-loop issues, it is essential to step back and look at what is causing the problem as well as what is motivating the problem solvers. Double-loop problem management is a corrective process that goes to a deeper level. Working with just the surface symptoms of a double-loop problem does no good.

Here is a brief case through which the principles of double-

loop learning and problem solving are illustrated. The senior managers of the electronic products division of a larger company handed
off a new marketing and sales strategy to the sales group. During
the first quarter of the new year, sales went down some ten points.
The senior managers swarmed all over the salespeople, accusing
them of sloppy work and dropping the ball. Even though the sales
personnel seemed duly chastened, sales dipped another five points
the next quarter. Alarm bells went off. A consultant helped the
problem-solving group apply the following double-loop principles:

- *Get the assumptions about the problem or issue into the
open; publicly test them.* In a series of meetings a consultant helped
the senior managers identify a number of mistaken assumptions
about the marketing and sales problem. Some of these assumptions
were that all key players, especially those in the sales department,
had been consulted during the formulation of the new strategy, that
everyone understood the new strategy, and that the current problem
was merely one of poor execution. None of these assumptions was
true.

- *Help the group reformulate any mistaken assumptions.*
Once the false assumptions had been blown out of the water, it was
time to formulate and test some new ones. One that emerged rather
quickly was, "This is not a sales strategy or execution problem but
a management problem." That is, senior marketing managers had
not done the groundwork needed to formulate the kind of strategy
that everyone, especially the executers, could work with.

- *Clarify the ambiguities in the motivation of the players
involved.* The testing of this new hypothesis uncovered the questionable motivation of several managers. Two of the senior marketing managers who led the charge in blaming the sales force for the
failure needed fall guys. These two bullies, the director of marketing
and a senior member of the director's team, had secretly conned the
head of the electronic products division into agreeing to the new
sales strategy before it had been discussed with the larger marketing
and sales group. Whenever an objection arose from a member of the
sales group, the two would intimate that they were carrying out the
wishes of the department head. If the strategy had succeeded, these
two would have been heroes. They would have taken all the credit.
Now that the strategy had failed, they wanted to blame the sales

force. While it was also true that the director of sales, furious because the strategy had been high-handedly pushed through, had dragged his feet and had inadequately prepared his troops, this was not a major cause of the failure. Even though he wanted the strategy to fail so that the bullies would get their comeuppance, it would have failed anyway.

• *See whether there are any incongruities in the processes being used to deal with the issue.* During one meeting, the bullies tried to get the division director to restrict the discussion to the ineptness of the director of sales. But when a consultant helped the group review the entire strategy formulation process, the faults of the secret planning process and of the sales strategy itself soon became clear.

• *Surface withheld information.* It was discovered that the data from a couple of marketing studies that challenged the direction of the new sales strategy had been withheld. The principal sponsors of the sales strategy claimed that this had been an "oversight."

• *Collect and put in order any scattered information that is relevant to the problem.* When all the data were assembled, the roots of the failure were clear. The bullies had tried to keep the information scattered—the results of the preliminary marketing studies were an example of this—but the consultant and, ultimately, the division director kept pushing for the whole picture. In the end, it was clear that it was a marketing management rather than a sales problem. While the bullies were not dismissed, they lost favor with the division director and lost face with their own troops. Both left the company within a year.

This kind of murky double-loop problem is not uncommon. The purpose of the double-loop process is not to find the culprits—poor problem solvers look for someone to blame while good ones look for solutions—but to uncover the dynamics that stood in the way of an institution-enhancing solution. Managing shadow-side issues often involves getting at false assumptions, surfacing incongruities, discovering hidden incentives, digging out hidden facts, and putting the pieces of the puzzle together. The importance of economic analysis is clear. Since all this work constitutes a substantive investment, the process must lead to some substantive payoff.

Emphasize Prevention

The economics of prevention are far more favorable than the economics of cure. In health care, better prevention programs would save the country billions of dollars per year. Some companies have learned this lesson. They have found that so-called wellness programs pay for themselves many times over in health care savings. The quality movement is an effort to move from cure to prevention. When well executed, such programs add great value.

Prevention makes more sense than cure in dealing with shadow-side activities and arrangements also. For instance, one company moved to team-based pay in part to put an end to the political self-interest games individuals were playing. While this dramatically reduced politicking on the part of individuals, managers noticed an increase in business-limiting interteam rivalry. In another preventive move the reward system was changed once more to include effective interteam collaboration.

What, then, keeps the world from moving en masse from cure to prevention? One key factor is that prevention is not very exciting. Bypass surgery has lots of drama. And its value is often seen immediately; that is, the incentives are loud and clear. But for many eventual heart patients, daily attention to diet and exercise is boring no matter what the advertisements for diet programs and fitness centers say. The incentives are not that compelling. Indeed, when a prevention program works, nothing happens. For instance, in shadow-side terms, it would mean that dysfunctional cultural norms don't take root. The challenge is to find ways of making prevention exciting rather than boring. The best preventive approach, of course, is to make the company, institution, or unit a winner. The winning spirit is often contagious.

Savvy managers, when starting a project or making an important decision, try to anticipate the consequences by asking themselves, directly or indirectly, the following prevention-oriented shadow-side questions:

- What are the hidden stumbling blocks?
- How will X (some difficult person) react?
- What silent arrangements will throw this project off course?

- How disruptive will this project be to current social arrangements?
- What power plays will be initiated by key individuals? key units?
- How compatible is this course of action with the covert culture?
- What inertia will we run into?

"Forewarned is forearmed" is a critical guiding principle. In the end, however, there are no magic formulas for managing the shadow side—just courage and hard work.

We now move on to the shadow-side categories outlined in Chapter One. Since culture is the broadest and most controlling aspect of the shadow-side system, providing norms for all the other categories, it is where we will start. Chapter Five outlines a framework for understanding culture and how it works. Chapter Six suggests strategies for challenging and changing the dysfunctional aspects of an institution's current culture.

REVEALING YOUR
ORGANIZATION'S
HIDDEN CULTURE

5

"THE WAY WE DO THINGS HERE": A PRIMER OF BELIEFS, VALUES, AND NORMS

T HE FOLLOWING TWO QUOTES tell the sad tale of the cost of an organizational culture that does not serve the business. The first is from a *Wall Street Journal* article dated April 7, 1986: "IBM towers over its competitors, the object of imitation, awe, envy, and accusations that it's just too powerful for the world's good. The advantages of size are especially clear now, as the [computer] industry enters a second painful year of slower growth. Downturns don't shake IBM's faith in the industry's future. It simply weathers the storm better than others. . . . Powerhouses in other industries once played similar roles, only to stumble before foreign competitors, tempestuous unions, bureaucratic management, or economic forces beyond their control. But IBM shows no sign of faltering" (Marcom, p. 15). In the second quote we hear Louis Gerstner, IBM's new CEO, talking about the company's culture in a *Business Week* article of October 4, 1993: "I have never seen a company that is so introspective, caught up in its own underwear, so preoccupied with internal processes. . . . People in this company tell me it's easier doing business with people outside the company than inside. I would call that an indictment" ("Rethinking IBM," p. 88). The company's culture played a key role in bringing the giant to its knees.

Culture—"the way we do things here"—has been called the broadest and most controlling shadow-side category because it dictates the norms for doing everything, whether related to business, organizational, managerial, or leadership activities. Cultural norms set limits to activities in all the other shadow-side dimensions. Managing culture is one of the manager's unwritten responsibilities. This chapter provides a framework for understanding the dynamics of culture. The next outlines practical ways of managing culture. Together they provide managers with a jump start toward making culture an asset instead of a liability.

Culture—What Is It?

Some years ago I was working with one of the Baby Bell companies. After the divestiture from AT&T, they needed to fashion a culture aligned with the new, much more competitive world into which they were moving. My contact, the vice president of human resources, noted that this task was so important that the company's president had included it among his key responsibilities. He went on to say that the senior managers of the company discussed the culture regularly at their executive committee meetings. After listening carefully, I said that I had two hypotheses. The first was that each of these gentlemen—at the time they were all gentlemen—had his own idea of what culture was, since the group had probably not taken the time to determine a common working definition of culture. A slight smile crossed his face. "My second hypothesis," I went on to say, "is that all of these personal understandings of culture are vague." His smile broadened but stopped short of a chuckle.

I asked him why I was talking to him rather than to the president, since the latter was taking leadership in culture transformation. After a bit of hemming and hawing, he said that "a lot of it" had been delegated to him because the president was "so busy." My fear was that the president did indeed believe culture was important but did not have the tools needed to understand and deal with it. And so he delegated the task.

If managing culture is a vague task, then managers will pay little attention to it. Therefore, it is essential that managers have a shared framework for understanding and working with culture. Few companies have such a framework. It is assumed that everyone knows what culture is.

Let's start with a simple definition of culture as it relates to behavior within a company or institution. Culture encompasses shared beliefs, values, and norms insofar as they drive shared patterns of behavior—"the way we do things here." Four principles summarize culture: (1) shared *patterns of behavior* constitute the bottom line of culture, (2) shared *assumptions and beliefs* are the foundation of culture, (3) shared *values* provide the criteria for making decisions, and (4) shared *norms* are the immediate drivers of the patterns of behavior that constitute culture.

Culture, then, has a "thinking" side—the shared beliefs, values, and norms—and a "doing" side, the patterns of behavior that this kind of thinking drives. Let's start with the bottom line of culture, the institution's shared patterns of behavior.

Shared Patterns of Behavior

The bottom line of culture is "the way we do things here," the habitual ways of carrying out business, organizational, managerial, supervisory, and leadership tasks and activities—the shared patterns of behavior. For instance, one manager said to me, "Strategy is king around here. If you're unclear about how to translate the strategy into practical guidelines for your unit, you had better clear it up quickly." In that company a division head was demoted; he had made a lot of money for the company but in doing so had violated the company's strategy. Failure to understand the real rules of the game did him in. Though the strategy itself had been freely discussed, the rules of playing it out in the organization had never been defined.

Culture permeates every behavioral aspect of the business— "the way we do strategy around here" or "the way we pursue quality around here," "the way we make decisions around here" or "the way we recruit people around here," "the way managers spend their time around here" or "the way supervisors relate to employees around here." Patterns of behavior in the following categories of organizational activity can significantly enhance or limit a company's effectiveness:

- A viable *strategy* provides clear-cut focus and direction for the entire enterprise and each of its units.
- A coordinated set of *operations*—work processes and programs—translates strategy into high-quality products and services that provide value for internal and external customers.
- A straightforward *organizational structure* serves the business by optimizing information sharing, decision making, and work flow.
- Flexible *jobs,* based on strategic and operational needs, are designed to channel value-adding work.
- Informed interunit and intraunit *teams,* with a solid understanding of both company and unit strategy, deliver value-adding outcomes.
- Well-designed *human resource management systems* are effectively used by managers and supervisors to get the right people, socialize them into both strategy and culture, equip them with the right competencies, and deploy them usefully throughout the structure—the right person with the right skills in the right job in the right unit.
- An effective *management system* is used to get and develop the right set of managers—that is, managers who are good at executing these master tasks and helping people give their best.
- There is a critical mass of *leaders* at all levels of the organization who play a critical role in fostering the kind of institution-enhancing innovation and change that keep the company on the cutting edge.

Cultural behavior patterns in each of these categories can either limit or enhance a business. Here are some examples, taken from companies in different industries, of *institution-limiting* patterns of behavior:

- *Strategy:* "We formulate strategy here, but then do little about it. It has always just floated on the top, disconnected from everything else. No one really takes it seriously."
- *Operations:* "We give lip service to customer service but never really do anything about it. We put up posters about it, but don't deliver, at least in a consistent way."

- *Structure:* "We continually let the decision-making process drag on and on here. At times it seems that no one is in charge. And I'm not sure that anyone cares."
- *Human resource management systems:* "We always get the best people, but then we leave them to their own devices. We almost *dare* them to succeed."
- *Management/supervision:* "You don't need 'people' skills here. If in doubt, be tough. No manager has even been fired for not listening to good ideas from subordinates."
- *Leadership:* "When leadership below the executive level emerges here, we squash it. So if you get some bright ideas, keep them to yourself."

Since these patterns of behavior remained undiscussed in forums that could make a difference, they inhibited the performance of the companies.

Of course, cultural patterns can also have a positive effect. Here are some examples of *institution-enhancing patterns of behavior:*

- *Strategy:* "We formulate strategy here by tapping into the wisdom of those middle managers who will be responsible for implementing it. As a result, most of our managers own the company strategy and sell it to the troops."
- *Operations:* "It's taken a long time, but just about everyone around here thinks in terms of quality now. It's in the bones and marrow of the company. But still, we never take it for granted."
- *Structure:* "We don't pay much attention to the organization boxes here. We readily cross organizational lines to get things done."
- *Human resource management systems:* "Development around here is a must. Just about every manager rises to the development challenge. The value of our human assets increases every year. People do more things and do them better."
- *Management/supervision:* "We choose savvy managers. They understand the relationship between productivity and quality of work life. They are good at achieving the right balance."
- *Leadership:* "Everyone around here tries to improve the work in

his or her unit. It's just in the air. The place is filled with improvement champions."

The expression "a culture of . . . " is a useful tool for describing specific patterns of behavior in an institution. In one company, there was a "culture of obedience"—that is, the working assumptions, beliefs, values, and norms of the firm conspired to produce consistent patterns of almost unquestioning obedience. There was relatively little grumbling when an unpopular directive came forth from senior managers. People tended to swallow hard and get on with it. There were practically no attempts to sabotage orders that came down the line. Workers were paid decently, and they saw themselves as "good soldiers" who rallied around the strategies of their commanders. At times this culture of obedience served the company's interests; at others it did not. As the company entered into more turbulent and competitive times—times calling for ingenuity and initiative—unquestioning obedience slowed the company down. The company needed to become much more flexible, but it was very difficult for it to rid itself of the old culture. It was in the company's bones.

On a more positive note, Pepsico is described as having a "culture of growth" (Magnet, 1994). International growth is so important to the success of the company that their managers "have growth stamped on their foreheads" (p. 70). The company's CEO points out how such a culture serves the business: "You need growth not just for its immediate financial reward but also to keep your management team energized and renewed with fresh talent, so you can stay vibrant for the future" (p. 71). In static companies, gifted managers leave, begin to focus on trivial bureaucratic details, or get embroiled in internal politics, vying with one another instead of with the competition. This is the beginning of the end.

Shared Assumptions and Beliefs

Undergirding behavior patterns is the "thinking" side of culture. Some say that the foundation, the deepest part of culture lies in the shared assumptions, beliefs, understandings, tenets, creed, philosophy, and dogmas of the system. The Johnson & Johnson mission statement begins with the company's central belief: "We believe our first responsibility is to the doctors, nurses and patients, to the mothers and fathers and all others who use our products and services." On the other hand, don't be misled by such high-sounding words as beliefs, tenets, and dogmas. A belief can be crass. A partner in a law firm, interviewing a candidate, shocked the young woman by saying, "No matter what you read in our fancy brochures, never forget that around here the dollar is king. The sooner you see that it drives everything we do, the better off you'll be."

Common beliefs espoused by companies include: "Our people are our most important assets," "Our customers are our primary reason for existence," "We believe that profit is not a goal but only a sign of how well we serve you," "Quality is everything," "Without trust we are nothing," and so forth. As you read these, you may well find the cynic in you stirring a bit. As we shall see later, there may well be a set of covert beliefs that temper this more high-minded set, or it may well be that these beliefs are only window dressing.

Sometimes the terms *beliefs* and *assumptions* are used interchangeably. However, unlike beliefs, which may or may not be published—the J&J belief noted above is published, while the crass belief of the law firm, for obvious reasons, is not—shared cultural assumptions are usually not stated publicly. Often they are not even noticed. And it can happen that there are as many assumptions as there are people involved. Take the case of a Midwest career-counseling center that targeted midcareer ministers. It was funded by a variety of Christian religious organizations. At one meeting of the board of trustees—composed of two or more members of each of the religious denominations that supported the center—the facilitator, perhaps in an off moment, suggested that the best way to clarify a problem being discussed would be to "take a few minutes" to chart the basic assumptions that the people in the room had about the center, its business, and the way it organized itself. The few minutes turned into a few hours. Dozens of assumptions leapt onto flip charts. Some were heatedly debated on the spot, even though the facilitator had asked the participants to "postpone discussion on the assumptions you generate till later."

It quickly became clear that the sponsors of the center held all sorts of conflicting assumptions about its purpose, operation, and organization. For instance, one group assumed that the center should help clients rethink their ministerial roles and make a decision whether they wanted to continue in the ministry or not. Others assumed just the opposite. The purpose of the center, in their minds, was to reinforce their clients' choice of a ministerial vocation. If the group had stuck to the basic Christian beliefs and values that were assumed to guide the work of the center, there would have been relatively little debate. Once the door was opened to any assumption that anyone had with respect to any dimension of the center, all hell broke loose.

The point is that assumptions generate patterns of behavior. These may or may not serve the best interests of the company. Therefore, uncovering assumptions can be an important part of managing culture.

Shared Values

Shared values are the ideas the company or institution prizes and therefore acts on. As such, values are both criteria for making decisions and drivers of behavior. For instance, a company for which customer service is a primary value constantly searches for ways to cement relationships with customers, meet their needs, and delight them.

Shared values serve the business goals of the organization. At least this is the ideal. I once asked the managers of an international agricultural center that focused on the irrigation needs of developing companies to declare what their business values were. They said that one important value was "working at the highest possible level within any given developing country." As a group, they believed that they did more good when they worked with the irrigation ministry, if there was one, than when they worked, say, with local farmer groups. Influencing changes in policies and practices in the irrigation ministry often took longer, but the impact in the farmers' fields was, in the longer term, better. However, they also discovered that a shadow-side entrepreneurial culture displaced this officially espoused culture. Many of their professional field workers, gifted with an entrepreneurial spirit, liked working with farmer groups and individual farmers. They hated the bureaucracies of the irrigation ministries. While they were doing good work, they were not having the total impact they could have. Entrepreneurialism did not add as much value as did focused country work.

Amoco Corporation, in reorienting itself strategically in the early 1990s, paid special attention to values as a way of refocusing its culture. The corporation first outlined what an explicit set of values would do for the institution. A set of values would define the fundamental character of the organization; create a sense of identity; provide guidelines for implementing company practices, policies, and procedures; establish a framework for assessing the effectiveness of this implementation; determine how resources would be allocated; provide both guidance and motivation; and reduce confusion and second-guessing throughout the system. The corporation then went on to describe what these values should look like. They should focus on a preferred state of affairs, avoid both generalities and specifics that are overly restrictive, be capable of withstanding "hard times," apply to all members of the system, and be consistently modeled by all managers, beginning with senior managers. Note the strong behavioral feel of the latter guidelines.

Amoco Corporation considers technology leadership one of its key business values or strategic drivers. Not only does Amoco pursue the development of technology in its own research centers but it also buys companies and establishes joint ventures to acquire needed technology. The company, through its R&D unit and its subsidiaries, develops technologies that serve new-product development and process improvement. They want to be technology leaders in the integrated oil business.

There is no values formula. Each company needs to establish and nourish the set of values that serves its business.

Shared Norms

Beliefs and assumptions interact with values and beget norms. Norms, in turn, stimulate behavior. Norms are the oughts, shoulds, musts, do's, don'ts, standards, policies, rules, principles, regulations, directives, laws, and taboos that govern the behavior of the system as a whole, of the subunits within the system, and of the

members of the system individually. Norms are extremely important because they sit on the edge of behavior. Norms and standards
spell out the kinds of behaviors that will be rewarded in the system
and set limits on the kinds of behavior that will be tolerated.

The interplay between beliefs and values ideally leads to
business-enhancing norms, as shown in the following examples
drawn from a midsize company putting its toes in the waters of
global markets:

- *Belief:* The company believed that globalization was a necessity
  for survival and growth.
- *Value:* A key value was open communication. The company
  valued the free flow of both creative ideas and corrective
  feedback.
- *Norm:* "Get everyone from top to bottom to think globally. Give
  a global twist to all internal communication. In coming up with
  ideas for new products, think of global markets and niches.
  Drive out parochial thinking wherever it surfaces."

Of course, the interplay between beliefs and values can lead
to institution-limiting norms, that, for obvious reasons, remain undiscussed. Here's how this dynamic played out in a telecommunications firm:

- *Belief:* There was an assumption, probably based on experience,
  that bosses did not want to hear bad news and would tend to
  "tar" the bearer in some way.
- *Value:* One of the primary unstated values in the company was
  personal security.
- *Norm:* "If anything goes wrong, look the other way. If you can't
  look the other way, don't tell anyone about what you saw."

This norm stifled communication and had an unnoticed but negative impact on productivity. Nothing was done about this until a
total quality management program was introduced. The consultants soon discovered the buried norm and challenged it publicly.
They pointed out that people needed to be *rewarded* for ferreting

out processes and procedures that stood in the way of doing things right the first time.

Overt and Covert Culture

The beliefs, values, and norms of a company's culture may or may not be published. Furthermore, even if they are published, they may or may not drive behavior. Covert or unpublished norms may be the real drivers of behavior. Culture has a distinctive shadow side. Let's take a look at what's out in the open and what remains undiscussed but powerful.

Overt or Espoused Culture

The espoused culture is the set of beliefs, values, and norms the company publicly endorses together with the policies and practices that flow from them. Beliefs, values, and norms are overt if they are in the public consciousness of the institution, noted in some public way, written down in public documents, discussed or even debated in a public forum, and/or celebrated in some public way. In theory this means that they can be challenged precisely because they are "in the open."

More and more companies publish their espoused beliefs and values. It is the company's way of saying, "This is who we are and what we stand for." Here is Johnson & Johnson's espoused culture, the Johnson & Johnson Credo, as published in a recruitment brochure.

> We believe our first responsibility is to the doctors, nurses and patients, to the mothers and fathers and all others who use our products and services. In meeting their needs everything we do must be of high quality. We must constantly strive to reduce our costs in order to maintain reasonable prices. Customers' orders must be serviced promptly and accurately. Our suppliers and distributors must have an opportunity to make a fair profit.
>
> We are responsible to our employees, the men

and women who work with us throughout the world. Everyone must be considered as an individual. We must respect their dignity and recognize their merit. They must have a sense of security in their jobs. Compensation must be fair and adequate, and working conditions clean, orderly and safe. We must be mindful of ways to help our employees fulfill their family responsibilities. Employees must feel free to make suggestions and complaints. There must be an equal opportunity for employment, development and advancement for those qualified. We must provide competent management, and their actions must be just and ethical.

We are responsible to the communities in which we live and work and to the world community as well. We must be good citizens—support good works and charities and bear our fair share of taxes. We must encourage civic improvements and better health and education. We must maintain in good order the property we are privileged to use, protecting the environment and natural resources.

Our final responsibility is to our stockholders. Business must make a sound profit. We must experiment with new ideas. Research must be carried on, innovative programs developed and mistakes paid for. New equipment must be purchased, new facilities provided and new products launched. Reserves must be created to provide for adverse times. When we operate according to these principles, the stockholders should realize a fair return.

Documents such as this are invariably high-minded. This credo describes preferred states, a set of ideals the company is striving for. These ideals also serve a very practical purpose. Johnson & Johnson was commended at the time of the Tylenol poisoning crisis for implementing this creed quickly and thoroughly. The fact that the company lived up to its espoused beliefs and values during a crisis greatly enhanced its public image.

The Shadow Side of the Espoused Culture

The shadow side of the espoused culture lies in a company's failure to get its publicly endorsed beliefs, values, and norms to drive behavior. Fanciful espoused values give way, in practice, to the real values, the company's values in use. One institution, deciding to push empowerment, set out a package of beliefs, values, and norms around this concept. The whole exercise proved to be a charade. Managers began using different language, but there was no real shared authority or decision making. Those lower on the totem pole began grumbling about this. But they were branded "cynical" and accused of not being "team players." Tacked onto the empowerment package was a covert rider that said something like this: "Anyone who complains about what we're doing is being disloyal and demonstrates by complaining that he or she is not committed to the empowerment process."

The actual patterns of behavior found in an organization tell us what the organization really believes, prizes, encourages, and sanctions. For instance, many organizations state that the people who work there are their most important resource. This does not mean that they live this out in the ways in which they treat their workers. A social service center claimed that its staff members constituted its most important resource, but managers provided them with little positive feedback, resisted innovative ideas that came from staff, and had a covert expectation that staff members would put in more hours than they were paid for. The espoused value—championing people—was not a value in use. It had little impact on managerial behavior.

A bit of humor to illustrate one further point: A conglomerate was in the process of choosing a new CEO. Since a number of people were in the running, they took advantage of meetings to do a little campaigning. One was giving a talk to middle managers. At the end he unfortunately asked for questions. "What do you stand for?" someone asked. Obviously what he stood for had not come across during his talk. A bit taken aback, he said, "Well, I stand for those seven values that this company has always proudly stood for." He began to name them. Getting stuck after three, he whined, "Come on, guys, give me a little help here." Needless to say, he was not the one chosen. The point is, even when the official culture is published, don't count on everyone's knowing what it is or is supposed to be.

Most individuals and most organizations from time to time espouse more than they deliver. There is nothing particularly sinister about that. Nor is it a cause for cynicism. It is part of the reality of the human condition. Few organizations look at the psychological or social economics of a pattern of failure to deliver on explicit promises. Such a pattern cheapens the workplace and creates a climate of distrust. Psychological anguish and social disruption, however, are often seen as free, without cost. In one hospital the cost was a lengthy and bitter strike by nurses that brought the hospital to the verge of financial collapse.

Covert Culture

Covert culture—the beliefs, values, and norms that are not named, at least not publicly, but that nevertheless drive patterns of behavior—affects all institutions. Because these beliefs, values, and norms are not publicly discussed, they lie outside ordinary managerial processes and often have a negative impact on the business. Here are some examples.

The CEO of a company with some six thousand employees published a document called "Managing People." It provided principles and guidelines to enable managers to help employees give their best. When asked in private, the CEO admitted that this document was something that he had to publish to "keep the company contemporary," but it was clear that he did not have much interest in the substance of the document. The management development group mounted courses to help managers develop the attitudes and competencies needed to implement the managing-people manifesto. The courses proved popular and were widely discussed and praised. About a year later an "inquiry" was conducted by the vice president of personnel into a "possible conspiracy" on the part of the management development group to subvert the "deeper values" of the institution. The newer overt values being pushed by the management development program were apparently counter to the entrenched covert managerial values. One can only imagine the hushed conversations behind closed doors that led to the inquiry. While the inquiry failed to prove any kind of conspiracy, it did sensitize the management development group and others to the shadow side of the company's culture. In that sense the inquiry backfired. The price of this culture-based conflict? The director of the management development unit quit. Three of the best members of the unit left shortly after. They were replaced by hacks. The quality of the development program plummeted.

Often, a culture embraces several covert, company-limiting norms. Most of the passengers on a large cruise ship had gone ashore to visit a Caribbean island. The crew held a fire drill. After it was over, one of the crew members asked an officer as he was walking by, "How'd we do, sir?" The only response was a reluctant "OK." There were looks of disappointment among the crew members who had heard the exchange. The same crew member shouted after the officer, "Hey, sir, it was good!" The officer, without turning, muttered, "Yeah, good," and walked on. The norm was clear: "We don't give positive feedback here." Later, poor service, sloppiness, and arrogance made it clear that the crew members had some norms of their own: "Do what is in your own best interest," "Treat passengers like the nuisances they are," and "Get away with what you can." Perhaps the crew culture was a reaction to the officer culture. At any rate, while the officers and the crew might have deserved each other, the passengers, in the middle, were the losers. They voted with their feet. This ship had one of the lowest return rates in the industry.

A common cultural norm is one that makes certain issues undiscussable. In a large urban hospital, department heads felt mistreated by a vice president but believed that they could do nothing about it. They discussed their feelings freely with one another and with a consultant, yet they refused to discuss their concerns in a retreat with higher management. "We don't talk about things like this here" was the unwritten norm. How costly was this distress? Turnover in this hospital was twice that of a sister hospital.

Such cultures are costly, but the costs, like the beliefs, values, and norms behind them, are hidden. According to industry-observer consensus, IBM has fallen in great part because it failed to see that it had a covert culture it could not afford, one that blinded it to the realities of the marketplace.

Strong, Weak, and Adaptive Cultures

The degree to which overt and covert beliefs, values, and norms actually influence and drive behavior can vary greatly. This gives rise to strong, weak, and adaptive cultures. Strong cultures, whether company enhancing or company limiting, drive behavior consistently. Weak cultures do not. Adaptive cultures are usually strong cultures that are flexible enough to meet the changing needs of the business.

Strong Cultures

A company's culture is strong if the following conditions prevail:

- A well-defined set of beliefs, values, and norms are firmly in place.
- The beliefs, values, and norms are shared by a critical mass of the members of the institution.
- The shared norms consistently drive behavior.
- The resulting patterns of behavior resist forces of change over time.

Craig Torres, writing in the *Wall Street Journal* (August 31, 1993), discussed technology companies called "cannibals." These are fierce competitors with a "savage entrepreneurial appetite" (pp. C1–C2). Such companies are quite willing to destroy the past in order to create the future. Intel, a world leader in computer chips, is such a company. It not only launched fierce legal attacks on companies that were cloning its 386 chips but also cut prices and cannibalized its own line by rolling out a new generation of chips. In the words of one industry observer, Intel not only moves fast but destroys the pavement behind it. Intel's entrepreneurial and competitive culture is very strong. It drives both corporate and individual behavior.

A company can be said to have a strong *overt* culture if its espoused beliefs, values, and norms consistently drive behavior.

United Parcel Service is said to have a strong overt culture. In the early 1990s, facing stiff competition, the company decided to overhaul its business culture. The covert norm was, "We know what's best for our customers. They should follow our guidelines." Customer service was poor, they refused to give volume discounts as their competitors did, and they focused on residential rather than commercial deliveries. This way of doing things, however, was stalling the business. And so UPS developed a new business culture. The new way of doing things includes premier customer service, flexibility, the use of improved technology, and a focus on commercial business. The organizational culture that backs up its business strategies—a culture that focuses, sometimes maddeningly, they say, on efficiency—has long been strong. The company's workers are expected to "sweat brown" to get ahead—that is, they must consistently put into practice the firm's clearly stated values and exacting standards.

Many institutions have strong *covert* cultures in that unnamed and undiscussed beliefs, values, and norms consistently drive behavior. In a company mentioned earlier, one with a culture of obedience, norms such as the following consistently drove behavior:

- "If in doubt, do not act until you check with your boss."
- "Try to find out what is in the mind of your boss and then act on what you find."
- "If your boss rejects a proposal of yours, keep offering new ones until he finally accepts the one he wants. But don't expect him to tell you what he wants."

For obvious reasons, these norms were never openly stated, but a critical mass of company employees, when asked, knew what the real rules were and they obeyed them. This state of affairs persisted for years. The covert culture of obedience was very strong. Obviously, strong need not mean good.

Weak Cultures

Some companies have weak cultures. Cultures are weak when the following conditions prevail:

- There is no well-defined set of beliefs, values, and norms.
- Relatively few people share whatever beliefs, values, and norms are in use.
- Any norms that are in use sometimes drive behavior and sometimes do not. They are wishy-washy.
- The patterns of behavior that are driven by shared norms are easily changed.

Weak cultures can have a decidedly negative impact. One company wanted customer service as a strategic driver. After announcing this, they halfheartedly tried out several programs for a couple of years and, not unexpectedly, their customer service scores remained consistently low. Finally, they realized that they were not going to get a culture of customer service by merely stating what they wanted. So they published a document outlining what top-flight customer service in their industry required and circulated this document throughout the company. Again, nothing much happened, because merely establishing a well-defined set of espoused beliefs, values, and norms did little to drive out a culture of indifference to customer needs and replace it with a pattern of customer-focused behavior. Few people within the company made the new norms their own.

One month, a significant drop in sales accompanied the lowest customer service scores in the company's history. This galvanized everyone. The top one hundred managers of the company were grouped into problem-solving teams around key areas of customer service. The groups came up with a clear-cut set of action programs around each key area. Implementation teams were assigned. The performance management system was changed to include specific objectives for everyone. Customer service champions were singled out and rewarded. A bonus system based on both internal and external customer service activities, output, outcomes, and impact was established. Modeling customer service behaviors was required of every officer of the company. Only then did customer service scores begin to improve, and sales with them.

Adaptive Cultures

Cultures—even business-serving cultures—can be too strong for the good of the company. The ideal is that a culture be both strong and *flexible*. The world is changing too fast. Companies and institutions cannot afford cultures that are set in stone. They may serve the company today, but not tomorrow. John Kotter and James Heskett, in their book *Corporate Culture and Performance* (1992), talk about "adaptive cultures"—strong cultures that have the flexibility to meet tomorrow's challenges. Oil companies have traditionally had strong cultures, but they have not been that flexible. Most of them have moved into substantive culture-change programs over the past few years. Kotter and Heskett see this pattern. Companies, entrepreneurially driven, achieve a certain degree of success. Over time they move from an entrepreneurial and leadership to a bureaucratic focus. They become preoccupied with the internal workings of the company and become arrogant. They lose sight of customers and markets. Initiative is stifled. All this adds up to an unhealthy, nonadaptive, and ultimately expensive culture.

There are four main characteristics of an adaptive culture. First of all, a culture of vigilance is at the adaptive culture's core. Companies and institutions with adaptive cultures are constantly scanning the environment for threats, opportunities, and trends. Second, adaptive cultures are proactive rather than reactive. The question is not How do we keep up? but How do we move to the edge? When AT&T bid for McCaw Cellular, it was giving expression to its proactive culture. The company had no intention of just keeping up with its competitors; rather it was moving to the competitive edge. Third, companies with adaptive cultures know how to let go of the past. Adaptive companies know what to keep and what to leave behind. A whining, "But we have always done it this way!" is not heard in the halls. If the Baby Bells were to hold fast to the "good old days" when regulation and ownership of telephone wires meant stability, they would die. With the emergence of deregulation and bypass technology, the good old days ceased to exist. Fourth, companies with adaptive cultures do not fall victim to faddish reengineering of work processes. They are *continually* reengineering them. They don't occasionally clear out the attic. Rather they keep the attic clear and use the space for something productive.

Economics of Culture

Appropriate cultures add value rather than cost. Consider AT&T. When AT&T's chief executive, Robert Allen, came on board, culture transformation was high on his list. He knew that culture was not soft-side nonsense. He understood the pragmatic economics of the workplace too well. He set out to change those parts of the culture that did not serve the strategy. The various units of the telecommunications giant needed to become more customer focused and to develop internal supplier-customer relationships. This called for a new mode of discourse. They started to discuss the undiscussables. For instance, internal customers began telling internal suppliers precisely what was wrong with wares and service. Culture change thus far has turned the company into a lean, competitive, risk-taking global giant, pushing aggressively into wireless services, a technology it invented but failed to capitalize on partly because of its outmoded culture. In light of AT&T's recent $12 billion bid for McCaw Cellular, it is evident that Allen is modeling the kind of competitive risk taking that he wants to characterize the new AT&T culture.

More and more managers are convinced that strong yet adaptive cultures that support the business add great value, while cultures that divert the energy and resources of the company add cost. They see it every day in their own companies. They see larger-than-life examples in the IBMs and GMs of the world. They see the benefits of strong, adaptive cultures in such companies as Wal-Mart, Intel, Pepsico, and Motorola. The Kotter and Heskett book mentioned earlier summarizes the results of their study of the cultures of some two hundred companies. The results show that companies with strong adaptive cultures prospered in ways that others did not. Over an eleven-year period, companies with adaptive cultures geared to satisfying the changing demands of critical stakeholders such as customers, employees, and shareholders dramatically outperformed nonadaptive companies. Culture-sound companies increased sales over that period by an average of 682 percent, while culture-problematic companies increased sales by 166 percent. Stock performance told the same story. Over the same period the stock of culture-problematic companies was up some 74 percent, while the stock of culture-sound companies increased over 900 percent. To be successful, companies need more than a sound business strategy. They also need a culture that supports that strategy.

The questions remain: What keeps dysfunctional or problem cultures in place? And what can be done to reform them? These are the subjects of the next chapter.

6

MAKING THE CULTURE
SERVE YOUR BUSINESS

MANAGERS OF COMPANIES with cultures that do not serve the business must ask themselves, What can we do to challenge and change the culture? This chapter addresses that question. For some companies, changing the culture can mean life or death. One company, faced with both decreased market share and eroding margins, opted for an entirely new structure to bolster its refocused strategy. This highly decentralized structure demanded an entrepreneurial mind-set in the managers chosen to head up the new lean and mean business units. The problem was that entrepreneurialism had never been a part of the company's mainline culture. Speed, exploiting niche markets, risk taking, and doing more with less were now essential behaviors, but they were not the average manager's way of doing things. Therefore, finding ways to challenge and change the existing culture were as important as bolstering the refocused strategy and planning the new structure. There are, of course, other culture-related issues that face managers. These issues can be summarized in two further questions: What does a start-up company or a new unit within an established one have to do to create a new culture that serves the business? And in a company that already has a culture that is, for the most part, serving the business, what needs to be done to reinforce, fine-tune, and maintain it? But since the shadow side permeates problem cultures, finding ways to improve them is of primary concern here.

Can Culture Be Changed?

In the early 1990s, facing a substantial downturn in profits in the face of stiff competition, IBM began examining and trying to change its own culture. Somehow the "way we do things here at IBM" was no longer serving the business. IBM needed a new way of doing things. It had to become more flexible and more nimble if it was to retain its stature. A 90 percent plunge in profits in the second quarter of 1991 underscored the problem. In an internal memo that was leaked to the press, John Akers, Louis Gerstner's predecessor at IBM, took people to task for their complacency. A culture of complacency was the last thing a computer company needed in order to move through the nineties into the even more turbulent twenty-first century. Though the CEO railed, little happened. This brings up two key questions: First, can an entrenched culture be changed? Second, if it can, how long does it take?

The first question can be answered with a resounding yes. There are many examples of companies that have overhauled their cultures. Of course, that in no way means that change is easy or that success is possible in every case. The trick is knowing what you want to accomplish. When British Airways began its move toward being a publicly held company, they knew that they had to change many things. But a top priority was changing a culture of indifference and arrogance to a culture of service. Without a culture of service they would not be able to compete in the global marketplace.

As to the second question, many say that culture change, although possible, takes a long time, because the deep beliefs and values of the company are so covert and entrenched. Let's draw an analogy. In counseling and psychotherapy there are different opinions about how deep constructive personal change can go. Some see therapy as the redoing of the personality, a deep and formidable process indeed. Others see therapy as a process of helping clients achieve sustainable constructive changes in behavior and in the kind of thinking that will support the new behavior. In the same way some who write about corporate culture see culture change as reforming the personality of the institution, while others take the "changeable patterns of behavior" approach.

If people are told that culture change will take five to ten years, many will lose heart or interest. Furthermore, many businesses in need of substantive culture change don't have five to ten years. When the head of IBM's human resources department resigned after being on the job less than a year, industry observers said that he was not "making fast enough progress in cutting the work force and remaking IBM's culture" (Hays, 1994a, p. A3). The marketplace is breathing down their necks. Therefore, it is necessary to challenge the truism that culture change takes a long time. It does and it doesn't. It does if we mean a total personality transformation of the institution. It is true that the stronger the assumptions, beliefs, values, and norms that drive patterns of behavior are and the larger and more complicated the institution is, the more difficult it is to get at and change the culture. The mildly dysfunctional cultures of smaller companies can be more readily changed. But in both small and large companies the goal of culture change is not a full personality transformation. The goal is sustainable changes in patterns of behavior that serve the business in key areas. The goal is enough change to make a difference.

In larger companies especially, the pace of change depends on the strength of the institution's resolve to change and the intensity of its focus. British Airways sent very clear messages to the troops that change was mandatory and that speed was necessary. The intensity of its focus on customer service enabled them to pull off the change in this dimension of their culture in a relatively short time. I heard customers say things like, "I hadn't flown with British Airways for a year or two. Frankly, I was amazed at the change and more than pleasantly surprised. It was like flying an entirely different airline." Furthermore, British Airways is still getting good marks for service, an indication that the behavior changes, while not easy to achieve, are sustainable.

In companies with deeply embedded dysfunctional cultures, like General Motors, a few quick wins can provide signs of hope that can in turn be leveraged for further gains. And, to be fair, the automotive giant has had a number of quick wins over the past few years. An executive vice president of the company spoke candidly at a trade conference in late 1993: "We'll have turned around by 1996. We'll be less arrogant. We will respect the customer. We'll love our people. And we'll have good quality" (White, 1993, p. A3). What he was saying was that the company would have the kind of culture needed to keep it in the globally competitive fray.

There are three parts to culture change: (1) auditing the embedded culture to determine what needs to be changed; (2) developing the beliefs, values, and norms of the preferred culture; and (3) formulating culture-change strategies that fit the character and resources of the institution.

Pragmatic Culture Audits

The first question to answer is, What kind of battle do we face? Challenging and changing the culture starts with a solid understanding of what the culture of the company or institution or unit is. Only then is it possible to determine which dimensions of the culture support productivity and the quality of work life and, therefore, need to be promoted and which dimensions limit the effectiveness of the enterprise and need to be changed. If understanding a culture is the beginning of the wisdom, then culture audits play an important role. Here are the generic steps in a culture audit:

- Identify key shared assumptions, beliefs, values, and norms, especially covert ones.
- Identify the institution-limiting patterns of behavior they generate.
- Determine what keeps these patterns of behavior in place.

The order of the first two steps is not cast in stone. As we shall see later, sometimes it is better to start with the second step. For instance, someone might say, "We never get projects completed on time around here." This person is naming a dysfunctional pattern of behavior. Then he or she might go on to say, "It's about time we find out what's behind this." That is, what are the beliefs, values, and/or norms that generate this institution-limiting pattern of behavior in the first place? Both the "thinking" and the "doing" parts of culture are important, but the patterns of behavior still constitute the bottom line of culture.

Of course, as in any audit, the reason for doing it should be clear up front. In this case, the audit should serve the purpose of promoting patterns of behavior that support preferred business outcomes, reinforce overall institution strategy, and improve the quality of work life. Furthermore, it is essential to keep in mind that culture is a dimension of the business—"the way we do things here"—not something that is separate.

Start with the Business

The starting point of a pragmatic audit is the immediate reality of the business itself rather than the underlying culture. Once it is clear that the business must be the focus, then it is possible to start with either behavior or the thinking that drives the behavior. In the following example, the approach is to dig out the cultural assumptions, beliefs, values, and norms from the patterns of business behavior.

I once said to a middle manager who had had little input into the formulation of his company's strategy, "I've read your strategy, and it's quite ambitious. Are you going to achieve the goals outlined in it?" He thought for a moment, shrugged his shoulders, and answered, "Not the way we do things around here." I pressed on: "Well, from your perspective, what are some of the things that are going to interfere with the execution of the strategy?" The manager went on to criticize the strategy itself. He said that the company had a tendency to create grandiose, unrealistic strategies that satisfied the ego needs of senior managers but ended up depressing the people who had to carry them out. Since the company was filled with "good soldiers," no one complained publicly that this or that part of the strategy was unrealistic. They complained privately to one another but then, like good soldiers, went out and tried to deliver the goods. He explained further that even a realistic strategy would demand a kind of risk taking that was not supported in the company. "In our company," he said, "you get no place by being an innovator or entrepreneurial. You only get hurt." The discussion of strategy led immediately to a discussion of culture—the working beliefs, values, and norms embedded in the company's way of setting strategy.

But if the business itself remains the starting point, another approach is to focus first on the "thinking" side of the business, that is, beliefs, values, and norms. Kilmann (1985) has described this approach. He would ask managers and other workers to name the norms that interfered with the business. He found that most managers could readily name any number of such norms. And, once named, they could be challenged and changed. One group of managers in a publishing firm did just that. They limited their focus to the company's marketing efforts. Instead of brainstorming them in a group session, however, each manager wrote down his or her list. The lists were collected and recorded on newsprint. Since certain norms were brought up again and again, a frequency count was kept. Here are the "winners"—that is, the norms that were judged to most severely limit the marketing efforts of the company:

- Treat all books the same.
- Use professionalism as an excuse for shoddy marketing.
- Work on the assumption that books should sell themselves.
- Turn down all marketing ideas from authors.
- Don't actively enter the marketplace. Keep a professional distance through catalogues and ads in the "right" journals.
- Do not crosslist books across company departments.
- Do not see a book as a product and then think of product extensions.
- Above all, remain conservative and above the fray.

The editors of this publishing house were both chagrined at their conservatism and heartened by the thought of so many untapped marketing possibilities. Some theoreticians claim that a process as simple as this does not get at the deeper issues. But not many managers are that interested in the deeper problems in the first place. Nor is it readily clear that getting at the deep issues leads to culture change.

Take the Pulse of the Culture When
You Take the Pulse of the Business

A culture audit can be the byproduct of a more formal review of the state of the business. Here is a process I use to help a company, an organizational unit, or a project group take the pulse, directly, of its business and, indirectly, of its culture.

Gather Business-Focused Data Through Interviews. Interview a sampling of key informants, managers, and other workers who know the system and are willing to talk candidly about it. Ask the informants about the problems, opportunities, and challenges the business is facing. Explore what they spontaneously offer with a range of probes based on strategy, operations, structure, human resource management systems, managerial and supervisory practices, and leadership. As you receive answers about business problems or unexploited opportunities, probe to get at the embedded culture. Sometimes it takes no more than the simple question, Why is that? to get at the underlying culture.

Manager: "We have never been able to achieve the margins that our competitors almost routinely do."

Interviewer: "Why is that?"

Manager: "I'll tell you why. We are so busy around here trying to compete with one another, trying to get ahead, that we don't stay focused. We're distracted."

Interviewer: "That doesn't sound very helpful. Why does it persist?"

Manager: "We get rewarded for what we accomplish. Pay-for-performance, they call it. They tell us it gets us working harder. It does—I mean, working harder against one another. But just try to say anything bad about pay-for-performance and you're accused of being a slug."

Notice that these "why" questions don't lead to theoretical specula-
tions and interpretations but to value-laden patterns of behavior
that, in the mind of the respondent, limit the business.

Organize the Findings. Use strategy, operations, and the other categories named above—the categories used to ask the questions—to
organize the responses. In each category, outline both strengths and
weaknesses and name the institution-limiting norms and patterns
of behavior that have been uncovered. In each category, include a
few very brief direct quotes, sometimes disguised to hide the identity
of the respondent, to let people know that this is their data, not the
speculation of the consultant. One manager said something like,
"One of the main reasons we don't improve in customer service
from quarter to quarter is that we don't have a customer service
attitude in our dealings with one another. We're too predatory. We
beat up on one another and then expect everyone to turn and smile
at customers. We give customers what we give one another—poor
service. We are so worried about looking good to our bosses that we
don't have the time of day for one another. And we don't talk about
it. In fact, those who do talk about it are considered weak managers." In the feedback, the interviewer included a brief summary of
this statement. Since other respondents said similar things, a cultural theme or pattern emerged.

Provide Feedback. Send a feedback document to each member of the
team a few days before a problem-solving and opportunity development session. Give team members a chance to reflect on the highlights of the feedback. The feedback should include specific business challenges ("Our competitors still have an edge over us in
terms of speed to market") together with factors in the culture that
contribute to the problem ("Even though we say we need to delegate
decision-making authority more readily, we don't do it; everyone
clings to his or her authority").

Mount a Challenge-and-Change Meeting. There is no use surfacing cultural norms and patterns of behavior unless you intend to
do something about them. After the convener of the meeting—

someone from inside the company, not a consultant—sets the tone and encourages both openness and a "let's do something about these issues" climate, the participants are divided up into corrective-action teams and assigned specific problems and opportunities along with a shared model of problem solving and initiating change (such as the process suggested in *Adding Value,* Egan, 1993). The teams are instructed to deal with the issues from an integrated point of view—that is, from a business, organizational, management, and cultural perspective. A consultant can challenge the group's attempts to sideline difficult or sensitive issues and help group members deal with the shadow-side dimensions of the issues that have been surfaced.

One company, totally dissatisfied with its new-product development program, used the above process to discover what was underneath their lack of success. They found, paradoxically, a culture of naiveté and a culture of arrogance. Their naiveté led them to

- Feel helpless in their search for new business possibilities
- Become overreliant on consultants who often proved to be inept
- Rehire the same consultants when new ventures did not work out
- Overestimate the importance of sheer size and technical competence
- Misjudge markets and competitors
- Lose heart after initial setbacks and allow projects to drift

Their arrogance led them to

- Promote only from within and therefore end up with a narrow range of both management and marketing skills
- Underestimate the importance of flexibility
- Dictate rather than respond to customers
- Fail to admit these mistakes and, therefore, to learn from them

They began to see that this lethal combination had been with them a long time. Since these patterns were so deeply rooted, they wondered how difficult it might be to root them out.

Use Intractable Problems as Triggers for Culture Audits

Recurring or intractable problems are windows into the culture. The fact that rational attempts to solve them get nowhere is an indication that something is going on in the shadows to thwart problem-solving attempts and to keep them in place. Therefore, the exploration of intractable problems and the attempts made to deal with them reveal shadow-side activities and arrangements.

One company felt that it was drowning in its own paper. No matter what people did, the mountains seemed to grow higher and higher. When a new CEO arrived, he issued executive orders limiting the production and dissemination of paper. This worked for a while, but soon the stacks began to grow again. It was evident that this paper flood was an intractable problem. A consultant involved in the company's management development program noticed that almost every document he read had the word "draft" on it. "Are there any finished documents?" he asked. Of course there were, he was told, but the word "draft" tended to disappear right before the document had to be at its final destination.

In working with managers, the consultant noticed two things: a culture of criticism and a culture of perfectionism, both reinforcing each other and both playing a role in the generation of the paper mountain. Since a perfectionist mind-set permeated the place, everyone tried to produce the perfect document. This led to many iterations of project proposals and a flood of memos sent to fine-tune previous memos. The whole place was substantially over-engineered. In view of the fact that the ability to criticize ideas and projects had been raised to an art form, calling a document a draft served as armor plating. If someone began to criticize the ideas in a draft version of a document, the author could cut him or her short by saying, "Good grief, it's just a draft, a few ideas I threw together and had intended to share with a couple of colleagues."

Project proposals were also overengineered to take into account and ward off any possible criticism. This added little value to the business of the institution, but it kept the critics somewhat at bay. The problem persisted throughout the six-year term of the CEO that had ordered the elimination of the paper mountains. The next president, early in his tenure, mentioned publicly that some-

thing had to be done about the mountains of paper the institution
was generating. But the problem would never be solved until the
institution had come to grips with the distinction between professionalism and perfectionism. The former added value; the latter
added cost. Furthermore, pandemic criticism had to give way to
constructive debate—that is, contention that improved projects instead of providing a forum for clashes of ego.

Audit the Infrastructure of Culture

Once the culture takes root in the bones and marrow of the system,
it tends to stay there, even when it does not serve the system well.
That is, the beliefs, values, and norms that drive patterns of behavior tend to be stable over time. The reason for this is simple: every
culture has a set of underpinnings that keep it in place. This is fine
if the culture serves the business but problematic if it does not. The
upside of this is that a dysfunctional culture can sometimes be
changed by identifying and removing its supports.

In any given company, of course, managers need to ask themselves, What keeps *our* dysfunctional culture in place? Why does it
persist? Adaptation to the culture, silent carriers, the covert incentive-reward system, habit and inertia as part of a culture system,
cloning, and the politics of self-interest, described here, are some of
the underpinnings. What keeps the dysfunctional elements of *your*
company's culture in place?

Adaptation. Part of the power of culture comes from the fact that
people adapt to it. It regulates their lives, but they no longer notice
it. In one organization the main complaint of new hires was that
veterans were so good at playing the "read what is in the boss's
mind and conform to it" game that they did not even know that they
were playing it and had no idea of how much it was costing the
company in lost opportunities. "This is a good company," the novices would say, "when it could and should be a great company."
Unfortunately, the CEO, and therefore his top managers, did not
like the term *culture*. He once said to a consultant, "Talking about
culture is simply a way of making excuses for poor performance."
"We don't makes excuses here," he added, not realizing that he was

talking about culture. In this company, as in others, cultural adaptation had become an obstacle to improving performance.

Carriers. The strength of a culture lies in the *shared* nature of beliefs, values, norms, and patterns of behavior. The people working in organizations are the carriers of its culture, even when they dislike the impact the culture is having on both business productivity and quality of work life. One manager who disliked the authoritarian nature of his company was deeply chagrined when he discovered, through an upward feedback exercise, that he was seen as authoritarian. He was a silent carrier of the larger culture.

Chris Argyris (1976, 1982) worked with business leaders who wanted to move themselves and their organizations toward a culture that would support both greater productivity and quality of work life. He found, however, that these leaders were often unaware that many of the strategies they were using to promote the culture change effort were contrary to the new culture they wanted to embrace. Paradoxically, members of Argyris's work teams tried to browbeat one another into encouraging greater freedom in their respective organizations. When challenged, they would deny that they had used such tactics. It was not until Argyris started to videotape the meetings that they began to see what they were doing. Even then they made excuses for their seemingly contradictory behavior. It is not easy to admit that one is a carrier of the very culture one resents.

The Covert Incentive-Reward System. It is not uncommon for companies, unwittingly, to reward behaviors they would like to eliminate and punish behaviors they would like to see in place. And so soul-destroying managerial behavior is rewarded because it is in keeping with a company's covert norm—"Get results at any cost"— and needed risk taking is punished because of the company's hidden no-mistakes-permitted culture. In one company a new delegation system was established to serve the newly espoused entrepreneurial culture. Managers were given much more capital to work with and were allowed to hire whomever they needed. However, when they were told, "You may now spend up to $1 million without going to the executive committee," there was a voice somewhere whispering,

"But don't do it." "You may hire the people you need to expand your business," was said out loud, but a silent message was, "Of course, you will really be rewarded for keeping your organization lean." Although changed on paper, the reward system from the old culture persisted, and people continued to do what they were rewarded for. It is estimated that this hidden process cost the company some $30 million over a three-year period.

Habit and Inertia: The Culture System. A body in motion tends to stay in motion in the same direction unless some opposing force interrupts its trajectory. The laws of thermodynamics are alive and well in corporate cultures. The interactive web of traditions, beliefs, values, norms, behaviors, and underpinnings constitutes a culture *system* that is not readily changed. Cultural inertia is rooted in the set of habits that guide organizational behavior. Inertia will win out unless real and clear-cut incentives constitute an "opposing force" to break up the system.

　　　Within an eight-year period, IBM managed to eliminate some 180,000 jobs, trim a billion dollars from its research budget, and write off about $28 billion. But while cost-cutting measures were being carried out, the company still operated three full-amenity country clubs for its employees, ran a state-of-the-art management school on a twenty-eight-acre campus, threw lavish parties featuring TV personalities and movie stars for its best sales personnel and their spouses, leased a satellite full-time to beam IBM programs to all its locations, and flew nine corporate jets (Miller, 1993). To the dismay of many, the company's appetite for the perks of success was motoring on despite a lack of success. What mattered was not so much the dollar cost of the items on this list but their symbolic value. The full culture web or system needs to be identified and challenged in order for culture management to work.

Cloning. The managers of many companies fall into the trap of hiring and promoting people like themselves. New managers take their cues from the old. This process is even more deadening in companies that have a covert policy of promoting only from within. Indeed, in one company the assumption was that hiring from outside was a sign of failure. They never said this, and it certainly was not written down, but it drove behavior. Cloning is a form of inertia. In the beginning this can be good because it means hiring people into the preferred culture and promoting them because they are carriers of the preferred culture. Down the line, however, the company runs the risk of inbreeding. They don't even notice that they are running out of fresh ideas. The world changes, and managers keep trying to face new challenges with outdated mind-sets. What was once a benefit is now a straitjacket. In one company you could feel this kind of culture in the elevators—men, white with few exceptions, dark suits, impeccable grooming, hushed conversations, from the right if not the best schools, politeness to the point of deference. It was obvious that they knew the ropes. This formula had worked for years. It had a momentum of its own. The problem was the world had changed.

The Politics of Self-Interest. Those who benefit from the current culture, even if aspects of it limit the effectiveness of the institution as such, will use their influence to keep it in place. For instance, one proud American company publicly proclaimed its commitment to "shareholder value." When another company wanted to take it over, however, a move that would have considerably increased shareholder value, management did everything it could to make sure that the merger never happened. Managers knew that the new CEO would be much more demanding. Their comparatively easy lifestyle would be in for a shock. From management's point of view, the values in use were managerial security, control, and business as usual. Eventually, market dynamics forced their hands. Faced with a falling market share and, for the first time in their history, losses, they brought in an outsider who turned the place upside down. The politics of self-interest produced short-term gains for those who played the "keep things as they are" game, but reality finally caught up with them.

A final point about audits: it is essential to avoid overkill in auditing the culture. If it is raining, it is not necessary to carry out a scientific experiment to determine whether it is raining or not. It is only necessary to use one's senses. In a similar way, those who work within a company often *know* what the dysfunctional aspects of the culture are, but they don't know what to *do* about them. In other words, a formal audit of a culture may not be necessary. Indeed, getting culture discussed in some proper decision-making forum may be more difficult than auditing it. Culture, like other shadow-side dimensions, often remains undiscussed or undiscussable in meaningful forums.

The Preferred Culture

The question here is: What kind of culture do we need to serve our business? There is no one formula for every company. This section will be relatively short because the elements of a preferred culture were covered in Chapter Five.

Over the past dozen years or so, a great deal of attention has been paid to the formulation of a company's mission, vision, and values. Since the term *values* here is shorthand for beliefs, values, and norms, the values named in the mission statement form the basis for the preferred culture. Johnson & Johnson's credo, presented in Chapter Five, is a statement of the company's preferred culture. The beliefs, values, and norms outlined there are meant to drive the business. The realities of the business constitute the starting point for formulating the preferred culture.

The values of the preferred culture are not meant to be window dressing but rather the drivers of behavior; they are meant to serve both business objectives and quality of work life. IBM's Gerstner replaced the three basic norms with a set of beliefs that he thought would serve the business better as it faces a much more complicated business environment (Hays, 1994b). The three basic norms were to pursue excellence, provide the best customer service, and show respect for each employee. The eight beliefs or principles of the new culture are the following:

1. The marketplace is the driving force behind everything we do.
2. At our core, we are a technology company with an overriding commitment to quality.
3. Our primary measures of success are customer satisfaction and shareholder value.
4. We operate as an entrepreneurial organization with a minimum of bureaucracy and a never-ending focus on productivity.

5. We never lose sight of our strategic vision.
6. We think and act with a sense of urgency.
7. Outstanding, dedicated people make it all happen, particularly when they work together as a team.
8. We are sensitive to the needs of all employees and to the communities in which we operate.

This set of principles is meant to drive out the covert values of entitlement, arrogance, inward focus, status quo, rigidity, decision by committee, and dependence. It is interesting to note that of the two principles that deal with employees, the first (number 7) emphasizes results and team effort and the second (number 8) focuses on two sets of stakeholders, that is, employees and communities. While some insiders saw this as downplaying the importance of the individual, industry observers saw this as Gerstner's way of moving away from the company's overly inward view of itself.

Here is an example of keeping a preferred culture evergreen. Jack Welch, the CEO of highly successful General Electric, had a lot about culture in his 1994 annual report letter (Hyatt, 1994). He stressed three values: stretch, speed, and boundarylessness. The concept of *stretch* would send most managers reeling. It means using, well, *dreams* to set business targets without an idea of how to get there. Incremental goals are out. They lack passion. The company is to reward stretch goals and "quantum leaps" toward them. Quantum leaps, by the way, are to be regular events.

Speed means a flow of new products with "drumbeat rapidity." There's a new product announcement from the appliances business every ninety days. Speed in all processes, Welch says, is allowing the company to shift its center of gravity toward the high-growth areas of the world.

Boundaryless means no more fiefdoms. Representatives of all functions are not to vie for the privileges of turf but for the honor of bringing to market "the world's best jet engine, or ultrasound machine, or refrigerator." And all of this is to be driven by leaders at every level who can "energize, excite, and coach rather than enervate, depress, and control." And if this package is not for you, a GE manager, no matter how impressive you are otherwise, then you're history. Better for you, better for GE. The principle is simple—fashion a culture that serves the business. This, of course, is the GE formula. What's yours?

The following questions are guidelines for this process:

- What is our mission? What business are we in?
- What is our vision for this business? What are our aspirations?
- What are the current needs of this business?
- What patterns of behavior should be in place to meet these needs?
- What beliefs, values, and norms are needed to drive these patterns of behavior?

Once more, the bottom line of culture consists of those patterns of behavior that serve the business and its stakeholders.

The preferred culture spells out the business-enhancing, desired state. Culture audits specify the current state, including the ways in which the current culture falls short of the preferred culture. Challenging and changing the culture assumes that the agents of change know what they want and what they have and that they possess the power, will, and strategies to close the gap.

Strategies for Challenging and Changing Culture

When the formal or informal process of auditing has provided sufficient intelligence, managers need to challenge and change the dysfunctional aspects of the culture. There are a number of actual strategies for doing so. As with any other set of action strategies, those that best fit the needs and circumstances of the company or institution should be chosen, packaged, and turned into a culture change plan. The approach that says, "This one sounds interesting, I think I'll try it tomorrow" will get the results it deserves. The following overlapping and interrelated strategies are presented in three groups: (1) business- and organization-based strategies, (2) change-linked strategies, and (3) frontal attacks.

Business- and Organization-Based Strategies

The culture change strategies in this group are based on categories we have already seen: strategy, operations, structure, human resource management systems, management/supervision, and leadership. Since culture is embedded in these processes, changing them can change the culture. For instance, setting up a new business structure should not only improve information sharing, decision making, and work flow but also change "our way of doing things" in these areas.

Change Strategy Itself. A change in strategy can be in itself a culture change tool. This may mean an entirely new strategy or a significant change in the current one. For example, a rape crisis center that specialized in direct services to the victims of rape had grown a bit stale. Some of the staleness came from an assumption that said, "The only real work is the direct service work with victims." This assumption had never been pinpointed or discussed, but it certainly influenced behavior. Counselors interacted very little with one another so that there was no culture of mutual learning.

A couple of the counselors, sensing the staleness, moved beyond this direct service orientation and assumed an advocacy role from time to time. They pleaded the cause of victims and potential victims with the courts, the police, local government, and the community itself. They finally convinced the board to make advocacy services another line of business. This breathed new life into the agency and helped the direct service group recommit itself. Those in the advocacy group still provided some direct services. They challenged the above assumption with a new, publicly stated belief that "service to rape victims and potential rape victims has many faces." Eventually, one more unit was added: education services. This unit focused on rape victims, potential rape victims, and the community. These strategic changes contributed greatly to a growing culture of learning within the center.

Use Contemporary Approaches to Operations. Many of the so-called business fads of the last five years are fads only in terms of the hype they have received. The best of them should probably be called "contemporary management approaches." Three of them that focus primarily on operations are total quality management (TQM), customer service (both internal and external), and reengineering. All of these, rightly executed, challenge outmoded culture paradigms. They work best as culture change strategies, however, when this focus is built into the program right from the start. For instance, reengineering should focus on both work processes and the culture permeating the old processes. Total quality management includes the quality of the culture.

This dual focus requires up-front planning. In one hospital, a nursing group, after using a TQM process to get its own house in shape, lobbied the administration for a system-wide TQM effort. Every group would be targeted: administration, doctors, nurses, lab technicians, the information system warriors, the pharmacy group, radiologists, business office personnel, and so forth. Since total quality demanded cross-functional teamwork, the change effort had to focus on such covert and undiscussed norms as, "Turf must be protected to preserve the professionalism of each functional group." The quality of health care would not improve until some of the walls came tumbling down and a team ethic pervaded the institution.

Use Restructuring. Much of the restructuring that goes on—centralizing and decentralizing, creating new boxes while eliminating old ones, putting people in new jobs, creating new positions, changing role definitions—is a veiled attempt at culture change. Restructuring is meant to shake up the system. It "unfreezes" old ways of doing things. One food processor built a new plant precisely because they had not been able to change the staid, business-limiting cultures of their other plants. The members of the management team of the new facility were given orders to create a new, more open, more entrepreneurial culture—the kind needed to stay alive in a competitive industry. After it was up and running, teams from the older plants were sent on scheduled visits. The task was to "infect" them with the spirit of the new culture.

"Skunk works"—covert think tanks or product development groups that often bend the rules and "steal" resources to promote innovations—have been created in many high-tech companies precisely to get around the limitations of the mainline culture. When Hewlett-Packard started its now highly successful laser printer business, the company purposely chose a site out of reach of national headquarters. They wanted to avoid any possibility of cultural contagion from the mother house. They wanted to fine-tune the HP culture, which at the time was considered robust, and adapt it to the new venture.

Use Human Resource Management Systems. Recruitment, socialization, promotion, training, and development are all potential levers for culture change. An old-line manufacturing firm promoted people whose work ethic differed from the work ethic of the sleepy mainline culture. These new managers brought a different outlook and spirit to their units.

Another company saw training and development as a possible lever of culture change. Many managers thought, and rightly so, that a lot of talent was going unused in the place and were distressed by the lost-opportunity costs. A massive employee development program was announced, consultants and trainers flooded in, pamphlets were published, but nothing happened. This was an indication of how strong the culture of non-development was. And so something quite different was tried. The top fifty managers—there were over four thousand managers in the company—were asked to pick two people they thought would add more value to the company and be more satisfied with their jobs if they were given the opportunity to develop themselves further. Each manager was asked to prepare a one-page write-up of each of the two development prospects. On the page was the name of the person selected, how this person might add further value to the company, what experiences the person needed to develop his or her talent, and how, specifically, this would add value to the business. This was then shared with the selected person, who reworked it. A final version was agreed on by manager and direct report. Then the direct report was asked to do the same for two people in his or her unit. It was a kind of pyramid scheme. But it fit the "doing" culture of the place much better than the formal program that failed. Focused training that is rightly planned, linked to the strategy, artfully designed, and professionally executed can be a potent force for culture change. But the culture change dimension must be built in right from the start.

Emphasize Competent Management. Since most people are promoted to managerial positions because they are good at some professional or technical specialty, taking management seriously by choosing managers precisely because of their potential as managers, helping them develop specific management competencies, and getting them to coach, counsel, and mentor others with a managerial flair is itself a substantive culture change. Managers should not only know how to manage but also should see themselves as guardians and promoters of the preferred culture. This should be an explicit part of the job specification.

Revamp the Company's Approach to Leadership. Leadership is one of those terms that is so soaked with meaning that it often ends up meaning nothing. Therefore, telling people what is meant by leadership in this company and developing a shared model or framework for leading would be a significant culture change in most companies. One company developed a model of leading that could be used by workers at any level of the company. This challenged the entrenched assumption in the company that headship and leadership were the same thing. Now leadership was to be assessed not in terms of position but in terms of results—specifically, results beyond the ordinary.

Any definition or model of leadership worth its salt will emphasize the role of leader as a creator and promoter of the preferred culture. Here are a couple of ways in which leaders can exercise cultural leadership:

• *Use the power of symbolic acts.* Once people are recognized as leaders, then even symbolic acts on their part can be very powerful. While such acts do not change anything in and of themselves, they send powerful messages. Effective leaders, knowing the power of such acts, use them sparingly but artfully. They capitalize on opportunities to send messages about culture change. Lee Iaccoca, former chairman of Chrysler and leader of its turnaround, seized such an opportunity. Or so it is reported. The workers of Chrysler, grateful for the part he played in turning the company around, took up a collection and bought him a gift—a Chrysler, of course. He was to accept the gift at a noon pep rally in one of the assembly plants. The plant manager made a short speech and then handed Iaccoca the keys to the shiny black Chrysler on the plant floor. Iaccoca looked at the key, looked at the car, and then said to the plant manager, "I can't take that car." A hush went over the place and the manager, obviously nonplussed, stammered, "But, sir, it's yours, it's a gift, you have to take the car." "Oh, I'll take a car all right," the chairman said, "but give me the next one that rolls off the line." In an instant everyone understood that every car that rolls off a company assembly line should be fit to present to the chairman.

• *Infect everyone with the preferred culture.* Leaders are good at getting others to buy into their business-enhancing agendas. If an institution's employees are the silent carriers of the old culture, as suggested above, then they need to become the vocal carriers of the new. Employees can be told explicitly which values are out and which are in. But the values must be expressed in specific terms. They need to be operationalized for *this* company in *this* set of circumstances. Instead of using the broad statement, "Be creative," one manager said to line workers, "Until now you have been told to follow the work process manuals slavishly, never to deviate from what is written down in them. But now it is clear that what is written down is not the best way of doing things. And so you are being asked to take a critical look at the work processes you are involved with and come up with ideas for doing them better. Those who designed the work mistakenly thought that you, the users of these processes, could not contribute ideas on how to do things better. We now know that that is nonsense." The adoption and use of the new values must be recognized, supported, and rewarded. Asking employees in some general way to take risks, for example, and then punishing them for not taking the "right" risks will quickly reinforce the old culture and breed cynicism around the new. On the other hand, providing them with the power that they need to accomplish the tasks of the new culture will go far in getting them to own the new culture.

If managers are to take a lead role in promoting, changing, and maintaining the company's culture and the subcultures that serve different parts of the business, then this role must be legitimized and managers must develop the competencies—those outlined in the previous chapter and this one—to fulfill that role. Large consulting firms like McKinsey are receiving more and more requests from companies to help them with culture change because the managers of these companies are not adept at it. But McKinsey admits that their consultants are also short on these competencies. Business schools ignore them. Therefore, the company that equips its managers with the competencies and tools to manage culture at the service of the business should have, at least in this regard, a competitive edge.

Change-Linked Strategies

The basic principle in this category is: link culture change to every key project, program, or change effort. This makes sense, since many change efforts fail because they do not factor in cultural realities.

See New Beginnings as Culture Change Opportunities. Every new beginning, however small, is an opportunity to reset the culture. Opening a new plant, launching a new project, announcing a new policy, introducing a new line of products, moving into a new market, opening a new store, mounting a new advertising campaign, repainting the office—the list goes on. Every change is a chance to say, "The change will add value to the company if. . . . " If *these* beliefs, values, and norms drive our behavior. If these *new* patterns of behavior take the place of the old. A small retailer that fell upon bad times finally emerged from bankruptcy. The new management team opened a new store as soon as possible. While the speedy opening did not make business sense in financial terms, it did make sense in terms of resetting the spirit of the company. In a rather stirring talk, the new CEO christened the store "hope." He went on to name the "demons" that did the company in—each a dysfunctional belief, value, or norm—and for each demon named a value that needed to drive behavior in the new company. This may seem hokey to some, but it worked for them. The small chain is flourishing once more. How many initiatives were there in your company or institution during the past year? How many of those were used to reset the culture?

Use Crises to Gain Leverage. Many culture change success stories start with a company in crisis. The system is more open, permeable, and vulnerable at such times. Normal rules are suspended, including the covert norms of the entrenched culture. The principle is: kick the dysfunctional culture while it is down. Sears, however belatedly, used the crisis in its retail business to mount an attack on its self-serving bureaucratic culture. With little fanfare the company flooded the place with workshops that focused on getting rid of outmoded practices and promoting work process reengineering, team building, and performance improvement. All of this was meant to serve changes in business strategy, including a new layout for furniture and a new drive into apparel. The economic payoff proved quite handsome. In 1993 the retailer did much better than the analysts expected. They surprised even themselves. It is not that Sears did a total transformation of its culture in eighteen months. But it was a good start, and there were some quick wins.

If there is no particular crisis, create one. One company over-dramatized, at least to a degree, the impact of the entry of a new competitor into its market. A highly visible get-the-invader campaign, including placards and pep rallies, was mounted. The whole process served to reinforce their merchandising values—value pricing, quality, customer service, added equities like same-day or next-day delivery, and the like—and put a battle-cry edge on them. The campaign went on for about three months. The fact that sales improved dramatically helped to no end. They celebrated their victory over the enemy. Another company merged two businesses that could have remained separate and used the ensuing turmoil to reset strategy and do battle against the culture of complacency that had crept up on it. In creating crises, however, we must take care not to dupe the work force. In both these examples a business case could have been made for the steps taken even though the goal was primarily cultural in nature.

Leverage Turnarounds. Every day in the business press we read of companies that need to turn their fortunes around. It is not that they are headed for disaster but that they have become mediocre. Turnarounds provide many opportunities for shaking up an entrenched culture. Since some rules, both formal and informal, are suspended for a while, certain robust interventions into the culture are permitted. One company used a turnaround period to get rid of deadwood. The covert belief was, "It's all right to be mediocre here." By moving into firing-hiring mode—getting rid of the drifters and hiring self-starters in their place—they blasted this belief out of the water.

Frontal Attacks

While many of the strategies previously outlined are powerful but indirect challenges to the culture, it is also possible to mount a more frontal attack.

Act Your Way into a New Mode of Thinking. When we think of change, we think of action. This action approach is borrowed from personal-change programs and is featured in some of the twelve-step approaches such as that used in Alcoholics Anonymous. The norm is, "Don't try to think your way into a new mode of acting; rather act your way into a new mode of thinking." In organization culture terms, this means supporting preferred patterns of behavior until a new set of attitudes, beliefs, values, and norms grows up underneath, making them self-supporting. The managers of a manufacturer realized that their inability to reduce waste was held in place by a set of shared cultural assumptions, attitudes, and norms. One norm was, "Don't worry about waste; speed is more important and entails a bit of waste." A corrective-action team spent six months studying "lean manufacturing" technologies and processes and visiting plants where they had been successfully adopted. Then, instead of attacking dysfunctional attitudes and norms, they flooded the place with action strategies for reducing waste. The formal campaign lasted a year. By that time there were enough converts to this new mode of thinking and enough champions of pushing this new way of doing things that the new culture drove out the old.

Use Guerrilla Warfare Tactics. In one company involved in a turnaround, the CEO hired as a consultant a man who had run his own company and had a reputation for being fair but tough. He reported directly to the CEO. His role was to be a kind of wandering guerrilla. He could show up almost anywhere at almost anytime and ask "naive" and even "impertinent" questions. "Why are we doing that this way?" "What purpose does this serve?" "How do customers feel about that?" "If that unit disappeared, would the company suffer?

Would anyone even notice?" This did not make him popular, but then he didn't aspire to popularity.

He described his role as follows: "There are many great younger people flooding into this organization. They want it to be a great success, and they bring lots of enthusiasm. At the top there are now some very creative people. In the middle there's a rock formation. My job is to wander around looking for chinks in the rock formation and then drop in a stick of dynamite." This gentleman annoyed a lot of people. They said little, because there was a culture of ladylike and gentlemanly behavior. But he did play an important role in unfreezing the culture of the place. He stayed about a year, and that was enough. Had he stayed longer, the new CEO would have suffered some kind of backlash.

Launch a Blitz of Programs That Promote the New Values. If you want a different culture, produce programs that promote it. At British Airways, many thought that senior managers were being profligate when a steady stream of mandatory meetings on "putting people first," customer service, and managing a service business flowed through the place from top to bottom. While these were presented as training programs, it was evident that they were actually frontal attacks on the entrenched culture. Although these expensive programs seemed to bring out the worst in both the naive, who swallowed them hook, line, and sinker, and the cynical, who predicted that "none of this nonsense will work," the flow remained unrelenting. The blitz was complemented by a new cabin-crew training program that focused not only on the "hard" issues of dealing with safety and serving meals but also on "soft stuff" like handling common service problems creatively.

One rather savvy flight attendant said something like, "I like all this stuff. It makes the flight go faster. When I'm greeting customers at the door and see Mr. Grumpy coming down the jetway, I say to myself, 'I'll have him in the palm of my hand by the time we hit Glasgow on our way to New York.'" The continued profitability of the airline even under the most torturous of industry conditions is due, in part, to the improved culture. Now no one, except the accountants, of course, remembers the cost of all those programs.

Keep Drawing Attention to Cultural Dissonance. In cultures that don't serve the business, the values in use differ from the espoused values. Drawing attention to this dissonance is annoying. It's the pebble in the shoe. And for that reason, it is effective. Sometimes people will act to move the culture in the right direction just to get rid of the annoyance. One of the subsidiary companies of a larger corporation took this approach. The values and norms that impeded the business were named and discussed at the beginning of every management committee meeting. A large chart was drawn up, one that looked something like the thermometers used to track the progress of fundraising goals, to measure the company's progress in fighting outmoded values and norms. Milestones were celebrated. For instance, a party was thrown when the degree of buy-in to the company's new team approach reached the halfway point on the chart. While tactics like this can keep the fight front and center in the consciousness of the company, they need to be combined with other approaches that deal directly with business and organizational realities. The company mentioned here celebrated team successes, rewarded team performance, and hired people who expressed a desire to work on teams.

An international agricultural research center that had been faulted by its financial supporters for being unfocused turned its new business values, which had been elaborated as part of resetting strategy, into a checklist. This checklist was shared with client groups and used to design projects, to track progress, and to evaluate final outcomes. Violation of these values had to be noted in reports, and actions had to be taken to bring the project back in line with the values. The economic results were positive. The center became more focused, more projects of greater substance were completed, and donor contributions went up.

Mandate the Kind of Culture the Company Needs. Why not save all the effort and indirection involved in the strategies outlined above and just go do it? "Let's make it simple," the person would say, "and do a few things." Here are some other examples:

- "We are going to take a revisionist approach to this institution's history and outline what should have happened and what should have been passed along as tradition. Here is the package."

- "I am declaring the following assumptions and beliefs dysfunctional, and the following correct set will now guide us."
- "Here are the values that keep getting us in trouble, and here is the set that we need to use to make decisions."
- "Here are some institution-limiting norms that drive behavior around here, but they are now invalid and inoperative. Here is the new set."
- "Now, with that mind-set, here are some of the things we're going to do. Furthermore, here are some behaviors that from now on are off-limits."

When, tongue-in-cheek, I suggested this as a primary approach to culture change to members of a class I was teaching, the general reaction was, "You can't do this. It's like *1984*. It is not the way individuals or social systems work. Managers might be able to carry this off for a while, but then it would all come down like a house of cards." However, a version of this can work.

Consider this example. In one midsize, family-owned bakery, the patriarch and majority shareholder got so fed up with the way the business was going that he simply announced a change in "the way we do things here" at a meeting of the extended family. His manifesto had the following four points:

- "You get paid for what you do and what you accomplish. This is a business and not a family picnic."
- "You become a manager only if you can manage. Reporting to a real manager is not a family disgrace."
- "We invest in the business. We don't bleed the business to make the family comfortable. If you want something for your children, create it."
- "We've got things backward. It's time to put things right. The family is the family. Its importance doesn't come from the business. It comes from love, commitment, tradition, relationships, crises, milestones—all the good family stuff."

He was amazed at how little opposition there was. What he had not realized was that there were other family members just as fed up as he was.

Are there other strategies for changing the culture? Certainly. The number is limited only by the limitations of your ingenuity. But whatever strategies are chosen should be right for the institution. What is the right package of strategies for *your* company or institution? By using some of these strategies, what kinds of quick wins could you get? What depth of culture change does your enterprise require? How long do you think it will take to make the kinds of behavioral rather than "personality" changes that will support your business more effectively?

MANAGING THE SHADOW SIDE OF PEOPLE

7

PERSONAL STYLES:
THE GOOD, THE BAD, THE UGLY,
AND THE AMBIGUOUS

A GREAT DEAL of the messiness of companies, institutions, and communities stems from the personal styles of the system's individual members, in all their complexity, idiosyncrasy, and unpredictability. The complexity of human beings is in turn charming and infuriating. We have all had bosses and co-workers whose personal styles both detracted from the business and caused us unnecessary misery. We have also had bosses and co-workers who did precisely the opposite. We have experienced bosses and co-workers who are inconsistent—charming one day and infuriating the next. The point is that the personal styles of individuals can add value or cost to the system.

Savvy managers understand the human condition and use their understanding to help individuals serve the business better and improve the quality of work life. Without becoming cynical, they are seldom surprised by eruptions of shadow-side behavior such as stealing, lying, and betraying. Nor are they surprised by individual creativity, commitment, and heroism. On the one hand, encounters with what is best in people encourage them without making them unwarrantedly optimistic about human nature. On the other, encounters with human venality do not discourage them or erode their basic optimism. They take people as they are instead of as they wish they were. They also know that people can be better than they are and thus constantly look at both themselves and others from a development perspective.

While much of the messiness and madness of human behavior is overt, there for all to see, more lies in the shadows. Understanding and dealing with personal styles, both in and out of the shadows, are challenges managers face every day. The economic consequences of meeting those challenges are substantial.

Categories of Personal Style

Personal style refers to all the qualities and characteristics of a person insofar as they are expressed in his or her workplace behavior. Personal style emerges not just from personality characteristics but also from an individual's *personal culture*—that is, the person's assumptions, beliefs, values, and norms insofar as they drive patterns of behavior.

In free countries, individuals are welcome to their personal styles. But usually they are also responsible for the consequences of expressing their styles in social settings. For example, an aggressive style that infringes on the rights of others is not to be tolerated. In the workplace, employees' styles may add value, add cost, or do a little of both, and the impact will be psychological, social, and financial. Yet personal styles are rarely discussed in formal settings. Even though personal styles are public, they remain part of the shadow side—perhaps because such things seem either *too* personal or simply inconsequential.

Various personal styles—good, ambiguous, bad, and ugly—are found in the workplace, and they need to be managed. But since the workplace is not a police station, a church, a social services center, or a mental hospital, human problems need to be managed from a work perspective. Let's take a look at the covert, undiscussed, undiscussable, or unmentionable good, ambiguous, bad, and ugly styles in individuals, but in reverse order.

The Ugly: Dysfunctional Personal Styles

On the extreme negative end of the personality scale are dysfunctional styles—dysfunctional, that is, in the sense of their profoundly negative impact on the workplace. Many people who found out that I was writing this book sent me shadow-side cases and examples of dysfunctional personalities from their own workplaces. Most involved individuals, and most were ugly. Envy, meanness, hatred, jealousy, prejudice, egomania, vindictiveness, stupidity, unfairness, neurosis, psychosis, blackmail, deception, manipulation, scams, conspiracies, bullying, harassment, lying, stealing, and cheating are all among the dark-side characteristics and activities of human beings that are found in the workplace.

Many of the ugliest examples hit the press. Story after story tells of the employee who finally blows up and goes on a rampage, engaging in either focused or indiscriminate slaughter. Others are caught in scams through which they have been bilking the company for months if not years. At the risk of appearing naive, however, I have decided not to spend much time on these kinds of examples, not because they do not exist but because they do not constitute the shadow-side mainstream. Examples of the darkest side of human nature, while titillating, don't provide managers with much help in managing the day-to-day idiosyncrasies of people. Yet when bizarre behavior erupts, the psychological, social, and financial costs are often enormous.

Chapter Eight focuses on strategies for managing the shadow side of personal styles and interpersonal relationships. However, since managers do run into ugly styles from time to time, here are a few suggestions on what to do when they surface.

Take Preventive Measures. The most economical approach to managing the ugliest dimensions of human nature is prevention. My bet is that employees who end up engaging in outrageous behavior in the workplace, whether it be the White House, the postal service, or corporate America, give some signs that they are approaching the breaking point long before they explode. But either nobody seems to notice or, if they do, they don't know what to do about it. Some suggestions: Stay in touch with the concerns, problems, fears, and dissatisfactions of workers. Talk them through. Help people solve, manage, or defuse problems before they go underground and then ultimately explode. In others words, be a good supervisor. Furthermore, while managers are not psychologists or psychiatrists, they

can still use their common sense to spot telltale signs on the part
of those already in place, such as sudden changes in behavior. One
gregarious worker went quiet. "He doesn't seem to be himself,"
some said. He later committed suicide. Telltale signs of impending
destructive behavior are more common than managers and supervisors are willing to admit.

Reform the Recruitment System. Some companies spend a lot of
money making sure that people have the technical competencies
needed for a job but ignore all those qualities and characteristics
that could make a person a disaster. I watched a company hire a
manager whose every pore dripped with ambition. They called it
high energy and enthusiasm. The next six months were ugly. He
sabotaged a viable strategy because he thought his was better. He
redid the information system to his specifications at great cost.
Later, more money had to be poured into redoing it. One key person
who foresaw the disaster quit as soon as the disaster-waiting-to-
happen was hired. Two more left during his six-month tenure.
Figure up the costs. Too many institutions operate on the assumption that technical brilliance outweighs everything else.

Reform the Promotion System. It is not that uncommon for people
with bizarre characteristics and behavior to be promoted. They are
usually very competent technically. It is almost as if the powers that
be are saying, "Well, if he were not so brilliant, we would probably
seek to have him hospitalized. But bizarre behavior is the price we
have to pay for such competence." Since in most companies key
people are also managers, there is no saying how much harm they
can do in skewing strategy, reducing operations to rubble, bringing
organizational structure to its knees, and destroying the human
assets of the company.

Act Assertively, Prudently, and Tactfully. This does not mean getting rid of people at the first sign of danger. It does mean finding
out what's going on. It does mean putting in place arrangements
that could prevent or contain further damage. In one company a
senior manager who seemed to be traveling excessively was given an
"assistant" because the former was "overworked." The assistant

soon discovered that the manager, overwhelmed with gambling debts, was involved in kickback scams with suppliers. He was fired and the suppliers dropped and prosecuted. While the company moved decisively when they discovered what was happening, there were any number of telltale signs around the manager's gambling that should have been spotted earlier.

The Bad: Defective Personal Styles

Defective here refers to the activities of individuals that limit the productivity of the institution and/or detract from the quality of work life. It includes more mundane human foibles rather than the bizarre behavior mentioned above. Lesser versions of the behaviors termed "ugly" infect the workplace to a greater or lesser degree: day-to-day laziness, venality, egotism, and the like. While soul-searing envy that ultimately drives someone to murder a colleague may not be part of the company's daily drama, milder forms of this human ailment are widespread. Though less dramatic, these kinds of personal styles can still be costly.

The costs of an undiscussed negative managerial style, for example, can be quite high. Consider the following instance. Kent saw himself as a tough manager. He had risen through the company ranks and was opposed in principle to what he saw as nonsense being written about empowerment, self-managed teams, and the like. "Tough but fair" was his motto. He made a point of not becoming too friendly with any of his direct reports lest this stand in the way of his objectivity. No one was going to get away with anything in his area. Whenever anything went wrong, he took a "guilty until proven innocent" approach to the workers involved. He was especially hard on his assistant, a competent young woman who had many ideas on how to improve the performance of the unit.

Since there was no upward, and little useful downward, feedback to managers in the firm, he knew little about the resentment and impaired morale among the troops. They ridiculed him behind his back and did only what they needed to do. When he started a project that they knew wouldn't work, they said nothing. They wanted him to fail. He had no idea of his effect on his assistant. She kept asking herself what she was doing wrong. In the end the project did fail, his assistant quit, workers in his unit asked for transfers, and his career was put on hold. The psychological and social costs led to substantive financial costs. Not only did a new assistant have to be hired and trained but the great potential of the disillusioned assistant was never realized; this translated into hidden lost-opportunity costs. The underperformance of the workers in the unit added hidden financial costs. The failure of the project was costly. And, since Kent's career was put on hold, there were even further lost-opportunity costs.

Of course, this was not all Kent's fault. The company's managerial culture played a critical role. Rising from the ranks does not automatically make someone a good manager. He rose because he was a good worker. And the company did nothing to give him the managerial competencies he needed to add value to the enterprise precisely as manager. This allowed Kent to pursue his own ill-formed and half-baked management ideas with no correction system in place to show him the error of his ways. The company's managerial culture was perhaps the key culprit, but it resided safely in the shadows.

Since the number of human foibles seems almost infinite, I am sure that each reader has his or her favorite stories, each focusing on a different package of style defects.

Ambiguous Personal Styles

While it is clear that managers and others should do whatever they can to drive both the dysfunctional and the defective out of the workplace, there are many individual idiosyncrasies that are ambiguous; that is, they may be two-edged or even three-edged swords. They may involve such workplace-influencing personality characteristics as ego, enthusiasm, drive, or entrepreneurialism. A deficiency or an excess in some characteristics and behaviors adds cost. The right amount adds value. And the "right amount" changes from time to time. A quality or activity that serves the business today may, when pushed to excess, limit it tomorrow. A case of entrepreneurialism pushed too far was discussed in Chapter One.

Sometimes it is not a question of the right amount of a personality characteristic but the right brand. Take intelligence. Academic intelligence does not help when street smarts are called for. Technical know-how cannot be substituted for social intelligence. Operational intelligence does not help the company in need of strategic leadership.

Ego in the Workplace. Ego is one of those personality characteristics that can add great value or great cost to the business. Even the degree of ego can be important. With too little, a manager might not influence anyone. With too much, he could do the organization in. The boss's ego—whether it is the big boss or any of the lesser bosses within the organization—often remains outside ordinary management processes, but it can add great value or great cost to the business. In the early nineties, the board of British Petroleum, after analyzing the impact of the big boss's ego, decided that it was too expensive, and they let him go. But other cases are not as clear-cut as this. In 1992, R. H. Macy & Company, a 136-year-old U.S. retailer, filed for bankruptcy. A rational analysis of this case would show that the company, like many others in the frenzied 1980s, courted excessive expansion and took on more debt than it could afford. A shadow-side analysis, reviewed extensively in the business press, indicted the ego of its chairman–chief executive. For years his ego certainly contributed to his merchandising brilliance and entrepreneurial flair. These added great value to the company. But ego also drove him to try to establish an empire overseen by a family dynasty. At this point his ego proved to be very expensive. The trouble is, who can sit down with the boss and help him do a balanced economic analysis of his or her ego? In this case, the board should have, but the shadow side of board behavior has only recently come under the legal, ethical, and business scrutiny it deserves.

Enthusiasm. Enthusiasm is frequently a part of personal workplace style. Even such a so-called positive trait, depending on how it is expressed, can add or subtract value. The best organizations are good at generating and maintaining enthusiasm. The enthusiasm of the entrepreneur helps the drive for success immensely, sometimes against all odds. On the other hand, the debris from failed start-ups that were all enthusiasm and no substance litter the business landscape. As one author put it, "My experience leaves no doubt that the failure of most new [enterprises] is contained in simplistic notions compounded of unbridled hope, the best intentions, and the denial of present or future conflict" (Sarason, 1972, p. 266).

Initial excitement is good because it drives people and helps them overcome inertia and initial obstacles. On the other hand, enthusiasm can create blind spots. If a project has less than a fifty-fifty chance of succeeding, then excessive enthusiasm can lead to debilitating depression if the enterprise does not succeed. Therefore, it is part of the work of a manager to encourage enthusiasm—create it even—and at the same time foresee and try to control its potentially limiting side effects. Finally, enthusiasm is so embedded in some people that they could be called "enthusiasts." Enthusiasts, as opposed to people with enthusiasm, tend to turn people off. Yet most managers hesitate to tell team members that they have too much enthusiasm. Misdirected and excessive enthusiasm, then, remain undiscussed, even undiscussable, and take their toll.

The Good: Healthy—Though
Unappreciated—Personal Styles

Healthy personal styles are addressed here not because they detract from the business but because the business so often suffers when the styles are not appreciated. It is not news that some workers have characteristics, qualities, and skills that could serve the business but are not identified and used. The cost of the failure to spot worker wisdom, talent, creativity, wit, drive, and determination is high. Indeed, the total cost of the failure to spot the good qualities in the shadows is probably higher than the failure to spot and deal with the bad and even ugly characteristics. This fact has spawned the so-called empowerment movement. Nor is it news that many workers have undeveloped potential that could serve the business but never does. Both skills and potential may escape the notice of those who can do something about them, or they may be unwittingly hidden from view by those who possess them. Though positive, they are still part of the shadow side because they remain unidentified and undiscussed in forums that can make a difference.

Overlooking Personal Qualities and Skills. Managers have a long way to go in appreciating and using the skills and qualities of the workers in their unit. Many have simply never been trained to do so, or they have never been asked. "Your job is to search out every last bit of talent in your people and put it to use" are words that were never heard, at least not until recently.

There is buried talent in every organization. Weston Agor (1988) found that the most typical organizational setting is one in which executives know each other primarily by formal job title, responsibility, or years of experience within the organization. Seldom do they know each other in terms of specific brain skills and abilities except in the most casual way. Therefore, assets lie fallow. He further discovered that managers frequently are not clear on what their *own* brain skills are. Therefore, companies and institutions that already have the intrapreneurial talent necessary to dramatically increase productivity often don't have access to it. Effective utilization of people's talents demands some kind of working knowledge of their makeup and skills. In my own practice I work on the assumption that the wisdom for handling problems and providing creative solutions lies within the company. My job is to help them discover that wisdom. The differential talents of individuals constitute a large part of that "buried treasure." Pooling that talent at the service of the business can increase both productivity and the quality of work life.

Ignoring Potential. Throughout the years, those involved in research on human potential have kept telling us that most people use only a fraction of their potential. In one way, this is very good news. It means that there is a great deal of unused potential in the workplace. I keep hearing managers recount stories in which they have spotted potential in some worker and helped him or her develop it. What is amazing is that they recount these experiences as *exceptions* even in their own managerial lives. I wonder what assumptions underlie their surprise. That if workers have unused potential they will identify and develop it on their own? That there is not much undeveloped talent in the work force? That people are not interested in developing their talent? It is more likely that the company does not have a culture in which talent is routinely identified and people are challenged and helped to develop it.

More sinister reasons for ignoring talent and potential are insecurity and envy. In one company a high-potential manager was asked to move from England to the main office in the United States. Not only was he good in his specialty but he also showed great promise as a manager. He was particularly good with people. But the American CEO saw him as a threat. And so he kept putting obstacles in his way. To put it simply, he made him fail. Then he fired him. The psychological, social, and financial impact of this was, of course, substantial. The life of the younger man and his family was disrupted. Onlookers did not intervene. Rather they learned that crossing the boss was dangerous. People were distracted from their work. The CEO later confessed his weakness and stupidity to a confidant and talked about how distracted from the business he had been. He was chagrined that no one in the company had the guts to challenge what was going on. Once more, no one won.

Imprinting Personal Style

Another reason why workplace style is so important is that it is contagious. In 1984, Manfred Kets de Vries and Danny Miller formulated an interesting hypothesis. In their book *The Neurotic Organization* they suggested that managers—and I would add, other key individuals—can "imprint" the organization with both their positive and negative attributes. If the characteristics and results are positive, that's fine, but that's not always the case. Sometimes the imprinting, usually undiscussed or undiscussable in itself, leads the institution in the wrong direction. The CEO of a data base software company was given to lavish theatrical gestures such as a press conference aboard a Concorde to tout the firm's products and highlight its growth. His style, it seems, rubbed off on his employees. One computer maker said that the typical employee was much more interested in his Jaguar and golf score than in serving customers having problems with products rushed prematurely to market. However, when Wall Street discovered that the CEO was exaggerating both revenues and profits, the company's stock collapsed. The CEO apologized for his arrogance and set about correcting the firm's many flaws. Customers, noting the change in attitude, began to respond. As of the present writing, the CEO has changed his ways, and the company has been moving from success to success.

If what managers model and imprint does not add value, this should be pointed out to them. Yet rarely is a manager told, "Your entire department, Joe, seems to have taken on your let's-be-careful and let's-wait-and-see approach to the business, but things are changing too quickly and we can't afford that style any longer." In many cases, however, managers who either cannot or don't want to model the required behavior grant themselves "exemptions." These exemptions, undiscussed shadow-side arrangements, are often very costly. For instance, a senior manager in one company did not have the guts to tell non-performers about their shortcomings. He kept talking to confidants about the dysfunctional behavior of two key people in his department. He should have fired both of them but never did. This weakness was imprinted not only on his department but on others. That is, managers said to themselves, "I don't have to be too demanding. After all, look at Joe. I may be soft, but I'm better than he is." Since it was in the shadows, no one figured out the costs of this imprinting until the company was bought out by a competitor. The new team was amazed at the sloppiness of the place. Not only did the two non-contributors lose their jobs but so did the senior manager who had imprinted his wishy-washiness on the company.

Imprinting is one of the vehicles for establishing and reinforcing the culture. "The way he or she does things"—with "he" and "she" referring to key imprinters—becomes "the way we do things here." This cuts both ways. If the personal styles of imprinters create or reinforce a business-enhancing culture, then all is well. But often all is not well.

Throughout this chapter there have been hints about how to manage the shadow side of individuals. The next chapter takes a more systematic view of such management, outlining competencies needed by managers and offering a set of guidelines.

8

WORKING WITH
PERSONAL STYLES
AND PROMOTING
PRODUCTIVE RELATIONSHIPS

J EFFREY PFEFFER (1994) studied the dynamics behind the success
of companies that provided the greatest return to stockholders
over a twenty-year period (1972–1992). The winners were companies
that had maintained sustainable competitive advantage over their
rivals by finding ways of distinguishing themselves from their competitors, providing positive economic benefits to their stakeholders,
and doing business in a way that their competitors could not readily
duplicate. The principal factor in the success of the five top companies, Pfeffer discovered, was *the way they managed people*. Company-enhancing and worker-enhancing human resource policies,
effective human resource management systems, and the ability of
managers and supervisors to use these systems are all ingredients in
this formula for success.

An important part of managing people and helping them
give their best is the ability to manage the shadow side of people's
personal styles. Effective managers and supervisors understand the
vagaries of people and know when to intervene and confront, when
to encourage and reward, when to coach and counsel, and when to
leave things alone. While this is only common sense—let's rename
it extraordinary sense—few companies make sure that their managers and supervisors have and use these capabilities. The fact that
they don't have these capabilities constitutes a major shadow-side

problem that has woeful psychological, social, and financial costs associated with it. Or, on a positive note, the lack of skills, strategies, and guidelines for managing the shadow side of individuals— or, even better, for helping them manage their own shadow side— constitutes a golden opportunity for companies wanting to develop cutting-edge managers and supervisors.

Four major issues are dealt with in this chapter: (1) developing the critical communication skills needed to help people manage the shadow side of personal styles, (2) understanding and using the principles of human behavior in the workplace, (3) uncovering and utilizing buried talent and hidden potential, and (4) developing strategies for managing the shadow side of individuals. All of these contribute to the kind of people-based competitive advantage Pfeffer is talking about.

The importance of a prevention mentality in using these skills and strategies to deal with the idiosyncrasies of individuals cannot be overemphasized. All the methods and strategies outlined in this chapter can be used at the service of prevention. Ask any manager who has to deal with people-related disasters. Hindsight is just too costly. "It's now clear that we should never have put Luis in charge of that department" is not just an expression of frustration. It is an unexpressed economic statement: "He has caused untold personal misery; he has totally disrupted the team approach we were trying to establish there; and the price is over $100,000." While some organizations leave no stone unturned in trying to make sure that the manager up for promotion will perform as expected and that the company will not be blindsided by whatever may be hidden in the shadows, many do not.

Consider the value of using people-related skills and strategies in prevention mode. A middle manager, interviewing someone for a kind of chief of staff position in his unit, outlined the role and indicated the amount of emotional energy that would sometimes be needed to make sure that certain key conversations and debates were actually taking place in the department. He gave the applicant a couple of cases and asked her how she would handle them. Still not satisfied, he took one of the cases and played the role of a resistant manager with her. She wilted. At least he knew. He did this a few more times with other applicants until he found someone who had both the technical skills and emotional fortitude needed for the job. Had he hired one of the other applicants, the cost of dealing with later disruptions would have been too high. Yet the people-related competencies needed to take either a preventive or a remedial approach are not widely distributed among managers.

Acquire Critical Communication Skills

Managers need to develop communication and coaching/counseling skills (Egan, 1994) that can greatly facilitate their interaction with one another and those they supervise. Of course, these skills should not be restricted to managers and supervisors. Any worker who gets his or her work done through communication with co-workers, customers, suppliers, and other stakeholders should develop the ability to

- Listen actively
- Respond empathetically
- Give both corrective and confirmatory feedback
- Challenge others forcefully but tactfully
- Help others engage in problem-solving dialogue
- Stimulate innovation-focused dialogue

As essential as these abilities are, most managers are really not required to have or develop them. But many people-related shadow-side issues will not be managed without them.

Listen Actively

An active approach involves the ability to listen to both the verbal and nonverbal messages of colleagues without distorting them through personal, system, or cultural filters. Total listening includes *contextual listening*—that is, picking up cues related to the other's competence and personal style. This is not an added task. Rather it is something savvy managers do in every interaction. But it is workplace rather than psychiatric listening.

Listening to others' points of view is, for the expert manager, not a chore but a source of business-enhancing ideas. I once said to a manager, "I have two hypotheses about your managerial style. The first is this: you feel if you listen carefully and sometimes patiently to others, take their ideas seriously, and open these ideas up to debate, you will lose a great deal of your power." "What's the second hypothesis?" he asked. "The second is that if you do these things, you will double your power." Leadership and empowerment begin with this kind of listening. The business literature is filled with cases of managers who end up saying something like what one chastened manager said: "When everything else failed I went to our employees and asked them what they thought. I found that most of them wanted to be more productive than they were. They wanted to tell me how I was screwing up the business." This kind of business-enhancing listening should not be a last resort.

Respond Empathetically

Empathy refers to the ability to communicate to another person that you have, to the best of your ability, understood what he or she has had to say from his or her viewpoint. Effective managers identify, appreciate, and learn from others' points of view. Empathy is the beginning of productive dialogue rather than self-centered monologue. Research shows that such empathetic responding—an objective, listening-based response not to be confused with sympathetic responding—is not common in human transactions. People's tendency is either to listen sporadically or to listen more carefully but evaluatively. Empathy is a skill that helps build relationships and gather the kind of information that is useful in managing human transactions. In one stroke the manager clarifies the idea offered and recognizes and reinforces the one who offered it. Both listening and listening-based responding are tough—tough to master and essential for tough managing. Yet without the use of such skills, so-called empowerment programs—not to mention attempts to build productive relationships—are shams. An important part of empowerment is listening with a truly open mind to workers' ideas on how to run the business more effectively.

Give Both Corrective and Confirmatory Feedback

Feedback sessions, both corrective and confirmatory, are, ideally, learning events. Corrective feedback works best when it is not a personal attack and does not pin the other person against the wall with no room to move; workers don't learn when they are pinned against the wall. The best managers allow team members to take the lead in learning from mistakes: "We all know the project failed, but I'd like to hear your analysis of what happened and what was learned from the failure." Merely giving employees chapter and verse on what they did wrong minimizes learning. Confirmatory feedback, recognition of a job well done, should also be a learning event. Most managers say something like this: "Good job, Nancy. Keep up the good work." There is recognition but no learning. A learning approach might sound something like this: "Great job, Nancy. Here's what you did, here's how you did it, and here are the results. In what ways could your approach in Project A be applied to Project B?" This approach leads to shared learning, and business-focused learning adds value.

Challenge Others Forcefully But Tactfully

The first three skills provide clarification and support for the other person. But support without challenge can be anemic, just as challenge without support can be harsh. Challenging means *inviting* others to explore assumptions, beliefs, values, attitudes, norms, and behaviors that are possibly system- and individual-limiting. Challenge is upbeat because it is future oriented. It addresses the unused potential of the person or unit challenged: "I bet that your unit could take the lead in this more-for-less initiative."

Challenge demands both assertiveness and tact. One of the reasons that performance management systems have such a poor track record is that managers save up their challenges and deliver them at the time of the appraisal meeting: "You did not step forward and champion the new marketing thrust." This is both cowardly and uneconomical. It is cowardly because the manager did not have the courage to challenge the team member at the right time. It is uneconomical because the now-challenged worker cannot change history. Both the psychological and the lost-opportunity costs are high.

Effective challengers know how to challenge themselves and

how to invite others to do the same. They also challenge unused strengths more than weaknesses. Research shows that this kind of challenge is not common among managers. Therefore, it constitutes an opportunity for developing a competitive edge. Managing shadow-side issues with others is inconceivable without the ability to challenge well.

Help Others Engage in Problem-Solving Dialogue

Effective managers know how to lead problem-managing discussions with team members. This means, first of all, that they have the guts to drag problems hidden in the shadows out into the light. Chapter Two discussed ways of moving shadow-side issues into the light. "Nobody's talking about the fact that our total quality management process is going nowhere right now. Let's name what's going on or what's not going on and see what we can do about it." Second, this process is greatly helped if, as noted in Chapter Four, the company or organizational unit has a shared problem-solving process in the first place. Having a shared process promotes a culture of problem-solving dialogue.

Managers need to know that dialogue can easily degenerate into self-serving debate. Those who moderate these discussions need to be familiar with the personal styles of the discussants, understand the ways in which these styles may corrupt the process, and challenge discussants when this happens. Both research and experience show that verbal, gregarious discussants can take over the meeting. When this happens, problem solving takes a back seat to agenda pushing.

Savvy managers engage disruptive personalities in problem solving rather than argument. Invitation to problem solving should routinely follow corrective feedback. Here is an abbreviated version of what one manager said: "John, in yesterday's meeting you talked more than the others. Some of what you said added value; some was your way of pushing your own agendas. I read the resentment on the faces of some of the other team members. I'm new here. This may be part of your style. If it is, what do you think would be the best way of managing it?"

Stimulate Innovation-Focused Dialogue

If opportunity development rather than mere problem solving is a managerial priority, then innovation-focused dialogue among managers and between managers and their reports is essential. Some problems need to be transcended rather than solved or even managed. If a company is losing market share to a competitor, "solving" the problem means winning back market share. An opportunity development approach, on the other hand, suggests moving to a higher plane—discovering new markets, finding niches, changing the product mix, and the like.

In my experience, managers do not consistently engage in innovation-focused dialogue with one another and with the members of their teams. Some companies now provide a specific time during the week—some as much as a half day—for teams to focus exclusively on innovation. When I hear managers say over and over, "I don't have time to stop and just think about the business," I hear the innovator within them stirring. There are all sorts of ways of encouraging such dialogue. One manager once said, "If we went to a zero-based company this coming year, what would we add back?" Another manager routinely asks the benchmarking question, "Which company does it best?" Then she adds, "And how can we do it better?" It is not necessary to take time out to focus on innovation-based dialogue. In companies with a culture of innovation, a critical mass of workers are asking themselves these kinds of questions all the time.

Some see this package of communication skills as too idealistic: "Let's get serious. Most managers don't have these skills. Let's stick with the real world." These communication competencies are not fuzzy amenities. They add value when linked to business issues. They stimulate results. Therefore, they are essential. Or at least they constitute competitive-edge possibilities. Without them, shadow-side issues will not be surfaced and addressed. Without them, managers will be neither smart nor wise supervisors. Without them, much of the potential of the workforce will remain unleveraged.

Understand and Use the Principles of Human Behavior

A couple of decades ago the term *behavior modification* frightened people. They pictured people being able to take control of their minds. In reality the principles of behavior modification—called here the *laws of human behavior*—are not the exclusive province of human service professionals such as psychologists. They can be learned and used by anyone. They deal with such everyday realities as incentives, rewards, and punishments. They are best used by individuals both to understand their own behavior and the behavior of others and, even more important, to control their own behavior more effectively (Watson and Tharp, 1993). Effective communication and problem-solving competencies are often referred to as *life skills*—that is, these competencies are essential to taking charge of one's own life and interacting creatively with others. Understanding the laws of human behavior and having the ability to apply them to everyday situations are also life skills. But, like communication and problem-solving skills, their acquisition is pretty much left to chance in our society.

Practical economists have long been interested in the principles of human behavior as a means of understanding and predicting group economic behavior (Landsburg, 1994). There were some attempts in the 1970s to get managers interested in the power that lies in what might be called the skills of behavior management (Luthans and Kreitner, 1975; Miller, 1978). But since they seemed faddish, and fears about psychological control in the workplace persisted, these attempts went the way of all fads.

Behind most fads, however, are realities that need to be understood and appreciated. The principles of human behavior remain in force in everyday life, including life in the workplace. Most of us use some of these principles, at least sporadically. For example, many astute managers and workers have an instinctive feeling for how incentives, rewards, and punishments affect workplace behavior, and they act on their instincts. But few managers have an in-depth working knowledge of behavioral principles that they apply consistently both to themselves and others. The purpose of this section is to briefly review some of these principles and apply them to the shadow-side behavior of individuals. Unfortunately the overview presented here is no substitute for the work needed to acquire a fuller understanding of these principles along with competence in their use.

Use Incentives to Stimulate Desired Behavior

An *incentive* is a promise that certain behaviors will lead to rewards and a warning that other behaviors will lead to punishment. Whether we know it or not, incentives are constantly shaping our behavior. Tom Gilbert (1978) said that the best way of creating *incompetence* in the workplace is to make sure there are no incentives for business-enhancing behavior. Here are some of his suggestions for creating the incentiveless and therefore unproductive workplace (p. 87):

- Make sure that poor performers get paid as well as good ones.
- See that good performance gets punished in some way.
- Don't make use of nonmonetary rewards such as encouragement and recognition.
- Design the job so that it has no future.
- Avoid arranging work conditions that employees would find more pleasant.
- Give pep talks rather than incentives to promote performance when business is tough.

Many of us might recognize this picture, or at least parts of it, in some of the companies where we have worked. Doing the opposite of what is outlined above would go far to creating a stimulating workplace. Successful companies tend to manage such incentives as fair compensation, benefits, the work itself, opportunities for achievement, recognition, promotion, increased authority and responsibility, education, training, opportunities for personal growth, working with congenial people, opportunities to choose preferred kinds of work, flextime, and participating in the decision-making process in such a way as to balance the needs of the business with the needs of employees.

When workers engage in company-limiting shadow-side activities, there are incentives for doing so. Some of these come from within—for instance, an attitude that "I can get away with almost anything." But managers sometimes unwittingly provide incentives for shadow-side behavior they deplore. In some insurance companies it was discovered that "rogue" agents were selling life insurance policies under the guise of retirement investments. While greed was probably an internal incentive, the compensation system itself provided some. Short-term pay incentives favored the sale of life insurance rather than investment products. In one company, agents got as much as $550 up front on a $1,000 premium for a whole-life policy, while they got 2 percent of a $1,000 annuity, an investment product, in the first year. Savvy managers would look at such an arrangement and say to themselves, "This might bring out the worst in certain people. What can be done to prevent it? And how do we monitor it?"

Therefore, with respect to company-limiting shadow-side behavior, managers need to ask themselves certain questions: What positive incentives do we unwittingly provide for the kinds of shadow-side activities and arrangements we are trying to eliminate? What negative incentives—a warning of probable punishment—do we fail to provide to help people avoid such behavior?

Use Rewards to Maintain and Strengthen Desired Behavior

A *reward* is the conferral of the "prize" promised by the incentive. "If you meet budget, there will be a 10 percent reward," is an incentive. "Here is the check for your 10 percent bonus," is the reward. While incentives stimulate people to engage in certain behaviors, rewards tend to *reinforce*—that is, maintain or increase the frequency and/or intensity of—the behaviors with which they are associated. In other words, rewarded behaviors tend to be repeated. If finding and developing market niches are consistently rewarded, such behavior will be maintained or intensified.

Of course, this backfires when undesirable shadow-side behaviors are unwittingly rewarded. When people get ahead because of political maneuverings rather than producing results, unwanted political activities will be maintained or even increased in intensity. In many companies, managers are rewarded for producing results.

However, in some of these companies, managers achieve these results by brutalizing the workers in their departments. In such cases, there is reinforcement not only of getting results but also of the undesirable managerial style that was used to get them. "I know Sue is a bit hard on people, but she does get results." In 1993, General Electric announced that managers would be rewarded for getting results only if they did so by implementing a set of basic managerial values, including people management values.

Use Punishment Sparingly to Manage Unwanted Behavior

While punishment tends to decrease or eliminate unwanted behavior, it does so at a price. Its effects are often temporary, it provides little opportunity for new learning, it often acts as an incentive for people to hide unwanted shadow-side behavior, it sours the relationship between the punisher and the person being punished, and it can have a *spread effect*—that is, it suppresses not only unwanted behavior but also desirable behavior. An example of the spread effect: A worker was punished for not getting permission to use some company resources to develop a new product. He became much more hesitant to use his creativity in the workplace.

This does not mean that punishment has no place in dealing with company-limiting shadow-side behavior. If there are no downside consequences for engaging in unwanted behavior, this can act as a stimulus for engaging in such behavior. One entrepreneur merely "cautioned" employees she discovered engaging in unwanted behavior such as petty thievery. Then she complained to me how difficult it was to get the right kind of workers and how people tended to take advantage of her. Firing the next employee found engaging in such behavior solved a lot of her problems. Very often it is not the punishment itself that is the culprit but the way it is administered. In the example above, the manager of the worker who used company resources without permission yelled at him in the presence of his co-workers. He needlessly embarrassed him.

Finally, even though there is a place for judiciously used punishment in the workplace, it is much better to make sure that there are sufficient incentives and rewards for engaging in business-enhancing behavior. The ideal, never to be completely achieved, is to drive bad behavior out by good. This is part of the prevention approach.

Develop a Respect for Internal Incentives and Self-Reward

You've heard it a thousand times: most employees, given the opportunity, want to do a good job. A lack of understanding of this internal incentive can create an unhealthy workplace climate. One company thought that it had to provide rewards for everything they wanted the employees to do. There were parties, good-service pins, pictures of good employees on the bulletin boards, congratulations galore in the company's weekly newsletter, small cash awards for incremental increases in productivity, and more. This created what I call a jumping-for-jellybeans culture: "If you don't give me something, I won't do it." While some system of such extrinsic rewards can be helpful, this company completely overdid it.

When it comes to managing shadow-side behavior, one strategy is to appeal to the person's internal incentive and reward system. One manager said to a worker whose continual cynicism was souring the workplace, "Down deep I don't think you're the kind of quitter your cynicism makes you out to be. I hired you because I saw more there. I think you do, too. Maybe I'm not doing my best to help you bring out your best." This led to a most productive discussion. Still, let us not be naive. If a person's internal incentive and reward system is weak, then strong external incentives and occasional punishment might be required.

Some take a very strong stand against the prevalence of extrinsic over intrinsic rewards. Alfie Kohn, in a book called *Punished by Rewards* (1993), claims that there is a shadow side to the administration of incentives and reward. The emphasis on external reward is manipulative and demeaning because it destroys intrinsic interest in the behavior being rewarded, such as work. The central points of his position are these: First, work is not in and of itself a burden; people live to work—that is, to grow things, solve problems, make things. Second, extrinsic incentives—that is, the promise of money, good grades, praise, and the like—constitute an inferior way of changing behavior. Third, the desire to do something well for its own sake is the only viable route to lasting, beneficial change.

While I admire the purity of this position, see it as an ideal to be strived for, and find it very useful as an effective antidote for a jumping-for-jellybeans culture, it is still necessary to deal with the workplace as it is.

Learn the Dynamics of Avoidance Behavior

Avoidance behavior underlies the failed potential of both individuals and organizations. Since shadow-side behavior often involves the avoidance of things that need to be done and the concealment of the avoidance, understanding and dealing with such behavior is critical. A central dynamic is that avoidance behavior is immediately rewarded. For instance, if a supervisor puts off giving feedback to a troublesome employee, the reward is the immediate relief of not having to experience an unpleasant situation. But, as we have seen above, behavior that is rewarded tends to be repeated. Avoidance begets more avoidance.

Furthermore, when workers fail to do what they are supposed to do, it often means that there are more incentives and rewards for *not* doing the required task than for doing it. Managers are routinely told to develop the people in their units. Many, if not most, fail to do so because developing people is not rewarded. Therefore, managers see developing people as a low priority. They first do the things they are rewarded for and then the things they are punished for not doing. Since there is no time left, development is left in the lurch. This is a system, not a worker, problem. Since the lack of development is not discussed in decision-making forums that could make a difference, it remains in the shadows.

Avoid "Social Traps" in the Workplace

John Cross and Melvin Guyer (1980) wrote an intriguing book on how failure to understand the principles of behavior and apply them to everyday situations make us prone to *social traps*—situations that seem to be rewarding, at least in the short term, but often lead to long-term misery. Both the addiction to immediate rewards and caving into the rewards inherent in avoidance behavior conspire to make individuals and organizations victims of social traps.

The smoker dying of lung cancer is an unfortunate example of this dynamic. Another is the office politician who finds each of her wins rewarding—"I got what I wanted" or "Boy, how clever I am"—only to find out too late that her political style has put her career on hold. Yet another: the manager who keeps putting off corrective feedback to a person with an abrasive style may well be creating a monster. The way to avoid social traps is to explore upfront the longer-term consequences of situations that are immediately rewarding. Managers do not do this instinctively. They need to say to themselves such things as, "If I don't give my direct report some corrective feedback, I will be temporarily relieved and have more time for other urgent matters, but the longer I let this go, the worse it will get."

This brief sampling provides some idea of the usefulness of the principles of behavior in dealing with the shadow side of individuals' personal styles. For an in-depth approach, see Aubrey Daniels' *Bringing Out the Best in People* (1994). The author points out that these principles are not tricks, gimmicks, or devious methods for digging into workers' psyches. They are managerial tools.

Uncover and Utilize Buried Talent and Hidden Potential

As Pfeffer (1994) noted, "Achieving competitive success through people involves fundamentally altering how we think about the work force. . . . It means achieving success by working *with* people, not by replacing them or limiting the scope of their activity" (p. 18). Working with people includes recognizing and using their talent and developing their potential. Since buried talent and undeveloped potential are both critical underperforming assets, it is essential to outline some skills and methods managers and supervisors can use to identify talent and develop potential.

Search for Unused Skills

Probe for competencies that lie unused in the shadows. Rotating people through different assignments helps them demonstrate skills that may not be noticed in routine assignments. One manager worked it something like this: he routinely asked team members about such things as hobbies and leisure pursuits. Very often these activities involved skills that could be put to use in the department. For instance, one technician talked about the extensive volunteer work she did with AIDS patients. Her brother had died of AIDS, and she had taken up this work in his memory. In discussing this with her, the manager discovered a tough-minded compassion, an ability to deal with difficult if not impossible situations, and communication skills that he had not noticed before. He immediately put her on the supervisory track. She had all the makings of an excellent supervisor.

Assume That People Can Be Creative

Studies have shown that even the slowest among us will, at times, have flashes of creativity and that almost everyone could be more creative than he or she is. Schools—at least the schools I went to— have a way of putting a damper on creativity. New ideas don't sell well in the classroom. They are often ignored or even punished ("Smart aleck!"). In many companies and institutions, creative ideas do not fare much better. A ray of hope in the workplace is the mini-explosion of employee empowerment and employee involvement programs. The jury is out, however, because companies and institutions not only have to create reasonable employee involvement processes but must also overcome the reluctance of people to be creative and the reluctance of managers to foster creativity. This is a new paradigm. The old will not give way easily.

Challenge the Culture and Structures That Inhibit Creativity

Individual workers, whether managers or not, might find their creative efforts hampered by the institution's structures and culture. If this is the case, then efforts throughout the company, from executive suite to shop floor, are needed to break through the impasse. Boeing's top team has a freewheeling weekly meeting to discuss the company's long-term challenges and to brainstorm ways of meeting them. Every unit in Amoco Corporation has been asked to fashion a "vision" for itself through team contributions. Both these companies realize that, despite their efforts, there are plenty of shadow hierarchical and command-and-control factors that inhibit individual employee effort. The trick is to flush them out and then absorb the best ideas of the empowerment movement into mainline culture.

Assume That People Want to Achieve More Than They Do

There is a rich humanistic and religious literature, backed up by countless examples, that suggests that even ordinary people are capable of achieving extraordinary goals. Ordinary workers have become product and program champions. Garden-variety managers have turned into exemplars and transformational leaders who have ignited the spark that set fire to the best in people.

Think Self-Development and the Development of Others

The starting point for helping others is self-development. If I don't realize that there are a slew of ways in which I can become a better contributor, then my efforts to help others will be hollow. The ideal is to help each individual maximize his or her contributions to the enterprise while he or she pursues legitimate personal goals in the workplace. As Jack Welch, the CEO of General Electric, once said at a meeting: "If you're not thinking all the time about making every person more valuable, you don't have a chance." Thinking is not enough. Having the competencies to do something about it is the next step. In many if not most companies, this entire issue remains in the shadows, undiscussed.

Develop Strategies for Managing the Shadow Side of Individuals

Using the skills outlined above, savvy managers become more and more able to do the following:

- Deal with the cultural foundations of shadow-side behavior.
- Do business-based audits of key individuals with whom you interact.
- Deal creatively with people's emotions.
- Deal with different people differently.
- Act assertively.

- Provide timely feedback.
- Recognize signs that people are getting into trouble.

Taken together, these principles constitute a system for preventing and dealing with institution-limiting idiosyncratic behavior. In the following discussion, explanations, mini-cases, and examples are provided for each.

Deal with the Cultural Foundations of Shadow-Side Behavior

Covert organizational culture often plays a key role in reinforcing institution-limiting behavior on the part of individual employees and in preventing them from engaging in institution-enhancing behavior.

A cursory reading of the daily press reveals company after company that has been caught engaging in either outright illegal and unethical or at least questionable business practices. It is almost as if they have covert cultural norms that say to their employees, "Do whatever you need to do to get ahead, but don't get caught." A Belgian-based food company with over a thousand stores in the United States prided itself on its cost-effectiveness. But it became a victim of its own culture. The company raced past competition with its no-frills stores and low-price strategy. But all was not rosy. The company's cost-cutting policies and practices drove individual employees to cut corners, to become unwitting rogues. The business press described the company as one that drove its employees mercilessly. One former employee said that he kept putting in more and more time—sometimes a hundred hours per week—but that he could never satisfy his supervisors. They wanted "100 percent conditions 100 percent of the time."

In late 1992 a major TV network did an exposé of the company. They showed secret video footage and claimed that some of the company's employees were cutting corners, for instance, by rewrapping fish and meat whose shelf life had expired. It may well be that the company pushed the cost control dimensions of the business so far that some employees began cutting corners lest they be seen as not conforming to the corporate culture. A norm evolved: "Do whatever you have to do to keep costs down." After the exposé, the company's sales plummeted. In 1993 the company paid the federal government over $16 million to settle the case, which also included violations of child-labor rules.

After the TV report, customers that abandoned its stores have been slow to return. Its growth pattern—the company had hoped to have two thousand stores in the U.S. by the end of the century—has been interrupted. Some unrest among its workers remains. The image of the company has suffered greatly. In the end, it seems that the company's driving culture did not bring out the best in its employees. Instead, it so encouraged company-limiting shadow-side behavior that we might well ask: At what point does a company in pursuit of profitability go over the edge? At what point does a company's culture turn employees into co-conspirators? Brokerage firms and insurance companies have come up against both criticism and legal action, supposedly because of the rogue behavior of some of their sales personnel. In one company, brochures with misleading information were said to be the work of individual operators. But it finally came to light that the brochures had been produced in the home office. In another case, a company blamed "a few bad apples" for the abuses. But a jury believed otherwise. They let the individual agent off, saying that the company was responsible. This was a question not just of a lack of due diligence on the part of the company but of something deeper and perhaps more sinister—a culture that may not promote but at least allows such behavior. The scams that have been discovered have proved to be costly in a variety of ways. The company gets a black eye, ethical sales agents are tainted, and there are litigation costs and fines to be paid.

Therefore, whenever you spot something that is dysfunctional in the personal style of any given worker, first ask, Is this just an individual problem, or is it a system problem? The culture can sabotage the work of otherwise effective supervisors and team leaders. I worked for one company in which many of the employees seemed to do what they wanted. My first instinct was to say, "They've hired the wrong people." But when I discussed this with managers and supervisors, most admitted that they had not even noticed how loose the place was. After that it did not take long for me to realize that it was not a case of poor employees or of managers and supervisors not doing their jobs. In dozens of different ways the culture reflected the principle, "We take care of ourselves here."

In all these cases, challenging the behavior of individuals without challenging the culture that supported them would have been blowing in the wind. A key question always is, What's behind the behavior that's inhibiting the business? The culture tools provided in Chapters Five and Six will help you answer that question.

Do Business-Based Audits of Key Individuals

Your job entails dealing with people. The better you understand them as they are in the workplace, the more effective your interactions will be. The key people you deal with—the boss, direct reports, peers, customers, and so forth—are company assets just as money, inventory, equipment, and buildings are assets. Human assets, like material assets, need to be audited. Figure 8.1 presents a self-explanatory human assets audit together with a suggestion on how to relate to each group, but it is limited to productivity and the use of work-related potential. It does not focus on shadow-side factors. Rather you or your company can develop your own audit process. The lead question is, What do we really need to know about people here? *Stars* are workers who are highly productive but still have large reserves of unused potential. These are the creative people. *Succession prospects* are highly productive workers who are ready to move into more challenging jobs. *Peaked performers* are highly productive workers who are using practically all the potential they have. *High-pot development prospects* are moderately productive workers who have not yet fully translated their rather substantial abilities into more value-added work. *General development prospects* are moderately productive workers who are capable of doing more. *Adequate performers* are moderately productive workers who are not likely to develop much further. *Problem high-pots* are workers with substantial ability but little to show for it. *Problem performers* have moderate abilities, but can't seem to get started. *Mismatches* are people who simply do not have the skill or the will for the job and do not seem likely to develop.

One manager developed an integrated audit process that focused on the competence, personal style, culture, relationship style,

Figure 8.1. Human Resources Audit Grid.

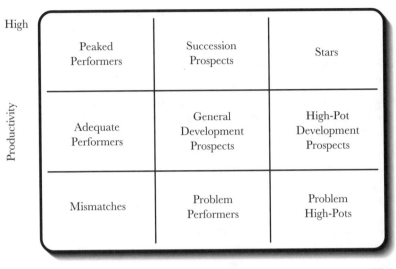

The Challenges

- *Mismatches:* separating them cost-effectively and with dignity.
- *Problem Performers:* helping them move into the General Development Prospects cell or moving them into the Mismatch cell.
- *Problem High-Pots:* helping them move into the High-Pot Development Prospects cell or moving them into the Mismatch cell.
- *Adequate Performers:* helping them stay at the task; not letting them drop into the Mismatch cell.
- *General Development Prospects:* helping members of this pool find ways to become more productive by, for instance, leveraging current skills, developing further skills, sharpening constructive attitudes.
- *High-Pot Development Prospects:* helping members of this pool move into the next tier.
- *Peaked Performers:* helping them remain motivated by, for instance, moving through company-enhancing career paths; not making the mistake of promoting them beyond their level of competence.
- *Succession Prospects:* grooming members of this pool for key positions; leveraging their talent and flexibility.
- *Stars:* helping them remain motivated, find new challenges, take the lead in company-enhancing innovation; not letting them become overly self-centered and use their talents in company-limiting ways.

and work performance of a colleague in another department with whom she had to interact a great deal. She said, "This guy is technically very competent. But he's a bit lazy. At least by my standards. And he's always filled with himself. In any meeting he assumes that he should take the lead, and he doesn't listen very well. He doesn't even know he's turning people off. He has great ideas but he does not follow through." She used her understanding to plan her interactions with him and to manage her part of the projects for which they were jointly responsible. She did similar audits on people who reported to her. Doing an audit of one's direct reports is the basis of value-adding supervision. The purpose of these informal audits was not to "psych people out," but to understand them at the service of optimizing the value of interactions with them.

Deal Creatively with People's Emotions

Shadow-side issues often have strong emotional undertones. Emotions act as drivers and as multipliers of the best and worst in people. The more interactive the workplace becomes in terms of teams, especially self-managed teams, the more important the ability to deal with emotional realities becomes. Emotions are two-edged swords in the workplace. While in and of themselves they are economically neutral, in practice they often add or subtract value.

Many managers shy away from dealing with the shadow-side idiosyncrasies of others because it means dealing with such negative emotions as anxiety, fear, anger, hurt, envy, and the like. Some workplace cultures forbid emotional expression, leading to shadow-side emotions that can do much more harm. Some of the bizarre behavior outlined in the discussion of dysfunctional personal styles in Chapter Seven arises because negative emotions are not identified or they are ignored. Since feelings and emotions do not go away simply because we don't want to deal with them in the workplace, here are a few principles that may help you deal with them creatively:

- Admit the existence and legitimacy of emotions. Don't drive them underground.

- Work from the general principle that people can be responsible for rather than victims of their emotions.
- Translate *victim* statements into *responsibility* statements. For instance, don't say, "He gets my goat." Rather, *"I let him* get my goat." Some people greet others goats in hand.
- Change "My fear of speaking in front of groups is hampering my career" to "I let my fear get the best of me."
- As needed, name one's own limiting emotions. Clear the air. "I see you as very competent. When I talk about a project with you, I begin feeling very inadequate. Because I let this get the best of me, I don't offer some of the good ideas I have."
- Turn negative emotions into stimuli for action rather than occasions for complaining. One team member said to himself, "I keep letting Jane take over the meetings, and then I resent her. The problem is mine, not hers. I'll come to meetings better prepared and give what I have to offer without apology."

Dealing with emotions, your own or others', and their consequences does not turn the workplace into an encounter group. On the other hand, *not* dealing with them can be detrimental. I doubt that emotionally sanitized workplaces are as productive as they might be.

Deal with Different People Differently

It is easy for supervisors to base their interactions with those they supervise on the assumption that a worker is a worker. The interactions will all be roughly the same. This, of course, leads to poor supervision, since the assumption is false. In fact, each worker is unique. Workers differ enormously in their kinds of intelligence, competence, personal style, emotionality, and shadow-side idiosyncrasies. However, spending hours poring over each worker's uniqueness can be a waste of time, since many of the ways in which A is different from B do not make a difference in the workplace.

Effective supervisors strike the right balance, dealing with others neither as cogs in a machine nor as totally unique. Rather they focus on differences that make a difference. If Jack is more sensitive to criticism than Jill, then a supervisor adds value not by coddling Jack but by being a bit more careful. This is true also of

shadow-side characteristics. If I know that Jack is constantly looking for deals that will get him ahead even to the detriment of the
business, and if I know that Jill has talents she is hesitant to reveal
lest she seem pushy, then I can challenge Jack and provide support
for Jill.

The best managers and supervisors tailor their interactions
to the needs of the individual. While this tailoring has been referred
to as *situational leadership*, I prefer the more mundane term
worker-centered supervision. It rests on the notion that workers
differ greatly in terms of their understanding of the business, understanding of their roles, understanding of the demands of the job,
skills needed to do their jobs, and willingness to work. It also assumes that dealing with individual differences is an economic
rather than a psychological exercise; that is, tailoring supervision
to each individual adds value. The audit process suggested earlier
should also provide supervisors with an understanding of each
worker's development needs. Then training and other forms of development can be tailored to each.

Willingness to work and the enthusiasm displayed on the job
is often a question of incentives and rewards. So let us return for
a moment to that topic. People differ greatly in terms of the appeal
of incentives and rewards. What is an incentive for Jane might not
be an incentive for John. It is difficult to provide incentives that
have universal appeal. While you think that assigning both Jane
and John to a special task force is an unalloyed good, Jane might
see it is the way ahead, while John sees it as a lateral move. A raise
in pay might leave a researcher relatively cold, but a new piece of
lab equipment is another story. One employee might focus almost
exclusively on increased direct compensation—more money in the
pay envelope—while another might be much more interested in the
right benefits package or getting the right promotion or lateral
move. Research has shown that members of product development
teams are more motivated by a sense of accomplishment and recognition and praise from their colleagues than by career advancement
and pay; visibility to top management, career advancement, pay,
and even peer pressure are also incentives, but they are not as important. Furthermore, for any given individual, what is an incentive
today may not be an incentive tomorrow. With some individuals

some incentives are entropic—they work for a while and then lose their bite.

If your interaction with those who work under your direction does not lead to an understanding of the reward preferences, then you are probably not listening very well. And so individual preferences are buried in the shadows. Supervisors take little time finding out what turns people on. When the incentives provided fail to have their effect, they blame "unresponsive" workers. Discovering which kinds of incentives appeal to different workers is not the same as coddling them.

Act Assertively

Managers rationalize their own unwillingness to deal with shadow-side behavior that is contaminating the workplace one way or another. "I did not want to hurt his feelings." "I thought that if I gave her time she would change." "We needed to have him finish that project and, yes, we do need him for the next project." "Her behavior isn't *that* disruptive." The list is endless. Managers often fail to act even when the personal, social, and financial economics demand action.

Dealing with difficult people often requires assertiveness. Difficult people are those whose competence, personal styles, and/ or relationships interfere with productivity and quality of work life. Every organization has them. More and more is being written about how to manage them. If they are in key positions, they have the ability to introduce massive inefficiencies into the system, even though these go unnoticed. But people in key positions are often exempt from feedback and challenge. This is a common shadow-side reality. For instance, Ted, the director of logistics for an automotive parts distribution firm, was a difficult person. He was opinionated, irascible, and committed to doing things the "old, tried and true" way. He had seniority, and no one ever thought seriously of replacing him. Other managers learned that they got nowhere when they tried to confront him directly. Therefore, they either went around him or put up with inefficiencies in delivery. When the company decided to mount a total quality management program, he fought it tooth and nail and tried to sabotage it once it started.

One of the TQM consultants focused not just on logistics but on Ted and his style. She did the economics of his style. She figured that Ted's style alone was costing the company about $2 million a year. While the TQM effort did not target Ted specifically, it did target all inefficiencies. Once inefficiencies were identified, managers were expected to clear them up quickly. Ted was gone within six months.

Recognize Signs That People Are Getting into Trouble and Provide Timely Feedback

Vigilance is not the same as paranoia. Paranoia is part of the shadow side, while vigilance is part of the solution. Early warning systems are much more economical than crisis management intervention. The "system" can be as simple as this: "I've gotten some hints that Fred might be beating up on his people because of that failed project. That wasn't their fault. And if he is doing that, it's just not right. You interact a lot with that unit. Monitor that a bit, would you?" The ideal, perhaps, would be to deal with such a situation directly, say, through Fred's boss. But that might not be as easy as it sounds. The relationship between Fred and his boss might be problematic.

It is one thing to be capable of giving useful feedback. It is another to actually do it consistently. Managers, because of the MUM Effect mentioned in Chapter Two or a lack of the skill to challenge effectively, keep putting off supplying feedback to individuals whose incompetence and personal style are detracting from productivity and the quality of work life. This entire situation remains undiscussed and therefore outside managerial control. Very often nothing is done until some crisis erupts or the situation becomes intolerable. The psychological, social, and financial costs of waiting until a crisis develops are very high but usually remain unexplored.

One manager, new to her department, developed the following business solution. She told people in her department that feedback given only at appraisal time was too late. She said that she was going to engage in informal "five minuters" with each member of the department. That is, whenever the opportunity offered itself, she would spend five minutes providing whatever confirmative or corrective feedback she thought might add value. No saving things up for the "big" discussion. This was also a time when they could provide feedback for her. If a critical incident came up, she did the five minuter immediately. Using this method, she got one very difficult person to quit, one lazy person to get up to speed, and one incompetent person to move to a less demanding job in another department.

The focus in these last two chapters has been on the individual. But since companies and institutions are also societies in their own right, we move on to the shadow side of group behavior in Chapter Nine.

9

IN-GROUPS, OUT-GROUPS, CLIQUES, AND CLUBS: FINDING VALUE IN YOUR ORGANIZATION'S SOCIAL REALITIES

T HERE ARE ONE-PERSON BUSINESSES: the self-employed consultant or marketing rep, for instance. But if there are two or more people in a business—a two-person consulting firm, for example, or a self-employed marketing rep with a secretary—then there is a social system. The social system consists of the individuals and units of the institution together with their social interactions. An organization is a social matrix within which people, individually or in groups, meet some of their social needs. The social aspects of a company or institution encompass such things as social structure, relationships, diversity, norms, cohesion, fad, fashion, and the like. Since these phenomena affect the business, they need to be understood and managed.

While business and social realities coexist and interrelate, they are not the same thing. There are business relationships, such as manager to direct report or team member to team member, but there are also personal relationships. Organizations do not just have departments, units, and functions. They also have in-groups, out-groups, and informal clubs. *Task force* and *cross-functional teams* are business terms. *Cliques* and *in-groups* are social system terms. Work teams are routinely discussed in the public forums of an institution. Cliques are not. Information sharing, business discussions, group problem solving, feedback, debate, and negotiation deal with business communication, while rumors, gossip, backbiting, and chewing the fat deal with social system communication.

The social system as a shadow-side phenomenon is outside the formal control of managers and supervisors, but its realities need to be understood, monitored, and dealt with for reasons relating to both productivity and the quality of work life. The following issues are considered here: (1) understanding the social culture, (2) promoting productive personal relationships, (3) managing the social system, (4) managing the shadow side of diversity, (5) managing shadow-side groups, and (6) managing social communication.

Understanding the Social Culture

If culture is "the way we do things here," then social culture is "the way we relate to one another around here." Since the social culture sets the norms for all social interaction, it needs to be understood. The social culture consists of the shared social beliefs, values, and norms that drive patterns of social behavior. This is the context in which specific social transactions occur. For instance, some companies pride themselves on their "family spirit." They publicly adopt and promote family-like values as part of their espoused culture. For them, such a culture serves the business. Some of them end the week with Friday "beer blast" social events. Other companies do not fare as well. Even though they may have espoused values and norms dealing with good relationships, the covert norms drive negative patterns of social interaction. Such companies or units within companies may be branded as having "predatory" or "cold" or "unfriendly" social cultures. As one worker in a shipping department put it, "I keep to myself and am glad to get out of there at night."

Overt Social Culture

Most companies do not publish their social norms. It's not that they don't have them. Rather they are not enunciated. Michael Maxtone-Graham (1991, pp. 12–13), believing that publishing a set of social behavior guidelines might help to improve morale and social cohesion, developed the following basic rules of social conduct:

- Be a good listener. You will stand out because, unfortunately, good listeners are a scarce commodity.
- Don't talk about confidential matters in public places.
- When you succeed, share the credit with others.
- If you must drink at lunch, have only one. If you have too many, don't return to work.
- Avoid office romances. If they go sour, the work consequences can be deadly.
- If you don't know the answer to a question, say so. Don't guess or bluff or bluster.
- If you make a mistake, admit it, but don't dwell on it.
- If you offend someone, apologize without apologizing for even existing.
- If you get in over your head, admit it. Trying to fake it will get you into deeper trouble.
- Stay well groomed. Your appearance can be an asset or a liability.
- Remember people's names.
- Don't discuss salaries with your peers. These discussions lead too easily to bitterness.
- Don't underestimate your boss.
- Don't use foul language. There are other ways of making a point.
- Be nice to people you don't like, especially if you outrank them. Don't make enemies unless it is absolutely unavoidable.
- Don't fall into lockstep with everyone else. Be yourself without making efforts to stand out like a sore thumb.
- Be ethical in all things.
- Take your lumps. Life is not fair. Taking your knocks without whining will get you noticed.
- Try very hard not to say, "I told you so." Ever.

In aggregate, this set of guidelines would constitute an espoused social culture. You may agree or disagree, even vehemently, with some of the norms on this list. Or you may see them as naive and superficial. That's not the point. If social norms are not explicit, then a covert set, whether benign, corrosive, or mixed, evolves anyway. Managers and other workers can do a great deal to establish an overt social culture that serves the business by discussing the social realities of the company more openly in decision-making forums. As we shall see later, this is now happening with respect to diversity in the workplace, with results that are enhancing both productivity and the quality of work life.

Covert Social Culture

Contrast the norms above with a more subversive, covert set found in the consulting division of a larger accounting firm. This company seemed to have a culture of civility, but it was a veneer. The visitor or the newcomer would think, "This seems like a nice place to work." However, behind the facade there was another set of less appetizing norms. Here are some of them:

- Share dirt on just about anyone, but not the CEO. He has a way of finding out who said what about him, and he will get you.
- Pawn work off on others if you think you can get away with it. Identify who's a sitting duck.
- Take as much credit as you can when things go well, but do it subtly.
- Get to know someone in the boss's office. You'll find out early which way the wind is blowing, and this will help you make a good appearance.
- Look sharp. If you do, then the people that count around here will think you are sharp.
- Don't let people get away with things. Send signals early on that you know how to retaliate. "Don't tread on me" is not a bad motto around here.
- On the other hand, don't make enemies unless you have to. Enemies around here are a big burden.

As a result of these norms, those who worked in the consulting division were always on guard. There was a sense of social uneasiness. As one junior manager put it, "I can never relax around here, but the tension has little to do with the work." Some people described this as a "tough" culture, intimating that a tough culture was needed for the tough business they were in. But this social culture did not really serve the business. Since the norms outlined above were covert, undiscussed, and in many ways undiscussable, people had to learn how to live within the social system, even though they didn't like its values and norms, especially the sleazy ones. Of course, expecting all norms to be logical and reasonable is—in light of the way social interactions evolve in any society—quite unreasonable in itself.

Promoting Productive Personal Relationships

We now move to the smallest social unit, one-to-one personal relationships. If individual employees are not fully appreciated assets, then relationships are even less appreciated. They are often even deeper in the shadows. The relationships that appear on organizational charts are technical or business relationships—the relationships of managers to their direct reports, of the maintenance engineer to the production group, of marketing to production, and so forth. The human side of these relationships does not appear on the charts. Yet these shadow-side relationships can add great value or great cost to the enterprise. They are seldom neutral. Karl Weick (1979, p. 252) once said that "whole persons aren't contained in the boxes on organizational charts. But managers forget that, which is why organizational charts are never the way things work—even though people invest enormous time in drawing, reviewing, pondering, and worrying over them."

A different way of saying this is that whole persons are there, all right, but many aspects of them lie in the shadows. It is one thing to discuss the organizational relationship between John Smith, director of marketing, and Sandra Jones, market representative and his direct report. This is on the chart. It is another to talk about a fifty-eight-year-old white male—insecure about his job, vindictive, highly political, and introverted—and his relationship to a thirty-eight-year-old aggressive black woman who is smart as a whip, successful, and very ambitious. This is not on the chart. Strange to say, the relationship described in this paragraph, despite its explosive possibilities, ended up serving the business. John was too smart to confront Sandra head on; Sandra was too savvy to make an enemy of John. They used each other in a variety of ways to get things done. Sandra kept John on his toes. John made sure that Sandra's maneuvers, while self-serving, served him and the business first. "Now that's a team!" John's boss would say when he saw them together. The real dynamics never crossed his mind. Nor did he hear what each said to their respective confidants.

There are a number of ways that relationships can be managed. First, an assessment must be made of whether the relationship adds value or cost to the business.

Relationships That Serve the Business

What does an *excellent* workplace relationship look like? In an excellent relationship both parties are competent, both have a positive personal style, both appreciate these factors in the other, and this entire package helps them interact in such a way as to improve both business productivity and the quality of work life. So Jill might say, "Jack and I have a great relationship. We see each other as competent, and we like each other. When we work together, we get things done quickly, and the results are inevitably good, even excellent. And we have fun, to boot." Such relationships are pure gold.

Tess and Jake, a husband-and-wife team, started their own interior decorating business. They called themselves "internal environment consultants." Their niche was small businesses. They offered cost-effective design and decorating packages that helped these companies, especially those that had customers coming to their offices, spruce up their images and send the right signals. They had an excellent personal relationship. Right from the start they based the division of labor on personal abilities and preferences. Tess, the more gregarious, spent a great deal of time with clients. Jake, less gregarious but more numbers focused, dealt with suppliers and the accounts. Like all married couples, they had their problems, but they worked them through. They even learned to deal more effectively with others by successfully grappling with their own problems. All in all, their relationship was one of the greatest assets of the business. On the other hand, they knew a number of entrepreneurial couples who had to abandon otherwise viable businesses because their relationship was an obstacle rather than an asset. Jake's sister and her husband ended up in divorce court after starting a business.

Wayne Baker (1994), in a book titled *Networking Smart: How to Build Relationships for Personal and Organizational Success,* provides many strategies for building company-enhancing relationships. Focusing on a wide range of relationships both within and outside the organization, Baker emphasizes personal relationship building and networking over what he calls the self-centered "cult of the deal" approach, which characterizes the politics of self-interest. Good relationships can help drive out bad politics.

Relationships That Add Cost to the Business

It is immediately clear that very many workplace relationships fall short of this ideal. Indeed, relationship hell would be the opposite of what is described above—two incompetent people who hate each other who end up damaging themselves, each other, and the business in the process. It is also clear why workplace relationships are often so difficult. There are all sorts of gradations and combinations. Jack may be highly competent but practically impossible to work with since he is an unfriendly and untrustworthy lout. Or vice versa. Then perceptions enter in. Jill may be very competent but not perceived to be so by Jack. Or vice versa. People do not behave in consistent ways. "I wonder what he'll be like today" is a common thought. And there are many other complicating factors. Still, since good relationships are good for both the business and the parties involved, it makes sense to do whatever we can to encourage good workplace relationships and limit the damage of poor ones.

But even the best of relationships are beset by problems that stem from personality variables. Despite a basic intention to collaborate, people keep getting in one another's way. A management training program at one large international development institution included a survey on personality types. The survey had nothing to do with pathology. Rather it dealt with different ways of seeing the world, relating to people, processing information, and making decisions. While the managers were in the training room quietly reading their results, one let out a yelp. When one of the trainers went over to see what the problem was, the manager said, "I've been thinking about Jane. We have been at odds with each other for years, and I have always assumed that she was just a difficult person. Now I realize that we have almost opposite personality profiles. She has probably been thinking the same thing about me. I am not a lousy person; neither is she. The source of friction is the way we each go after life and work. I think that knowing this will help me develop a working arrangement with her that will be better for both of us—and the business, too." He was right. Jane came to the same conclusion when she participated in the training program.

Poor relationships usually subtract value from the company. Even in cases where two people manage to contain their dislike for each other, some of it inevitably leaks out. Poor relationships are costly. The protagonists spend a lot of time and energy engaging each other antagonistically or keeping themselves under control. The work they do is often contaminated. And more often than not they bring others into the fray. Therefore, there are both direct psychological, social, and financial costs and lost-opportunity costs. A poor relationship does not necessarily imply that two people are screaming at each other all day every day. It may be that they simply ignore each other whenever possible. But if their working closely together is necessary for the good of the company, then a poor relationship adds cost. Lost-opportunity costs that never hit the balance sheet are involved. One does not have to talk with many people to realize that there are many poor and even bizarre relationships in the workplace.

Here is a case where personal styles and social realities conspired to subtract a great deal of value from a company. A highly qualified electronics engineer was chosen to head up the product development function for a computer company. He reported to the director of research and development. For those who notice such things, it was clear within weeks that the director could not stand his junior's brilliant, abrasive, know-it-all style. It was also clear to onlookers that the younger man had little respect for his boss and his rather patrician style. Neither invested anything in building a decent relationship. In a sense, they deserved each other. Furthermore, the new man was alienating some of the best engineers on the product development team. But since his boss had no real relationship with him, he provided the younger man with no feedback.

Within two months the newcomer was gone. The R&D director was embarrassed that he had personally recruited him. The human resources director was angry because he had said that the man should not be hired. Team members resented the fact that the R&D director let them endure three months of hell. Products were behind schedule. And no one knew what the man fired would do with the intelligence he had gathered during his short stay. It would be easy enough to figure out, in round numbers, the money this poor relationship, caused and compounded by personal defects, cost the company. The psychological and social costs are extra.

Of course, managers should intervene in a preventive or remedial way only when they have to. Workers often quietly manage their own difficult relationships quite well. Here is an interesting case. The relationship between Ruth, the boss, and Rosalie, the direct report, looked good on the surface. It had a mentor-protégée look to it. In reality, Ruth had become quite dependent on Rosalie and needed a great deal of reassurance from her. Her marriage was rocky, and her three children had all left the nest. The problem was that Rosalie was not growing in business skills and acumen through her relationship with her boss. Here's how she dealt with the dynamics of all this. She continued the personal relationship with her boss, providing whatever support she could. Ruth was hardly a basket case, and the support she was getting from Rosalie helped her to continue to add value to the company. But the younger woman quietly found a real mentor, a man who understood the dynamics of the situation and made no fuss. Since they often worked on projects together, their relationship attracted no particular notice.

It is important to note that many workplace relationships sour not because of personal characteristics but because of lack of competence. This is the "he's a nice guy, but . . ." phenomenon. This often happens between direct reports and their managers. The manager is incompetent in either his or her technical or managerial role. The subordinate has to do double time to make up for the other's deficiencies and resents it. Positive personal characteristics do not make up for business deficiencies. But they often do make the situation more difficult to handle. "How can I tell her that I can't stand working with her when she is such a decent person?"

Strategies for Addressing Disruptive Relationships

What can be done if a personal relationship is interfering with the business and is not being managed by the parties themselves? Here are some guidelines:

- *Link relationships to the business.* Work from the principle that dealing with relationships that are hurting the business is a legitimate *business* necessity. For some this means overcoming a reluctance to "interfere in other people's personal affairs."

- *Determine degree of disruption.* Determine how disruptive the relationship is mainly by estimating its impact on both the business and quality of work life. In one company the leading salesman was more than meeting his sales targets, but his relationships with his two closest competitors were so mean-spirited that it cast a pall over the entire unit.

- *Act if economics warrant it.* Since you cannot legislate personal relationships, intervene only if the direct or lost-opportunity costs have some substance to them. In the case just mentioned, it was clear that the lead salesman was the aggressor. He intended to stay number one at any cost. Therefore, despite his record, he was eased out of the company.

- *Act with both tact and speed.* If you determine that a relationship needs attention, act carefully but act with dispatch. "Eased" is the operative word above. There are both legal and social dimensions to be considered. When relationships sour, there is usually some fault on both sides. Acting fairly, then, is important for the health of the larger social system. The sales manager discussed the issues with each of the two surviving competitors separately. He wanted to help them see how they made a bad situation worse. He wanted them to learn something about the social realities of the company.

- *Deal with relationship-damaging incompetence.* If the relationship has soured because one party is incompetent, move quickly. Prevention or immediate cure is the best approach. The boss of the incompetent party should know of the incompetence and deal with it before it contaminates relationships. One week into a new arrangement, a manager said to a worker of moderate abilities whom he had paired with a star, "Ron, this is not going to work.

You and Beth are a mismatch. It's not good for you, her, or the company. I made some mistakes in assigning partners.''

While personal relationships are in the shadows because they are not discussed in decision-making forums, they are widely discussed in informal settings. There is a delicate balance between the privacy of a personal relationship and its impact on the business. Companies and institutions that have developed a *culture* of good working relationships complemented by a solid set of good working relationships have leveraged this part of the shadow side at the service of the business.

Let me end this section with a light-hearted piece from the *Harvard Business Review* (1989, May–June, p. 221) that has more to do with the importance of personal relationships in the workplace and shadow-side wisdom than humor. Although it is called *The Law of the Lunch,* its wisdom goes beyond the lunch hour.

> The general rule may be laid down that in all humankind's institutions, especially in business, government, and the priestly employments, there is an inverse relationship between how much their literature and instructions attend to a particular activity and the importance of that activity. The greater the attendance, the less important it is; the less attendance, the more important.
>
> By that principle, few things in business are as important as the business lunch, about which absolutely nothing can be found in textbooks, casebooks, MBA programs, seminars, or conferences.
>
> The business lunch is a pervasive institution, virtually obligatory, and everywhere conducted according to a fixed ritual. He who invites pays. Conversation starts and for a long time remains in the realm of seemingly idle chatter about personal interests in recreations, entertainments, family matters, and mutual acquaintances. Business is finally and gradually crept up on with careful avoidance of any implications that the lunch exists specifically to enhance

the lunchee's opinions about the lunchor and the lunchor's assessment of the lunchee.

The business lunch and its rituals are based on the established fact that important buying decisions are rarely made on price alone, or alone on specifications, technical service, delivery, or vendor competence and reputation. The lunch exists to learn about things that are not said, to help establish and cement relationships of personal trust and understanding, to create commercial friendships and reciprocities, to facilitate favors hoped for and favors given, to go beyond technicalities and legalities in getting and cementing some sort of sale.

So don't knock it.

We won't knock it. Instead we will move to the next section, dealing with guidelines for managing the larger social system.

Managing the Social System

Savvy managers learn how to intervene in the social system with both tact and business acumen. Dealing with the social realities of the workplace, especially those that are covert, undiscussed, or undiscussable, is not just a "nice thing to do" but an economic necessity. Managers who deal with social realities poorly add cost, while those who deal with them well add value.

Principles for Managing the Social System

Here is a set of principles or guidelines for dealing with the social system issues found in the workplace, together with highlights of a specific case. In this company, two competing cliques, one with loyalty to the president and the other with loyalty to the chairman, stood in the way of the implementation of a strategy to which both camps had publicly agreed.

Uncover the Social Culture. Get a general reading of the institution's social culture—"the way we interact socially here." A courageous human resources manager once said in a high-level meeting on HR strategy: "In this company there seems to be an assumption that social arrangements and transactions are neutral and a norm that prevents them from being discussed in decision-making forums." In the case above, this type of openness was difficult to achieve because the company was located in a country where the discussion of shadow-side issues is even more taboo than it is in the United States.

Audit Social Dynamics. Informally, do a common-sense audit of the specific social dynamics that permeate the business. Discover which dynamics are adding value and which are adding cost. In the case at hand, a manager said in an off-the-record meeting with representatives of two of the banks that provided financing for the company: "We let cliques form and pursue their own interests even when this interferes with the business. Two of these cliques are currently taking different approaches to the implementation of strategy, but no one is doing anything about trying to reconcile these different points of view. Not just individual but group ego is at stake."

Determine the Business Impact of a Social Dynamic. Determine if a social system arrangement or activity is causing a business problem. In our case the problem—the roadblock to strategy implementation—was aggravated by the personal styles of two key players. One player observed, "Our problem lies with these two very strong personalities [the chairman and the president]. They both command great respect and loyalty. But they have different views of the business world." In our case the social dynamic is leading to the business problem.

Determine the Social Impact of a Business Problem. Determine if a business problem is causing social disruption. Poorly run businesses often cause social distress. Another insider said, "The lack of coherent strategy implementation means that we are falling behind our competitors. This is causing a morale problem. Everyone knows that we are better than we are performing. People are beginning to worry about the business, and their fears are contagious."

Act Assertively. Do not allow social system problems to fester. They sabotage the business in covert ways. The members of the board, in a meeting without the chairman, decried their lack of assertiveness: "We have been at fault here. We have allowed this to go on for years. But the changing business environment demands that we act."

Find Business Solutions. Keep in mind that focusing on social system problems in and of themselves can cause embarrassment and make the overall situation worse. Whenever possible, use good business practices to deal with poor social dynamics, especially when the social dynamics are as sensitive as they were in this case. The board moved to combine the office of chairman and president and to restructure the role of the board itself in order to avoid similar impasses in the future. This restructuring was seen as part of the overall revamping of the company.

Balance Business and Social Solutions. Do not be heavy-handed. Strike a balance between business strategies and intervention into the social dynamics themselves. Focusing narrowly on business solutions may mean that the unresolved social dynamics may go underground and cause further problems down the road. Some months after the restructuring, one of the board members said, "In solving the problem, we made no reference to the cliques. We made the outgoing chairman honorary chairman with a great deal of fanfare. This not only soothed his ego, but it was the right thing to do. He did not lose face. He was also retained as a consultant in charge of a project he will handle very well. Also, another important message drifted out through the grapevine: no one was to be covertly punished because of loyalty to the outgoing chairman. But the new norm is clear: loyalty is to be to the business, not to personalities."

Practice Social Realism. Become a social system realist. Do not try to create a perfect society within the business. Be neither naive nor cynical. In general, see both yourself and other workers as adults responsible for their own social interaction. A final remark from one of the managers in the company was, "Different cliques and other kinds of social groupings are always forming around here. People are free to do so. This will never stop. However, since some add value and some cost, we need to monitor what's going on. We cannot afford the kind of stalemate that has just been resolved. Because of global competition we cannot afford such social luxuries no matter what our company or our national culture is."

Let's see what happens when these principles are violated and when they are used effectively.

Adding Cost by Managing the Social System Poorly

A manager—the new director of customer service—was politically astute but naive with respect to social system realities. Not a happy combination. During the first week of his new job he was told that one of the members of his team was going to quit. He thought that this would reflect poorly on him. He immediately had a talk with her during which she recited all her frustrations with her job. Since he listened sympathetically, something his predecessor had not done, she poured out all her woes. He then asked her what she wanted in order to stay. She outlined a couple of experiments she wanted to undertake in the field to help the supervisors of frontline salespeople promote high-quality customer service. He agreed on the spot.

What he failed to realize was that the person he was talking to was considered a pain in the neck by her associates. The fact that her "whining" had put her in a favored position did not sit well at all. The new manager had taken pains to understand the structure and work goals of his department but not its social dynamics. It was certainly not a mistake to listen to her, but giving her special attention without first exploring the social dynamics of the unit was a blow to morale. Excellent customer service initiatives began to grind to a halt. The new "star" began to act like a prima donna, and this galled her colleagues even more. The social and lost-opportunity costs were high. He never got over this first misstep. The members of the team simply did not trust him. And this without knowing anything about his political maneuverings.

There are a number of lessons that can be drawn from this case. Get a fix on the social dynamics of the unit. Find out what the social climate is like. Determine which relationships add value, which cost. Explore the social consequences of favoring one person or one group over another, even for business reasons. In summary, if this manager had followed the guidelines outlined above, he would have avoided the mess in which he ended up.

Adding Value by Managing the Social System Well

Another manager in the same company added value by understanding and managing the social dynamics in her department well. See if you can determine how she used the guidelines outlined above. She had inherited a human resources department with a history of discord. Before she took the job, she took the time to ask a number of informed people what the department was like from both a business and a social perspective. She talked to a couple of HR veterans who had recently moved to different departments. Through these and other off-the-record conversations she began to stitch together a picture of the department, including its social culture.

Here is one problem she stumbled across. It seems that one group of personnel managers, more or less on their own initiative, had moved into an internal consulting relationship with their line managers. They discussed not just personnel problems but also better ways of implementing strategy and of getting HR initiatives to serve the business more effectively. Some of this group had even begun taking business courses on strategy and operations management at a local university so that they could discuss these issues with line managers more intelligently. Line managers liked this approach. But in the eyes of some HR department members, this group had taken on some "airs" by intimating that they were contributing more to the business. They had, in the eyes of some, become convinced of their own self-importance and were looking down their noses at those doing "mere" personnel tasks. Morale sagged.

Armed with this understanding, the new manager designed an off-site "resetting HR strategy" meeting. The central question was, Who are we and what do we need to do to serve the business? This meeting helped reset the direction of the department. Task forces were established to find ways of getting HR to link its efforts to the business more effectively. Therefore, instead of getting the personnel managers who were engaging in internal consulting to temper their zeal, she helped others find ways of updating their jobs. For instance, the labor relations group spearheaded a task force with key union members to find new win-win strategies for union-management collaboration. The spirits of those who had been left behind began to revive. They saw that internal consulting was only one way of helping line managers make the business better. In sum, the new manager took a *business* approach to doing something about the social dynamics. She did not call a meeting to deal with the morale problem. She helped the group transcend it. Unlike the director of customer service, she did understand the social dynamics of her unit and did something creative to help manage them. The department's new look and strategic approach added a great deal of psychological, social, and financial value.

I am sure that by now you have noted that the HR director instinctively used most of the principles of managing social realities outlined above. Some managers are "naturals" when it comes to dealing with both the personal styles of individuals and the social dynamics of their units. But do not expect to be able to handle social realities automatically. If the social dynamics of your company are important, then choose people to be managers who have the interest, tact, and skill needed to deal with them. Furthermore, take the time to bring current managers up to speed in this tricky shadow-side area. The benefits might well outweigh the costs.

Managing the Shadow Side of Diversity

Currently, conferences, seminars, and workshops on "managing diversity" are springing up everywhere. It is impossible to open a magazine or journal without finding an article on the topic. There are countless consultants and programs available to bring your company up to speed in terms of understanding the upside of diversity and managing it at the service of both increased productivity and the quality of work life. Some observers of this scene decry what they see as incompetent, bullying diversity entrepreneurs hyping the social equivalent of snake oil. In their eyes, the movement subtracts rather than adds value. Others, seeing diversity as a positive force in the workplace, welcome the opportunity to explore it through such workshops. While the diversity movement may have the feel of a fad, diversity itself is here to stay. While it always needed to be dealt with, there is a growing imperative to leverage its upside and contain its downside. The question to be asked from a business point of view is: What do we need to do to make diversity serve the business in terms of both productivity and the quality of work life?

Managing diversity can mean different things. When managing diversity focuses on *fairness*, then it is a moral, political, and legal issue reflected in such phrases as "common decency," "getting our piece of the pie," and "achieving quotas." When managing diversity focuses on *relationships* between groups with different characteristics, then it is a social issue reflected in such phrases as "getting along," "appreciating differences," and "cultural richness."

Kleiman (1994) reported the results of a study of diversity sponsored by the Human Resource Management and Commerce Clearinghouse. Between 1983 and 1993, white men in the work force increased only by about 10 percent, women by 69 percent, African-Americans by 59 percent, Hispanics by 49 percent, and Asians by 44 percent. And yet human resource executives, those who commissioned the study, were 91 percent white with about half being white women. Of course, other kinds of social groupings—by education level, sexual orientation, religious affiliation, and so forth—make diversity an extremely complex phenomenon. Certainly, the workplace has always been diverse. But today there is greater diversity along with a higher degree of awareness of and sensitivity to issues of fairness and equity in the workplace. There are also programs to address diversity-related issues.

Different social groups within companies are making their voices heard through networks. While such groups usually begin informally and focus on social interaction, many have developed into sociopolitical forces. They provide support for their members and become advocates for the group in such areas as recruitment, development, and expansion of career paths. Avon Products has three strong groups: the Avon Asian Network, the Black Professional Association, and the Avon Hispanic Network. Each has a clear mission, meets quarterly, and has a member who is a senior officer in the company. This officer keeps senior management informed about the viewpoints and needs of the group and, in turn, keeps the group informed about the needs and direction of the company.

Overlooking diversity can be costly. The diversity/fairness issue erupted a few years ago in a Catholic diocese in a large U.S. city during a reorganization effort. Church officials grouped organizational units and agencies that lay scattered around the landscape into six major areas or categories, each with a "moderator." The moderators chosen all had Irish surnames—this in a city with great ethnic diversity. All hell, if you will excuse the expression, broke loose. Dozens of complaints were received from different ethnic groups. As a result, the appointments to the governing board had to be changed so that the board had a more representative ethnic mix.

What should have been done? After the six moderators had been tentatively chosen, someone should have said, "All right, let's take a look at this slate. How will the diocese react to it?" It would have been immediately obvious that people would be up in arms. Too often questions like, "What kind of social sensitivities are involved in this issue?" and "Given the social dynamics of this company, how will this decision play?" are never asked. The social dynamics in question are not limited to racial, ethnic, and gender issues, but include all significant groupings within the enterprise.

The managing-diversity movement has much to recommend it. It has helped to move critical covert, undiscussed, and undiscussable issues from the shadows to center stage. But there is much more to social diversity than is openly discussed even in this new improved climate. That is, social diversity still has a strong shadow side.

The Disturbing Dynamic Underlying Diversity

There is an ominous dynamic underlying diversity that, uncontained, can lead to the kind of racial, ethnic, class-based clashes we continue to see here and abroad. Diversity can breed distrust. Distrust breeds fear. Fear breeds protective behavior. Protection turns to aggression. A comparatively benign form of this dynamic is illustrated by an experiment conducted in Europe some years ago. It went something like this: People were asked to fill out some kind of pre-employment form at tables in a room. They were asked not to interact with one another. As they entered the room, they were given, randomly, either a red pen and a red-bordered name tag or a green pen and a green-bordered name tag. Afterwards they were debriefed one by one about the form-completing exercise. During the debriefing they were asked about both the form and, incidentally, any feelings they might have had about the others in the room. It was discovered that the "reds" did not much like the "greens" and vice versa. Recall that being a green or a red was a random event and that the difference between the two groups was external and insignificant. If random, insignificant differences can lead to intergroup hostility, imagine what real differences can do. We do not need to imagine it at all. We need only to review history and look around the world today.

It is as if people who see others different from themselves engage, at some level of their being, in some form of the following monologue: "She's different from me in this regard. That makes me wonder. It could mean that she has chosen to be different. Therefore, she does not like my choice. Or, if it was not a case of choice, she is glad that she is different. This means that she feels that she is better than I am and probably looks down on me. I bet she doesn't like me. This means that she is a threat to me. It could be that she wants to do me in in one way or another. Well, at the minimum I should be on my guard. I don't want her to get away with anything. Perhaps I should be more aggressive. Maybe I should get her before she gets me." The precise words here are not the issue, and, of course, there are both more benign and more malignant versions of this monologue.

Principles for Managing the Dark Side of Diversity

This dynamic, however mild and hidden, is part of the human condition, and the workplace does not escape its impact. Attempts to deal with diversity—whether by the UN in Bosnia, through diversity workshops in the workplace, or by managerial intervention in specific cases—are based on two principles: interrupting the dynamic and putting a different dynamic in its place.

- *Interrupt the dynamic.* Develop strategies to prevent,

challenge, and rectify the kind of monologue outlined above. Diversity programs in the workplace are attempting to do precisely that. Indeed, direct challenges of the covert prejudices of participants are included in some programs.

- *Put a different dynamic in its place.* For instance, celebrate diversity and its capability of making institutions richer in both human and financial ways. The new monologue might start something like this: "I notice that you are different from me in a number of ways, and this helps me expand my view of the world and appreciate its richness more fully."

Of course, no matter what we do, the old dynamic is likely to reassert itself. It can be contained, not conquered. A brief review of human history will make that clear.

Some companies avoid the mistake of suggesting that one group is better than another in certain respects by highlighting the pleasant and uplifting aspects of mingling different cultures. In one company some of the employees complained that the company made "too big a deal" of St. Patrick's Day. Before the work force had become so diverse, everyone joined in and became "Irish" on March 17th. Instead of banning St. Patrick's Day celebrations, the company encouraged other social groups to celebrate their days. And so, Latino Day and Black Pride Day were established. After all, there were enough days in the year to accommodate all groups. In fact, the more the merrier. At the World Bank, more than a hundred nationalities are represented in the work force. Celebrations of cultural diversity are common. Art exhibits, lectures, and ethnic foods in the cafeteria add zest to the place. People who work there come to appreciate one another's cultures more. But no attempt is made to link cultural characteristics to productivity or the lack of it in the bank. At least not in the formal settings of the institution.

Companies and institutions are culturally richer because of their diversity. This does not necessarily make them better competitors, although if workers actively embrace, celebrate, and are proud of their diversity, it can certainly add to the quality of work life and indirectly aid productivity. Business sociologists are currently trying to determine whether diversity in and of itself tends to be a business enhancer.

Does this mean that everybody in these two institutions saw

themselves as one, big happy family? Hardly. There are plenty of disquieting stories in both places to discount such naiveté. But both had overall social cultures that supported the business. The World Bank also counted on a business solution. That is, the mandate of the bank to help alleviate poverty around the world acted as a strong cohesive force, helping many transcend social differences.

Managing Shadow-Side Groups

While the company bowling league is quite visible, other groupings are less visible and sometimes less salubrious: covert clubs, cliques, conspiracies, tribes, cabals, sororities, fraternities, and other groupings that spawn dynamics that can either help or hurt a company. They hurt the institution when their agendas conflict with those of the institution. They also hurt a company when others feel excluded. Let's take a look at two kinds of groupings: covert clubs and tribes.

The Club

In some companies there is the Club, an unnamed and undiscussed group of individuals belonging to the "inner circle." It is not always clear what is required to become a candidate for membership. It is often a mixture of ability, social characteristics, and knowing the right people. Entry comes through sponsorship by a Club member, often someone who has become the candidate's friend or mentor, even though neither the Club nor membership is ever discussed. Membership in the Club carries with it undiscussed privileges, not the least of which is an inner track to promotion. Even when there is a public, formal succession-planning system, the Club can work its magic. In this case, every once in a while there is an outcry. "Why did Jill get the job instead of Jane? Jane was obviously more qualified." Well, Jane was not a member of the Club, while Jill was. This, of course, is undiscussable.

Groupings such as this can cost a company plenty, even though most of the costs are covert. Inbreeding leads to myopia and groupthink. Making sure that members prosper is an agenda that can conflict with the best interests of the business. And since others know about the existence of the clubs, envy is spawned. Some people spend time jockeying for entrance into the club, time that could be better spent on the business.

A manager in a large European company who was very successful by all the usual criteria—position, accomplishments, compensation, and relationship with his boss and even his boss's boss—talked to a consultant about his "depression" that was interfering with the quality of his work. It soon became clear that his malady stemmed from the fact that, despite all that he had, he still felt that he was not a full-fledged member of the Club. But there was a strong cultural norm forbidding even naming the Club, much less discussing its membership or how one felt excluded from it. What were the costs of this? The manager suffered personal turmoil that distracted him from the business. He began to make mistakes—small ones, but still mistakes. In this company, some highly skilled managers who were not members of the Club were promoted, but reluctantly. And promotion did not bring with it Club membership. The social malaise persisted.

Review the guidelines for managing the social system outlined earlier in the chapter. They are pertinent here. Here's how the above case was handled. The board, aware of what managerial inbreeding was costing the company, chose a new CEO who was not a member of the Club. While promoting from within had been heralded as a morale builder and as a sign of confidence in the managers of the company, it in fact helped preserve the status of mediocre Club members. Failure to get new blood into the company was one of the reasons it was in the doldrums. The new CEO, with the backing of the board, reversed that policy. He knew that if only a handful of managers came in from outside, they would be coopted by Club members. He did not forbid promoting from within, but he demanded that the heads of the various businesses and departments find the best managerial talent they could. That was one of their strategic objectives. In very many cases this meant going outside. This was a business solution to the social system problem. No mention was ever made of the Club.

Tribalism and the Caste System

Neuhauser (1988) used the term *tribes* to refer to social and cultural diversity among the various functions of companies and institutions. In a health care facility the tribes include the administration, doctors, nurses, lab technicians, the information system staff, the pharmacy group, radiologists, and business office personnel. The tribes in an airline include pilots, flight attendants, ticket agents, the catering group, the ramp staff, baggage handlers, human resource personnel, reservation clerks, and others. From a completely rational point of view, these groups constitute various interactive subunits of the business. But they are also different tribes or societies within the structure, each with its own variations in language, values, thinking patterns, and rules.

There is an upside to tribalism. At its best, it promotes professionalism. For instance, in one company the information technology personnel ardently pursued professional goals. They were learners in their fast-changing profession. They kept up on the latest technology and how it might add value to the business. They represented their views in the decision-making forums of the company. "We want to be the best" is a sentiment that should be heard from marketing, financial, human resource, sales, engineering, and manufacturing professionals. All of this adds value.

But there is a dark side to tribalism. It often happens that certain units develop chronic tribal conflicts with one another—for instance, between manufacturing and sales. They have different world outlooks. Manufacturing does not want to contribute to a costly inventory problem, while the salesperson wants immediate delivery to satisfy customers. In one hospital, overworked nurses were looking for ways to lighten the pressure. Many said that they were sometimes too tired to provide adequate care. Admissions, on the other hand, was trying to keep every bed occupied. Clashing work priorities ignited emotions. Name calling and finger pointing erupted. Nurses began implementing strategies that kept admissions from knowing whether a bed was empty or not. Things got more complicated when a new information technology system was proposed that would inform admissions of empty beds the moment they became available. Since the clashes between these two "societies" were never discussed in formal decision-making settings, they kept up their running warfare.

Tribalism often leads to a covert caste system. Those who work in marketing may enjoy higher status than those who work in manufacturing. Workers in the human resources department may be much more marginal, approaching the pariah state in some companies. In other companies the financial hotshots may constitute the social elite. Salaried workers may constitute a privileged class, with hourly workers more marginal. The problem is that these societies have a dynamic of their own. As they develop, there is no assurance that they will do so in such a way as to serve the business. If, because of these dynamics, the "elite" in marketing or R&D interact less effectively than they should with, say, the "lesser mortals" in manufacturing, then the business suffers.

Principles for Managing Shadow-Side Groups

Companies cannot afford to have second-class citizens, marginalized groups, and "ins" versus "outs." Social exclusion is too costly. What, then, are some business approaches to moving beyond clubs, tribalism, caste systems, and other groupings that inhibit both productivity and the quality of work life?

Use Strategy. Bartlett and Ghoshal (1990, p. 140) suggested that "the surest way to break down insularity is to develop and communicate a clear sense of corporate purpose that extends into every corner of the company and gives context and meaning to each manager's particular roles and responsibilities." A company without a clear strategy is not only rudderless but also a kind of vacuum that fosters the development of shadow-side processes. If the business itself is not interesting, workers will find other ways to interest themselves. Social shenanigans are a favorite substitute.

Reengineer Work Processes. Teams focusing on reengineered work processes can drive out shadow-side social groupings interested in their own rituals. In companies driven by integrated work processes, the focus is no longer on functional units and the walls between them but on work flow as a translation of strategy. And work flow, such as the processes involved in high-quality customer service, transcends clubs and tribal boundaries.

Decentralize. If decentralization makes business sense, it can help limit tribal aspirations. Decentralized functions like human resources, engineering, and information technology tend to lose their tribal characteristics. Also, if there is a concentration of Club members in one area of the company such as marketing or finance, then decentralization disperses and thus limits the influence of Club members.

Set Up a Reward System That Favors Results Rather Than Groups. Rewarding strategy-enhancing rather than unit (tribal) accomplishments can make it worthwhile for tribes to collaborate. Promotion on demonstrated merit rather than Club membership diminishes the importance of the Club.

All of this can be summed up in a single principle: Running a really good business tends to drive institution-limiting behavior out of the system.

Managing Social Communication

One dramatic way to get a feeling for the company or institution as a social system is to review the kinds of communication that characterize the business versus the kinds of communication that characterize the social system. Business-enhancing communication includes business-focused information sharing, feedback, problem-solving and innovation-focused dialogue, negotiation, and conflict management. Social system communication, on the other hand, includes social chitchat, the sharing of personal problems, informal counseling and advice giving, gossiping, griping, rumor sharing, lying, conspiring, social-activity planning, backbiting, flirting, excuse making, complaining, and so forth.

Of course, both kinds of communication go on all the time, but books on communication in the workplace focus almost exclusively on the first set. It is not that the first set is "good" and the second set is "bad." Social communication, whether complaining about managers or the sharing of personal ups and downs, is a "lubricant" for the social system just as much as feedback and problem solving are "lubricants" for the business. However, griping about bosses, while it may act as a safety valve, is dysfunctional if it takes the place of feedback to bosses. If there is no meaningful feedback loop between boss and direct reports, then nonproductive griping is likely to increase.

Sharing rumors is a very common form of social interchange. In some companies it is a daily event. At crisis times, however, the ability to manage rumors is critical. Consider the case of a large bank. The new president decided to put his stamp on the system by reorganizing it. A consulting firm was hired to work with an internal reorganization committee. A classic mistake was made. Most of the work of the consultants and the committee was done in secret. All staff members knew that the work was going on and that the new structure could have a profound impact on their lives. Since there was an information vacuum, rumors filled the void. Wild rumors. Rumors about everything—which functions were to be consolidated, who was to be laid off, what kind of separation package would be offered, who the new power brokers would be, and so forth. The day-to-day work of the institution was severely impaired. The institution was in turmoil for about a year. When the new structure was finally announced, more turmoil ensued.

Since getting rid of the rumor mill is impossible, managing it is sometimes necessary. Rumors should be addressed only if doing so adds value. Rumors can be divided into two categories—true and untrue. True rumors are commonly vigorously denied one day only to be presented as fact the next. This can make a company look stupid. If the rumor is true, but the time for divulging the truth is not right, then it is better to say that the company has no comment to offer at the time. Most unfounded rumors can be ignored. However, if a rumor is damaging productivity, morale, or both, it may be important to squelch the rumor. For instance, one company took out a full-page ad in the business press saying that it was *not* being sold or merged with another company. Squelching can, of course, take less dramatic forms. In any case, it should be used sparingly and, when used, done quickly to contain as much damage as possible.

The grapevine is an interesting social phenomenon. It is more than just a conduit for rumors. A study cited in the *Wall Street Journal* (Hymowitz, 1988) suggested that the office grapevine is 75 to 95 percent accurate and often provides managers and staff with better information than formal communication. With few exceptions, companies and institutions tend to be leaky. What is said in private or even in confidence has a way of leaking out into the grapevine. Therefore, it makes sense for managers to listen to what is being said in the grapevine. Even though the facts sent down the grapevine may not be accurate, it does give some insight into attitudes. Also, the grapevine is not a bad place to garner a few creative ideas. Some managers use the grapevine to send messages they would rather not state publicly or to test the reaction to possible policies and programs. Savvy managers feed the grapevine selectively and carefully instead of complaining about it.

A senior manager in one institution used technology to get the grapevine to serve the business. Anyone who wanted to was allowed to post messages and queries on the company's electronic bulletin board. This manager responded to key messages on-line. One of the things he did was kill off rumors that would otherwise have caused unrest. One message poster said that he or she had heard that a key function of the institution was going to be outsourced. "Baloney" was his reply. Not all social communication, however, can be managed. The electronic bulletin board became a bit unruly, with biting criticisms of management intermingled with queries. When the manager who started it moved to a different department, his successor pulled the plug. This was too countercultural for him.

This, then, is a sampling of shadow-side social issues that may need managing. And, as we have seen in a number of cases, the personal styles of individuals further complicate the social scene. As mentioned in Chapter One, the shadow-side categories discussed in this book are interactive. Depending on your point of view, this makes things either more challenging or more chaotic. The next two chapters complicate things even further. Organizational politics are added to the individual and social stew.

POSITIVE
POLITICAL SKILLS
AT WORK

10

TURF, POWER, AGENDAS, AND RESOURCES: THE ANATOMY OF ORGANIZATIONAL POLITICS

T HE ESSENCE OF POLITICS is competition for a prized and scarce commodity or resource. Only one person at a time can be president of the United States. We are used to watching potential candidates on television vie for that position. We even understand that a lot of deals are being cut off-camera behind closed doors. When it comes to the workplace, however, some are more aware of the political nature of the organization than others. A frequent complaint voiced by workers is: "My organization is *so* political." A frequently asked question is: "How do I cope with the politics of this place?" Often what they really mean is, "I feel powerless. I don't know how to play the political game. I don't know the rules. What can I do to exercise more influence in this system?"

Decrying the fact that the system is political is like complaining that water is wet. While some companies and institutions are less political than others, all systems have some kind of politics. Where they differ is in the degree of virulence. When government agencies, businesses, churches, and educational institutions are ranked for the virulence of their politics, churches tend to be the easy winners; educational institutions are the runners-up, followed by businesses and, finally, government agencies (Yates, 1985). Political maneuvering tends to be most virulent where it is most vehemently denied and least so where it is freely admitted. When did

195

your company or institution last have a formal meeting to discuss internal politics? Never?

Since everyone agrees that politics can be costly in terms of human anguish, social disruption, and financial loss, it makes economic sense for managers to get a clear idea as to what is meant by the term *politics* and gain competency in managing political issues.

The Elements of Organizational Politics

In the world of organizational politics, players compete for prized commodities that are scarce, such as budgetary resources. Here is a breakdown of what is involved in a political struggle:

- *Competition for scarce and prized resources or commodities* is the essence of organizational politics. If the commodity is not prized or is in abundant supply, there is no need to compete.
- *Self-interest and/or institutional enhancement* are the principal driving forces of politics. Some organizational players push their agendas out of self-interest. Other players use political maneuverings to make the business better. Still others, perhaps most, have mixed motivation.
- *Power* of some kind is needed to compete. Since influencing others is central to the competitive process, some power base is needed to get people's—or the right person's—attention.
- *Political strategies* are the means players use to get what they want. A political campaign involves organizing and sequencing a set of political strategies. Some players have power but use it poorly.

Here is a brief case that includes all these elements. It demonstrates that politics should be viewed not as an abstract concept or another box on the chart but as a way of achieving either business or personal objectives. Josh, the director of information services in a midsize manufacturer, was fuming. His plan for the organization of the firm's information systems had just been defeated. In offering his plan, he had taken what he thought was the high ground. He showed just how the new system would benefit the company even though individual units would have to cede some of their power.

Other organizational players, he mused, had not played fairly. They had twisted his words; cast doubt on his motivation, intimating that what he really wanted was to become the czar of information services; lobbied senior management; cobbled together figures that showed that the current arrangement was most cost-effective, at least in the "near term"; and easily deflected any suggestion that their motivation focused on anything but the good of the company. He was particularly annoyed at Sheila, the director of marketing, who he found out had led the effort to stop the reorganization. She had convinced colleagues to lobby senior managers, while she herself targeted the CEO. We'll let Josh stew awhile and then, in what follows, show him what he should have done.

All companies and institutions, including families, are political. They differ only in terms of the quality and intensity of their politics. Politics is a shadow-side phenomenon because many political "ingredients" are unnoticed, hidden, undiscussed, or undiscussable. Politics, like other shadow-side activities, can add cost or value. It depends on how the game is played.

How to Analyze Internal Politics

The individual elements of organizational politics can be turned into tools for exploring the politics of any given situation or transaction within an institution. A political issue cannot be managed unless it is first identified and analyzed. Here is a process that can be used by anyone in the organization to understand its politics more fully: (1) note activities surrounding prized resources that are scarce, (2) uncover the motivation behind competitive activities, (3) identify the sources of power, and (4) observe the strategies of political players. Of course, the depth of this audit or analysis will differ from person to person, since some organizational players will have access to more information, especially insider information, than others.

Note Activities Surrounding Prized Resources That Are Scarce

Since politics revolves around resources that are both prized and scarce, keep your eye on activities surrounding them. Of course, if the object sought is not scarce, there is no need to compete. At the time of a substantial expansion in one institution there were more desirable new positions to be filled than internal candidates to fill them. And so the succession process was relatively apolitical. There was little reason to compete. Furthermore, if the object sought is not prized, then no one will be interested in competing for it. A managerial position opened up in a company's Anchorage office. But no one wanted to go to Anchorage, so there was no squabbling to get the position. The same position in the home office would have had many contenders.

If certain critical resources are scarce, reason dictates they be put to best use. How can they be used to best add value? should be the central question. Capital should be employed where it does the most good. Scarce promotion slots should be allocated to those who will add the most value. But we all know that such principles are violated at every turn. Here are some of the scarce prized commodities for which organizational players compete: capital, desirable positions, benefits, turf, and influence over policy and decision making.

Capital and Other Budgeted Resources. A company has only so much money for capital investment. It is a scarce resource. An R&D group may lobby senior managers on a particular project or product, not to expand their kingdom, but because they believe that the product or project will enhance the fortunes of the company and its employees. Managers in manufacturing offer a competing scenario. They believe that the expansion and globalization of the firm's commodity business is the key to the future. They want money for plant expansion, new equipment, and the exploration of lucrative joint ventures with foreign companies.

Sometimes the more rational the process is thought to be, the more extensive the shadow side. What could be more rational than a budget? It is the primary tool for institutionalizing a company's goals and monitoring performance. Yet, since budgeting is not a precise process, the door is open for manipulation. If we could but look inside the shadows, budget time might look more like feeding frenzy time. Doing the budget is hardly a manager's favorite activity. Yet some managers see budget time as a political opportunity to acquire resources. Others see budget politics as critical to surviving in a hostile organizational climate characterized by unrealistic demands.

Bart (1988) studied the games that product managers in a range of firms play. He defined budgeting gamesmanship as "the deliberate and premeditated manipulation of current year sales, cost, and profit forecasts by product managers to project an overly conservative image into their product budgets" (p. 293). On the other hand, he did find some firms in which there was practically no budgetary gamesmanship. In these firms, bosses tended to trust their subordinates to work hard and strive to meet targets. In a word, they were less paternalistic in either the soft or the hard sense of that term. They treated their managers like adults. There might be a message here. In sum, a well-targeted incentive and reward system coupled with a climate of trust can go a long way toward reducing budgetary politics and their associated costs. Psychological value comes from rewarding those who play it straight. Lost-opportunity costs are the result of allocating more resources to those whose needs are less but whose political skills are greater.

Desirable Positions. It used to be that one out of about twenty to twenty-five people became managers in organizations. Now, however, given the push toward downsizing and structural leanness, it is one out of fifty to fifty-five. Since managerial positions together with the power, authority, and prestige that accompanies them are more scarce than ever, competition for them is keen or even ruthless. Once more, the business press is filled with horror stories of those who have climbed over the backs of their colleagues in order to reach a higher position. This differs radically from those who wanted the position because they thought they were best equipped to make the position work and add value.

One upside case belongs in the record books. The importance of preparing one's successors was being emphasized in this retailer. The manager of one department hired a woman who he thought could be on the succession track. After two months he went to his boss and said something like this: "She's very good. Not only did she bring a lot with her [she had been hired away from a competitor], but she has learned very fast. Given our focus on succession,

the mind-set I started with when I hired her was to let her compete
with me for my job, even though I did not say this to her. To tell
you the truth, she's better than I am. Here's my proposal. We're
having trouble with furniture. I'd like to move over there because
I think I can clean up the mess and get us back on the right track.
And she should have my job." And that's what happened.

When competing for positions, some players, adopting the
poet's suggestion that "it is better to reign in hell than serve in
heaven," choose a lesser position where they can exercise maximum
power. The head coach of a very successful high school football
team declined the job as assistant coach at one of the better state
universities. He was too used to being the boss, and the university's
head coach made it clear to everyone that *he* was the boss. One
business school professor declined a dean's job, saying to a friend:
"Who wants to be king when the barons have all the power?"

Benefits. Since benefits often constitute a scarce resource, how they
are to be distributed is politicized. Something akin to class warfare
can break out in the effort to get a fair slice of the benefits pie. In
the early 1990s a worker in Boston asked his boss for the same three-
months paid child-care leave she herself had taken advantage of
some months earlier. His request was denied by both his boss and
her boss. While he thought that his being denied was probably
illegal, he did nothing about it and later left the company. He said
that there was an unwritten rule stating that paid child-care leave
was given at the discretion of managers, with men being excluded.
This creates a kind of class struggle: "The covert conflict pits men
against women, mothers against other mothers, professional wom-
en against nonprofessionals, and children's needs against those of
employers" (Guyon, 1991, p. A1).

Often, favored employees get the perks like child-care leave,
while the out-of-favor see themselves left out in the cold. This leads
to the politicization of the workplace with private deals being cut:
"Winning benefits—particularly the coveted perk of flexible
hours—has become a delicate, stealthy art, played best by working
parents in positions of power" (Guyon, p. A7). When these private
deals leak out, colleagues resenting special treatment accorded to
some try to blast them out of the water.

The "ins" and the "outs" are part of every social system. However, given a new militancy in the social arena, companies need to explore the legal consequences of social decisions. While it is ridiculous to expect managers to become sociologists, it probably makes sense to have them learn how to assess the impact of both company policies, especially covert policies, and their own decisions on the social system.

Turf. While there is some relationship between the terms *turf* and *tribalism,* they are not the same. Tribalism often leads to vying for scarce resources such as turf and influence, but turf has a broader meaning. A manager might have a number of tribes within his or her domain, but the influence of the unit rather than of any given tribe within it is the most important political issue.

Ruling over this exclusive territory—turf—and having the ability to control what goes on within it are prized and scarce commodities. In these days of downsizing, flattened hierarchies, and cross-functional teams, turf is an even more political issue. Turf is about sovereignty, borders, gatekeeping, buffer zones, and state secrets. Invasions are to be warded off. Outside interference in internal affairs is not allowed. Intelligence gathering by outsiders is discouraged. Hands off. Turf can be as small as the classroom. University instructors love the autonomy they have. Whether this serves the common good of the students and the institution itself is another issue. Units within a larger organization can be as ferocious as jackals in protecting their turf. Empires take a long time to build and in the course of time become quite resistant to change. Those with an expansionist mentality take a "spheres of influence" approach. Not only do we protect our turf from encroachment, but we want to influence how you act in yours.

Of course, each unit, wanting to be master of its own destiny, justifies its political moves and countermoves by claiming that another unit is "interfering" with its work. Therefore, when marketing wants R&D personnel to go out to meet customers in a team effort, there is grumbling about "interfering with research," "failure to understand the needs of an R&D department," "short-term thinking," and the like. While there may be some truth in these allegations, the reaction also stems from fear that the empire is in jeopardy.

This kind of political posturing and jockeying comes with a price tag. Since there are no accounting categories for interunit politics, no one knows how much it costs. But if segmentalism is the bane that many think it is, the price tag is hefty. A consultant watched the jockeying that went on between the marketing and logistics group of a mail-order computer firm. He figured that the costs of political infighting that led to such things as order delays, the need to expand hotline services for disgruntled customers, lost business, and the like was some $2 million per year—unforgivable in a business in which fierce competition keeps eroding margins.

Creating cross-functional teamwork, now a necessity rather than an amenity for most companies, demands that interacting units transcend their differences. IBM instituted a work-process reengineering effort as part of its Operation Bootstrap. In individual units, reengineering went relatively well. In the PC market, where speed is essential, components were modularized and processes streamlined with relative ease. However, reengineering of cross-functional or cross-divisional processes did not fare as well. Divisional jealousy was getting in the way. Organizational units cannot continue to score victories over one another while less balkanized competitors race ahead.

Influence over Policy and Decision Making. Shall we take this strategic direction or that one? Shall we adopt this set of human resource practices or that one? Shall we use this set of means or that set? Who calls the shots? People often espouse different ideologies, sets of beliefs that define what outcomes are important in the institution and the best ways of achieving them. If my vision of the future of the company is to prevail, then yours cannot. A firm cannot be driven by competing visions. Or, if we share the same vision, we may differ in how to get there in terms of strategy, approaches to quality and customer service, how departments and jobs are to be structured, the kinds of human resource management systems to be adopted, approaches to performance management and appraisal—the list is endless. The political issue in this instance is convincing or forcing others to share one's philosophy or world view.

In monitoring activities surrounding prized resources, consider the following:

- What prized and scarce resources would be on the current list in your company?
- What kind of jockeying goes on?
- What scarce resources evoke the most political infighting?
- Which individuals or units are best at playing the political game?
- To what degree does political contention add value or cost to the institution?

Uncover the Motivation Behind Competitive Activities

Naked self-interest, pure-form institutional enhancement, or some mixture of the two are possible driving forces in the competition for scarce resources. The trick lies in determining which.

A distinction can be drawn between two kinds of politics, even though, in practice, they are intermingled: (1) the politics of individual or group self-interest and advancement—that is, the politics of vested interests—and (2) the politics of institutional enhancement. Unalloyed versions of the former are negative, while the politics of institutional advancement can be quite positive. If I cut deals to get my man or woman in a position simply because he or she is my person, even though someone else would be better for the institution, I am into the politics of self-interest. On the other hand, if I have a job candidate who I believe is the best person for that job, then my fighting for him or her is an instance of the politics of organizational enhancement.

Negative Politics: Individual or Group Self-Interest. According to a national survey reported in the *Wall Street Journal* (October 8, 1991, p. A1), more than 50 percent of those polled picked "personal ambition and motivation" as the top trait for getting ahead. Only 2 percent cited "dedication to the organization." Few will deny that there is a lot of me-first embedded in human nature. Miletich (1988) described the rather unsavory picture of a company with a culture of self-interest: "From the moment you were 'welcomed aboard,' they began circling, the office sharks, the jackals, the vultures, the whole business bestiary, all looking for an opening through which to curry favor, consolidate a position, block a rival, or lobby for a pet project or against a pet peeve. All of them jockeying for position and your attention" (p. 11). There is something within a percentage of human beings that whispers, "Maximize winning, minimize losing." Even if I win a lot but you win more, I feel as if I have lost. To focus too much attention on this "bestiary," especially at the expense of the many solid citizens that populate a large number of companies and institutions, would lead inevitably to cynicism. To pretend that these types do not exist would be naive.

The politics of self-interest and associated costs can be found all around the globe, even though it might be necessary to look below the surface. But not far below. To the naked eye, Lot Polish Airlines has improved remarkably since the dissolution of communism in that country (Michaels, 1993). There is a brand-new Boeing fleet, modern catering facilities, and the best service in Eastern Europe. Dig a little deeper, however, and it is a different story. Most of the changes have been implemented by young, eager second-tier managers who have to fight the system to get things done. While such outlandish practices as a government official's being able to commandeer a plane are gone, there are struggles over ideology; that is, how the airline is to be run, both internally between older managers who grew up in the now-outmoded system and younger managers who have taken their cues from the new politics of Eastern Europe and externally between the airline itself and government officials tied to old ways. There is a reluctance to privatize the carrier, because that would mean the end of both managerial and government perks. The quick physical transformation was relatively easy. Making inroads against old coalitions, self-serving organizational practices, influence peddling, perks, and the like is a different story. Let's face it: it is not easy to give up the politics of individual self-interest for the politics of institutional enhancement.

Positive Politics: Institutional Enhancement. At the other end of the continuum, players practice the politics of institutional enhancement. That is, players lobby for agendas that they believe will advance the fortunes of the company and compete for the resources needed to accomplish the goals of their projects. It is not naive to say that many people in organizations have this mentality. They see their fortunes, the fortunes of their colleagues, and, indeed, the fortunes of all the institution's stakeholders tied to the fortunes of the company.

I know one researcher who pursued the development of a product he was convinced would be a winner. He received little support from within the company. One of his colleagues, also into institutional enhancement, lobbied for the purchase of a plant being sold at a bargain price. This plant could be used to make some of the company's mainline products, but it could also be used to pilot the researcher's product. Again, he received little support. But he persevered, and the company bought the plant. The rest is history. Not only did demand for the company's mainline products go up but the new product proved to be an outstanding winner. When the researcher was near retirement, he belatedly received a monetary reward, a paltry one, it would seem, in light of the success of the product.

Mixed Cases. Picture a political continuum. At one end the motivation is pure-form self-interest. Vested interests are to be pursued even if this means limiting or destroying the company. The pages of business journals are filled with examples of executives who became rich at the expense of the fortunes of their companies. At the other end the motivation is pure-form institution advancement. While it is easy to point to pure-form examples of either positive or negative politics, most cases are probably mixed, with negative politics predominating in some and positive in others. When institution-enhancing agendas compete, their sponsors tend to ignore the merits of others and push their own. That is only human nature.

Consider this case. The COO of an airline, in agreement with his human resources manager, decided to use special assignments and job rotation to develop a number of the firm's high-potential employees. The COO recommended to the corporate director of reservations that he appoint a woman that he, the COO, believed to be a high-potential employee to be director of reservations in a large city. She was not the very best candidate for the job, but he liked her and believed in his heart that she would develop nicely. The director of reservations went along with the COO's plan even though he had some misgivings. Then he left the airline suddenly. His replacement wanted his own reservations team in place and believed he had a better candidate than the woman already appointed. Though even in his mind she was "good enough," he replaced her with a man he thought could do a better job. Somewhere in the back of his mind his intention was also to test the COO. He thought that the latter was not tough enough for that job and saw himself as an ideal replacement. The COO did not intervene.

In this case we have deals, maneuvering, hesitation, and veiled challenging. Some of this is motivated by care for the institution, some by self-interest. It's the kind of mixed bag found frequently in most institutions.

In determining motivation, consider the following:

- Where does your institution stand on the continuum between the politics of self-interest and the politics of institutional enhancement?
- How does it manifest the politics of self-interest?
- How does it manifest the politics of institutional enhancement?
- What is your own political approach?

Identify the Sources of Power

Power, the ability to get things done, is dangerous in the wrong hands. "All power tends to corrupt," said Lord Acton, "and absolute power corrupts absolutely." Rather than an outpouring of cynicism, the good lord's dictum can be taken as a warning. Although power should be used for the common good of the company or institution, sometimes it is not. No one knows how often. No one knows the cost of the misuse of power. Some individuals or groups, however, love executive power and glory in its use. Sometimes this adds value; often it adds cost. While the business press is filled with examples of power struggles at the top, competing for power itself is an institutional staple. Always has been and always will be. Those who complain about organizational politics tend to say, "I feel powerless. Many things around here affect me and my destiny, but I have no say in them."

Power of one kind or another is at the core of political maneuvers. Without power it is impossible to compete. Since power is the essence of politics, then getting it is part of the political process. Common sources of power are position or authority, competence or expertise, the ability to persuade, personal attractiveness or charisma, and connections with those possessing these kinds of power. Effective politicians know how to acquire power and use it to get what they want. People differ radically in their feelings about power. Some relish and strive for it. Others feel guilty about acquiring and using it. Others fear it, even if they possess it. Studies show that negative feelings about power outweigh positive ones by a wide margin.

When people are hesitant to acquire and use power, those who have no such feelings can have a field day. I was talking to a nun who was a member of a religious group that operated more than a dozen hospitals in the United States. She believed that the order was not living up to the spirit of its founder, a man with a passion for the poor. "The poor," she claimed, "receive no better treatment at our hospitals than they do at other hospitals." Since policy was set by the religious superior and her council, influencing them was one avenue toward change. She was not a member of the council. "How does one become a member of the council?" I asked. "They are elected," she replied. "Well, then," went my logic, "why don't you run for a seat on the council?" She was horrified. "We don't 'run' for places on the council!" "Ah," I said, "the Holy Spirit makes the choices." Never having it heard it put so starkly, she hesitated. "Do you mean to tell me," I went on, "that the sisters don't talk about possible candidates in private—perhaps late at night behind closed doors? Or is it that the day of the election, the Spirit moves through the house whispering, 'Vote for Sister Gertrude'?" "Well," she said and then stared off into the distance, wondering, perhaps, about all the years of her disenfranchisement.

In analyzing power, consider the following:

- How do you feel about power and its use?
- What are the principal sources of power in your institution? Authority? Expertise? Personal attractiveness? The ability to persuade? Connections?
- What is the source of your own power?
- To what degree do people in your institution glory in its use?
- How do you use the power you have?

Observe the Strategies of Political Players

Many different strategies can be used to promote a political agenda. We have been exposed to most of them in national, state, and local campaigns. While these strategies are blatant when writ large on a national or local screen, the same strategies are more covert within organizations. This is not to suggest that all maneuvering in public politics is there for everyone to see. That conclusion would be extremely naive. It is rather a question of degree. In public, political maneuvering is the name of the game. In organizations, since politics can come in many disguises, many political strategies are deeper in the shadows.

Some political strategies are neutral, some are dirty. The term *dirty* refers to the legal, moral, and ethical character of the means used to achieve political goals. Some extend the term to political strategies that are carried out in secret even though they are not illegal, unethical, or immoral. Cutting a deal to get my boss's job by bribing my boss's boss is dirty in both senses. Political activity is also dirty if the competition itself is a sham. For instance, in some companies, candidates for promotion are led to believe that a certain position is open and that the best person will get it, while in truth a decision has already been made. Some companies welcome competing agendas even after the ultimate decision has been made. Common political strategies are listed in Chapter Eleven.

In observing strategies, consider the following:

- What strategies do political players in your organization use to accomplish their goals?

- Which ones are allowed by the culture? Which are forbidden? Which ones do you use?
- To what degree are political fights fair?
- What kind of political strategies do you find distasteful?
- What principled people in your organization are also good politicians? How do they carry it off?
- On a scale of 1 to 10, how political is your organization?

One manager used an innovative way to get one of his direct reports to use his considerable political skill at the service of the institution. This manager was very effective in using the communication skills outlined in Chapter Eight. "Luis," he said, "you're one of the savviest political players I've seen in a long time. I don't have to tell you that this company is filled with personal politics. I want you to be my adviser on how we can get politics around here to serve the business rather than just hidden agendas. It's not a question of eliminating politics. We'll never do that. But we can redirect all this political energy. I bet you could give me a couple of tips right now." In a flash he let the other know that his political maneuverings had not eluded him, that the covert culture promoted the practice of personal politics, that he respected his direct report's abilities, and that he wanted to work with him.

Recognize the Ethical Implications of Political Activity

By now it is probably clear that many shadow-side activities and arrangements have ethical implications. Some shadow-side activities, such as theft, are unethical in themselves, while others are unethical in terms of the ways in which they are pursued, and still others are unethical in terms of their impact or consequences. In the following case, a young man, let us call him Jake, becomes a pawn in an organization's internal political warfare. Jake, an English major at a small Eastern college, visited a range of newspapers and magazines in a large Midwestern city before finishing college. Though the interviews seemed to go well and people mentioned positive things, there were few openings at the time. One magazine had a senior writer named Mark who spent a lot of time going over Jake's work. He liked Jake, and, although he wasn't sure if there were any openings, he said that he believed the magazine might make an exception. Realizing that the recruiter didn't care much for his opinion, Mark arranged for Jake to meet with a writer who had been with the magazine a long time. This writer, Elizabeth, took a real liking to Jake and his work and promised to set up a meeting with the recruiter.

The interview, however, took several weeks to be arranged, and when Jake finally met with the recruiter, she seemed to feel that Jake wasn't yet prepared to carry the work load. Upset, Jake went back to Mark and Elizabeth, who both expressed surprise and said they would see whether they could get some money allocated to employ him. By this time, the winter holiday season had rolled around. After the holidays, Mark told Jake that he and Elizabeth were going to try to schedule a meeting for Jake with Martha, the woman in charge of their particular section. The meeting took dozens of calls from Jake to set up, was canceled twice, and finally was conducted in late March. It turned out at that point that Mark and Elizabeth had written a letter of recommendation to some of the higher authorities in the magazine's system and had said that the decision would be up to Martha, with whom Jake finally had a meeting.

Martha also seemed to like Jake and his work, and in fact told him she wanted to hire him. Since Jake had been told by Mark that Martha had the right to decide, he expected to be offered the job shortly. However, the magazine felt that, because Jake was so young and inexperienced, they ought to double screen him. A head of the writing department, who was also one of the chiefs of the magazine, asked to meet with Jake. Again, the meeting took several weeks to set up, and again, when it finally took place, it went well. The man, Timothy, said that he would let Martha decide. Martha told him the paperwork was in personnel, but for a week and a half Jake heard nothing. Finally, he received a call from the director of recruitment, the same woman with whom he had met in the fall. Mark and Elizabeth seemed to feel that this was a good sign, and told Jake to get ready to negotiate his salary.

When Jake went in, something entirely different took place. His work was examined again, and he was told that maybe, possibly, he would be given some freelance work. He told the recruiter, who noticed his disappointment, that he had been led to believe that he was going to be employed full time. The recruiter responded by saying that Elizabeth and Mark were certainly *not* the decision makers. By this point Jake was very upset. He went and spoke to both Mark and Martha, who were shocked at his treatment and claimed they had been told nothing to contradict their expectation that he would be hired.

Jake had become a pawn in the running war between line and personnel. Those who worked on the line thought that they should have final say in hiring staff members. The director of personnel had his own empire, and the chief recruiter was his staunch ally in this. In Jake's case, the director of recruitment was upset about being circumvented. Mark, Elizabeth, and Martha were using him as a test case without telling him what was happening. Personnel won and the line writers lost. Of course, the real victim was Jake.

In this chapter we have explored ways to analyze the internal politics of the organization. One of the best ways of driving out institution-limiting politics—a task that will always be with us—is to champion and pursue positive politics (Block, 1987). The next chapter suggests ways of doing precisely that.

11

HOW TO PRACTICE
POSITIVE POLITICS

INCE, AS MENTIONED EARLIER, it is impossible to avoid organizational politics—as a natural form of human behavior it
is a natural part of the institutional landscape—it is important to
harness the system's political energy and focus it on making the
business better, to the degree that this is possible. Here is a model
or framework for engaging in politics positively. As with frameworks presented in earlier chapters, managers may use it in the step-
by-step fashion presented here or refer to it as a set of guidelines or
a checklist for practicing politics positively, promoting prevention
over remedy, and establishing a culture of positive politics. Bear in
mind that, given human nature, this model, even if fully implemented, will never eliminate the politics of self-interest or dirty
politics. Use it as a way to function effectively in a dimension of the
shadow side that will always be present.

The trick is embedding the values of the model in the culture
of the system and seeing to it that the skills needed to implement
it are shared by a critical mass of the institution's players. A sponsor
for a project in one company, after being exposed to the model, said
that if he had used it, getting the institution-enhancing project
accepted "would have been a piece of cake." The project was ultimately accepted, but only after needless anguish caused by a lack of
an upbeat political outlook and some positive political skills. The

model includes the following steps: (1) start with an institution-enhancing agenda, (2) welcome open scrutiny and entertain competing agendas, (3) promote positive political values, (4) acquire the power needed to compete, (5) do a stakeholder analysis, (6) choose the most viable political strategies, and (7) organize a political campaign. Not all of these steps will be used by every political player around every organizational agenda. In a sense it is the spirit of this process that counts. The spirit should pervade the company's political processes.

Start with an Institution-Enhancing Agenda

Political activity is about shepherding agendas through the organizational maze. Agendas include such things as resetting the strategy, choosing and developing projects, proposing new products, altering the company's structure, changing human resource policies, adjusting procedures and systems, and the like. Decisions need to be made about which agendas to pursue and the kind of capital to be invested in those that are given the go-ahead. A positive approach to politics starts from a different point than one based on self-interest. The starting point for the latter is "I" or "we" or "our unit." Any given agenda is favored to the degree that it benefits us. Hidden agendas are central to the politics of self-interest. The starting point of positive politics, on the other hand, is the common good of the institution. The chosen political agenda or proposal should benefit the institution directly. The enhanced institution then provides benefits for its stakeholders, including the sponsor of the agenda.

Consider the following case. A consultant was asked by two senior managers of one of the divisions of a company to help them review a divisional strategy. Their purpose in hiring her was to help them sell the president of the company on their strategy. He was a visionary and tended to have little time for strategies rooted in the past. He wanted to move away from commodity businesses and move into high-tech products. The point of these two managers, however, was that the company was going through a transition. Viable commodity strategies, with new twists such as the involvement of foreign partners, were needed to complement high-tech

strategies during this period. Joint ventures with foreign partners—
even in commodities—were needed to open up foreign markets.
These partnerships could be used later to set up channels for the
newer high-tech products.

Their starting point was not vested interests but what they
saw to be an institution-enhancing strategy. Their job was to sell
the president and other key stakeholders in the company on the
value of the strategy. In fact, there was some concern in the company that the president's push into high-tech products had more to
do with the advancement of his own ego than the strategic development of the company. He wanted to be known as the leader who
brought the company into the new high-tech era.

A second example. A professor in a university wanted to start
a new master's degree program. There was a growing market for the
kind of professional program he envisioned. Since no other university in the area had a program like the one he was proposing, he
saw this as an opportunity for the university. Because of the content
of the new program, however, it did not fit well into any of the
university's existing departments. Therefore, he proposed having
the innovative program report directly to the dean of the graduate
school. The professor knew little about institutional politics at the
time, but what he was proposing was an institution-enhancing
agenda. He thought that the program should be accepted because
it was a good idea. "How naive," some of his more cynical colleagues said to themselves.

He was not prepared for the harshness of the response from
the academic community. Hidden agendas abounded, even though
cleverly disguised. Some players did not want any new program,
however effective, because in a time of diminishing resources there
would be one more mouth at the trough. But they objected because
the program did not "fit into the cohesive strategy of the university." Others objected not because they disliked the new program
but because it was not to be located in their departments. They
complained that the new program challenged a structure that had
served the university well and that it could well suffer from lack of
"proper oversight." Organizational players who had been enemies
for years collaborated to stop the program. In the end, the program
squeaked through the scrutiny and decision-making process, par-

tially because a few very respected academics supported it because they thought it was a good idea and would further the cause of interdepartmental collaboration, and partially because a few people voted for the program to annoy the "loudmouths who think they run this place."

The notion of a positive political agenda is a powerful one. It legitimizes "political" struggles insofar as they contribute to the well-being of the institution.

Welcome Open Scrutiny and
Entertain Competing Agendas

All agendas need to be open to challenge and disconfirmation. It must be clear that the agenda will further the fortunes of the institution. To the degree possible, hidden agendas behind the public agenda need to be ferreted out and scrutinized. Who will the real winner be? must always be asked, however tactfully. Hidden agendas are usually hidden not because they serve the balanced interests of institutional stakeholders but because they serve vested interests. Hiding agendas from competitors is understandable; hiding them from colleagues is another matter. Even if by all criteria an agenda is institution-enhancing, there may still be a better one. It is as if players were to say, Yes, this is a worthy cause, but is there a better one, one that would add even more value to the institution? Players who have the institution's best interests in mind welcome competing agendas. The competition gives them an opportunity for making their own agendas even better. And, in the end, the institution wins if the best agenda is chosen.

Too many companies have gotten into trouble because some agenda was not studied and questioned. Here is a case in which this was not allowed to happen. The head of marketing for a small computer company that assembled and marketed PC clones tried to convince the executive committee to buy a troubled software company because it was a bargain. He was a strong personality and lobbied vigorously. The firm had some cash to play with, and the issue was the best use. A competing agenda from the director of operations was "bigger, better, faster." That is, he said that the route to greater profitability was to become one of the premier clone suppliers, not just in the U.S. but also in Europe. He, too, lobbied strenuously. The executive committee finally decided that buying a software company would, at this juncture, be a distraction. The company invested the money in improved quality, better service, and European marketing ventures. The company emerged as one of the premier clone makers in the United States and abroad. Open scrutiny of competing agendas helped keep the company on the right track.

Unfortunately, many institutions have cultures that limit debate. It is too messy, causes dissension, sets one group against another, takes too much time, infringes on the authority of decision makers, delays projects, and so forth. Others have cultures that see constructive contention at the heart of the decision-making process. One inventive manager never offered just one proposal. He would say, "Here is what I think the best strategy is." After explaining his position, he would go on to say, "And this is what I think the second-best strategy is." That is, he primed the pump for debate by starting with alternatives.

Promote Positive Political Values

Since political campaigns are about vying, contending, competing, winning, and losing, it helps to understand the "rules of combat." In some companies, or at least in the hearts of some of the players, it is almost as if there were but one rule: "Do whatever you have to do to win." Such a philosophy obviously does not serve a positive political approach. If, on the other hand, the principal value is compromise, then mediocre decisions will be the order of the day. Several positive values contribute to institution-enhancing politics, among them collaboration, entrepreneurship, and stewardship.

The Value of Collaboration

Even though internal political activity involves competing and internal debate, the concept of evolutionary economics, which focuses on the nature of competition, offers some lessons for those pursuing positive politics. There is some evidence that a degree of collaboration between competing companies may make more sense than brute, beat-their-brains-in competition. Here is what evolutionary economics has to teach us:

- Competition is not always a zero-sum game, even though zero-sum psychology drives many players. If they play it right, multiple players can win by increasing the size of the pie.

- More than naked self-interest drives the economy and, by extension, the internal economy of organizations. Profit, while important, is a sign of the company's success rather than success itself. There are other success components, such as quality-of-life values. To be blind to the needs and interests of multiple stakeholders these days can spell the beginning of the end.

- Economic benefits can often be optimized through some form of collaboration, even among competitors. The business press is filled with discussion of alliances among competitors. In high-tech businesses, the cost of research and development is so great that it has to be spread over a number of players. If they do this right, it creates new products that in turn create new markets.

These principles make as much sense when applied to internal competitors. In one smaller eight-office accounting firm there were two good candidates to take the place of the retiring president. The firm decided on an upbeat competitive approach to succession. Each candidate toured the offices and presented his vision and platform. This was followed by lively debate about the platform between himself and the local partners. Each partner had one vote, and the ballot was secret. Part of the platform consisted of what each would do to make sure that the other did not leave the firm if not elected. The outcome pleased everyone. One became chairman and the other president.

Entrepreneurial Values

Peter Block (1987) outlined the value foundations of positive politics in part by describing two different political cycles. The negative cycle is based on bureaucratic values. It starts with a covert patriarchal contract, benevolent or otherwise, that breeds myopic self-interest in the work force. Workers, manipulated by paternalistic managerial approaches, themselves use manipulative tactics to get what they want. This fosters a culture of dependency. The positive political cycle, on the other hand, is based on entrepreneurial values. Its basis is an implied or explicit entrepreneurial social contract that tends to foster enlightened self-interest. Institutional enhancement leading to benefits for all stakeholders is the way forward. Political tactics that respect the rights of others are encouraged. This approach fosters a culture of autonomy. The game is autonomy, courage, and risk taking versus dependency, caution, and maintenance.

Stewardship as a Value

In a new book, Block (1993) deals with *stewardship,* which he defines as "the willingness to be accountable for the larger organization by operating in service, rather than in control, of those around us." He is reexpressing the idea of "servant leadership" found both in Plato and in more contemporary writings. Power is about opportunities for service. Therefore, if an institution-enhancing agenda is one that takes into account the needs of key stakeholders, then the "steward" moves into collaboration mode. Knowing that the greatest benefit for all will be achieved not through self-interest but through open debate and collaborative give-and-take, the steward acts as an endorser, coordinator, and facilitator of this process. Stewards are not naive flunkies. They are principled realists. "Wow!" some will say, "that's about as far from what goes on in this place as you can get." And they are right. What is needed in some institutions is a total culture change in this regard.

What values would you like to see permeate the exercise of politics in your own organization?

Acquire the Power to Compete

One of the first tasks of those who already have power is to audit it. What kind of power do we have? How useful is it? What further power do we need? One of the first tasks of the powerless, disenfranchised, or politically weak is to *acquire* the power needed to push their institution-enhancing agendas. We have already named some of the common sources of power: position or authority, competence or expertise, the ability to persuade, personal attractiveness or charisma, and connections with those possessing these kinds of power. Others can be added, such as control over resources that can be swapped for other resources.

Here are some hints on acquiring power. Of course, in positive politics the way power is acquired should be in keeping with the espoused values that are to drive the political process. There are the self-serving approaches to acquiring power at one end of the continuum and stewardship approaches at the other.

- Review the *authority* you already have and the power it entails. Don't forget the incentives over which you have control. Many managers do not use the power associated with their positions. Either they are not aware of what they have or they are "keeping it in reserve" for the right moment—which, of course, never arises.

- Take stock of your *competencies*. Determine the demand for what you have and then leverage it in sponsoring and promoting institution-enhancing agendas. Develop further competencies that are in line with the strategy of the institution. This kind of self-development serves personal, institutional, and political goals.

- Develop *the ability to persuade and influence* others. Often enough this means assertiveness rather than ability. Those unwilling to enter others' lives, in a business sense, or the life of another organizational unit, lose a lot of their power.

- Review the qualities that make you *attractive* to others. If you are a self-deprecating sort of person, this will be hard. One reason we use only a fraction of our potential is that we are not in touch with it. Get in touch with the best in you and see how it can be used to touch others.

- Review your *relationships* with others. If you can't push a value-adding agenda on your own, see how you might push it through those with whom you have good relationships.

- Do an audit of the *institutional resources* you control and determine their political value. See which resources can be validly and usefully swapped for resources you need to pursue a political agenda. One manager controlled a warehouse that he no longer needed. A manager in another division needed the space desperately. He called him and said, "I've got a warehouse that you might need, but I also need a bit of your time." What the first manager needed was the expertise of the other so that he could hone a marketing agenda that he believed would add great value to the company. The second manager listened to the marketing agenda, offered suggestions for improvement, and pushed it at the next management committee meeting. He also got the warehouse.

Developing power from more than one source or base can increase power exponentially. For instance, the technical expert who is a communication klutz may exercise relatively little power. However, add persuasive ability to positional authority and the package may be overwhelming. If all of this sounds too crassly utilitarian, remember that you are serving the institution through all this and not your narrow self-interest. Remember also that others who might not have the same motivation as you are doing just these things.

Do a Stakeholder Analysis

A stakeholder is an individual or a group whose life will be affected by the agenda and who can, in turn, affect the agenda and its accomplishment. Institution-enhancing agendas affect different individuals and different groups in different ways. Block (1987) developed a useful taxonomy of political stakeholders based on their view of the proposed agenda—for it or against it—and on their feelings toward the agenda's sponsor, including their degree of trust. What follows is my version of that taxonomy, with several changes and additions. Remember that as agendas change, the stakeholder mix also changes.

• *Partners* are those who, either formally or informally, believe in and actively support the agenda and have a good relationship with the sponsor. They are self-starters. Players like this are pure gold, and care needs to be taken not only to avoid alienating them but to give them scope in the promotion of the agenda.

• *Allies* are those who believe in the agenda and, at least with the proper encouragement, will support it. Allies must be cultivated. The biggest mistake with respect to allies is to take them for granted. Often this is not clear until they fail to speak up at a meeting or do not show up to vote. A manager once said: "Kim, the head of finance, told me that he was behind the proposal. But he also said that he might work more effectively for the agenda if he were to work 'in the wings.' Well, he was so far back in the wings that I would have needed binoculars to find him." Either Kim was never an ally in the first place or he had not been cultivated properly.

• *Fellow travelers* are players who like the sponsor and therefore support the agenda, at least passively. Their lack of personal commitment to the agenda can be a problem. Lacking a clear understanding of it, they can go off in the wrong direction. Or they can push your personal stock instead of the agenda, thus alienating people. Suggestion: don't be beguiled by those who like you. Instruct fellow travelers on the merits of the agenda itself. Get them to speak about it, not you.

• *Fencesitters* are players whose position on the agenda and/or feelings toward the sponsor are not clear. It is a mistake to see them as neutral or indifferent. The trick is to find out where they stand or help them move in your direction. Some fencesitters sit on the sidelines until they see which party is to be the likely winner. They are driven by self-interest.

• *Loose cannons* are difficult people who cause a great deal of damage even though they might not be specifically against the agenda or its sponsor. They come from nowhere and wreak havoc. They may vote against agendas they have no interest in. In one accounting firm a partner spoke out strongly against a new marketing proposal even though he had never even read it. If the sponsor had done a careful stakeholder analysis, when she came to this particular partner, she would have said, "This guy is dangerous because you never know what he's going to say. Yet, because of his track record he has a great deal of credibility in the firm. We need a strategy for managing him."

• *Opponents* are players who oppose the agenda but not the sponsor. They may feel that some competing agenda has more merit or have some personal hidden agenda, institution-enhancing or not, that will be thwarted by the sponsor's agenda. In cases like this the sponsor can use the good relationship to get a heart-to-heart discussion with him or her on the issues. One sponsor did so and discovered that the opponent really did not fully understand the proposal. If opponents cannot be converted to the agenda, then steps should be taken to neutralize them. You may not be able to convert an opponent, but someone you know might. Otherwise, find out what they are offering instead of your proposal and discover its flaws.

• *Adversaries* are people who don't like the sponsor and therefore reject the agenda. Or they may be at odds with the institution itself and therefore don't like the agenda *because* it is institution-enhancing. One sponsor, realizing that a key manager from the financial department was an adversary, got a colleague to sponsor the proposal. Suggestion: find ways of clearing up the relationship. If this is not possible, find ways of using their poor relationship with you against their efforts to do you in. "Of course, since Mr. Smith does not like Ms. Jones, it is difficult to determine how seriously his remarks should be taken."

• *Bedfellows* are players who like the agenda but may not know the sponsor well enough or distrust him or her. In this case, the relationship itself needs attention. The sponsor for a new product took a member of the new-product review team to lunch the week before the review. Her approach was straightforward. She said, "My best bet is that you like the product, but you're not sure if I'm the one who should manage it. I may not be. I would really appreciate hearing from you what your misgivings may be." Suggestion: with bedfellows, keep their attention on the issues rather than the sponsor.

• *The voiceless* are stakeholders who have little power. They are people whose lives will be affected by the agenda but have no voice in either espousing it or opposing it, and they have no power to affect the outcome. They are people who lack advocates for their causes. The disenfranchised may not be as powerless as they seem. For instance, disaffected employees can easily engage in a "silent conspiracy" to block the progress of an agenda. Suggestion: do not be duped into thinking that the voiceless have no power. They may be used by your adversary. Pay attention to their concerns.

I once met a manager who had just returned from an important meeting. He was furious. "What's wrong?" I asked. "I can't believe that guy!" he exclaimed. "Believe what?" I countered. "He manages that division and he didn't have the votes! They rejected the proposal. Why would anyone call a meeting like that without having the votes?" In other words, here was someone who had not done a stakeholder analysis together with the political work needed once the stand of each stakeholder was known.

The stakeholder analysis process is straightforward. First, draw up a full list of stakeholders. Get someone to do this with you so that you don't fall prey to your blind spots. Second, star key stakeholders, those whose behavior toward the proposal could make a significant difference. Third, write down what you think their interests are with respect to the agenda and toward you, the sponsor. A manager doing this exercise said at this point, "Sue will think that this proposal is not in line with the overall strategy. I had better make the linkage clearer." Another said, "The ones who count like me well enough." Fourth, briefly indicate what action should be taken, if any, toward each key stakeholder.

Choose the Most Viable Political Strategies

Political strategies involve shepherding ideas, projects, visions, and agendas through the organizational maze. Some of the following strategies apply to the direct promotion of the political agenda itself, while others deal more specifically with managing stakeholders. Since these means are, for the most part, neutral, their value character comes from the cause they serve. For instance, one manager as part of his campaign delayed his proposal until three others had been reviewed. When a colleague intimated that this was sneaky, he replied something like this: "I believe that my proposal best serves the interests of this company. Its true value is better seen when contrasted to the alternatives. Being last in line will put the proposal in the best light." He did not lie, steal, bribe, or cheat. He did jockey, and his proposal was approved.

• *Understand the business needs of the institution.* Your agenda has to fit into a larger picture. The more informed you are about what the company needs in order to survive and thrive, the more likely your agenda will be seen to fit.

• *Get to know the playing field.* Become familiar with the informal or hidden organization (discussed in Chapter Twelve). Get a feeling for the informal communication networks. More specifically, understand the context in which you'll be pushing your agenda. A manager was appointed to the strategic planning committee. The first thing he did was get the minutes of the meetings of that committee for the previous two years. He studied them, looking for themes, flaws, and possibilities. Needless to say, he exercised a great deal of influence on that committee.

• *Learn the name of the game.* Learn how politics are played in this company generally and how they are played specifically in the departments involved in or affected by your proposal. What political strategies work here? Which fail? In one company, appeals to reason worked, while overly emotional appeals failed. In another company, consensus was the name of the game. In a third, analyzing the economics was critical. In a fourth, getting the ear of the CEO was all that mattered.

• *Identify the key players.* Sometimes the key players are not the most obvious ones. The director of human resources in one company was pushing empowerment programs. A couple of managers saw him as the key player and stonewalled him. "We don't have time for that stuff," they said. However, several savvy managers discovered early on that the chairman of the board and the president were behind the HR agendas. Therefore, they decided that they were going to do whatever they could to tailor the empowerment process to serve the business.

• *Identify the interests of key players.* Astute political players also know the interests behind agendas. One manager in the company saw in the push for empowerment programs a dynamic that cut deeper. Like the others, he knew that the president and the chairman of the board both wanted a company that was up-to-date managerially. But he believed that they began the updating with sessions on empowerment as a way of finding out who would be willing to champion a program that involved distributing decision making more widely. They were testing the managerial waters.

• *Address the self-interest of key players.* The politically astute, even when pursuing an institution-enhancing agenda, appeal to the self-interest of those they are approaching. "Do it my way and you will get what you want."

• *Get organized.* People who are politically astute are good at organizing campaigns and enlisting people in the service of a cause, whether it is the institution's cause or their own. They know that there is power in numbers.

• *Develop and use communication competencies.* Politicians know how to talk to people, or, if they don't, they gather around themselves people who are adept at communicating. Politicians are good at persuading and selling. They are assertive: they do not hesitate to sell their ideas, opinions, values, goals, and programs.

• *Establish and use informal communication networks.* These networks, mentioned in Chapter Twelve, can be used both to gather intelligence and to send messages unobtrusively. They can be used to "float" ideas or agenda possibilities and get feedback that can then be used to fine-tune proposals.

• *Enter into alliances.* One way to gain power is to ally yourself or your group with a group that already has power. This may mean swallowing one's pride, but loss of pride may be a small enough price to pay for the cause.

• *Form coalitions.* Pull together several relatively powerless groups and form one group that has a strong voice. Keeping the group together, at least long enough to get your agenda passed, usually takes effective communication and negotiation skills.

• *Develop both champions and followers.* Champions are players who understand the cause, believe in it, and don't have to be told how to promote it. Every agenda needs some champions. But political campaigns also require foot soldiers. Followers, in the best sense of the term, are not sheep but individuals who understand the cause and offer their services. However, followers who believe that they are being used can ruin a campaign. Developing a critical mass of followers who believe in the cause is critical for longer-term campaigns, for instance, those involving culture change.

• *Develop and back causes.* The politically astute know how to turn their agendas into causes around which their colleagues can rally. Or they know how to tie them to causes that are already being pushed. They find parades, get in front of them, and then lead them where they want. Politicians are forever listening to polls and even taking them, formally or informally. They know which way the political winds are blowing, and they know how to set sail with the wind. They know that, historically, the ideas or ideals that have captured the imagination of people are basically simple.

• *Know who "owes you one."* Politicians do not hesitate to call in owed favors when this will help. This calls for tact. Over-doing this strategy can cheapen your image. And remember, if you call in favors, others will do the same. Do a cost-benefit analysis of favor exchange.

• *Learn how to use trade-offs well.* If you understand both the agendas of your colleagues and the interests that underlie them, you are in a position to barter. If you shortchange your colleagues, they will find ways of getting back at you. Be an honest trader.

• *Maximize flexibility without becoming slippery.* Politi-cians know many different routes to the same destination. They also know when to modify an agenda to get it through. They know when to bail out and can do so with their integrity intact.

• *Balance overt and covert action.* Effective politicians know when to work in public and when to work behind the scenes. If they cannot organize people openly, they do so quietly. Learn when to work quietly and when to go public. Public discussions about your proposal may be most effective if they are simple. Deal with more complex issues with key stakeholders privately.

• *Use drama and theater, but sparingly.* Sometimes a stir-ring speech or a dramatic gesture helps. Too much drama cheapens the agenda. Whenever possible, let the substance of the agenda speak for itself. "Less is more" is a good campaign slogan provided you know when more is more.

• *Make haste slowly.* This adage is borrowed from the an-cient Romans who used it to create and govern their empire. Know when it makes sense to push and when it is better to bide your time. Timing is a critical political tool.

• *Get the votes.* If you need votes to get your agenda passed, then learn how to get votes. Pay attention to key stakeholders. Don't be blindsided. Count only the votes that are sure.

This is not an exhaustive list of political strategies. While it includes none that is clearly "dirty," it may include a few that seeem unsavory to you, especially if you are not naturally a political player. The point is this: if you are not willing to use strategies like these, others are. Remember that neutral strategies such as these take on the value character of the goal to which they are directed. Since we are talking about positive politics, the goal is the accomplishment of an institution-enhancing agenda. This is not the same as saying the end justifies the means. That principle is used by some to justify strategies that are immoral in themselves.

Organize a Political Campaign

The organization and sequencing of a set of political strategies constitute a campaign. While not all political transactions involve a campaign in the extended sense, selling an important agenda—an agenda that will use significant institutional resources—usually requires one.

Campaigns can have many different faces, whether the objective is self-interest or institutional enhancement. There is the ongoing campaign to protect turf or the one-time campaign to get a promotion. The campaign may be addressed to a single stakeholder or to many. It may be sufficient to convince the boss, or it might be necessary to get approval from a succession of committees.

Organizing a political campaign involves taking many of the steps discussed previously, as shown in the following example. The vice president of marketing of a fast-growing telecommunications firm felt that the company was plagued by many sloppy work practices. They were overlooked because of the booming nature of the industry. He used a little money from his slush fund to hire a consultant firm to help him with the economics of these sloppy practices. While he did not believe that downsizing made sense in the company, cleaning up the mess as a part of the process of strategic positioning did. In a word, he thought that the company would benefit greatly from a thorough reengineering effort. However, if he were to say that baldly at a management council meeting, he knew that he would be accused of pursuing the latest management fad. He wanted to see two things happen: a total reengineering of the company's work processes, including both soft and hard areas, and a complementary business-based training effort to provide all managers with work-design skills. He was convinced that if managers had and used work-design skills in the first place—if ongoing work design and redesign were part of the continual improvement process—then costly reengineering would not be needed down the line.

His first tactic in the political campaign was to put his own house in order. The consulting firm helped him do an in-depth study of marketing and sales practices and to reengineer them. While he was a bit ashamed by what he found, it reinforced his belief that it was economically wise to pursue a company-wide effort. Sharing what he had learned in his own shop would help him be seen as a "humble petitioner" rather than a johnny-come-lately management guru. A "see how good I am" approach would be deadly.

The key strategies in his campaign included establishing an informal coalition with a couple of other interested department heads, helping them "do the numbers" in their own shops, quietly developing a few champions of reengineering two and three levels down in their departments, getting the president interested in the idea of reengineering and its economics, mounting a small benchmarking effort with a couple of companies that had undertaken similar R&D projects, getting his colleagues to unobtrusively sow seeds in their own departments and with their friends, doing a stakeholder analysis of key managers and opinion leaders, identifying areas of the company where the most economic gain could be achieved, and mending fences with a couple of adversaries. All this culminated in the president putting reengineering on the agenda of one of the management council meetings. He opened the meeting by saying, "I've been taking a closer look at our work practices over the last six months, and I've asked Paul to share a couple of experiments he's been carrying out in marketing and sales. What he's found will, I believe, be of strategic interest to all of us."

Organizational players cannot afford to be naive. The politics of self-interest are here to stay. But they can be contained. Effective players are not cynical about politics. Rather they learn to practice them in a constructive way.

Audit the Politics of Your Organization

Approaches to politics differ from company to company. Take an inventory of the attitudes toward and practice of politics in your own organization. Then use your findings to determine the kind of player you would like to become.

- What are politics like here? How would we describe the political culture?
- To what degree do politics serve the company? In what ways do they limit our effectiveness?
- What are the rules of "combat" and conflict management currently in place? How do we currently handle competing agendas? How do we go about settling disagreements?
- How do we manage vested interests? What do we do about those who work consistently from self-interest?
- How do we feel about working secretly on agendas, especially those with a strong vested-interests component?
- What values permeate the negotiation process?
- To what degree are debate and negotiation seen as learning events—as discussions of different points of view and interests that enable us to make institution-enhancing decisions more effectively?
- How do we feel about employee empowerment and involvement? To what degree are we a paternalistic organization?
- What do we do with the good ideas of those who are naturally less political? What happens when one individual has a cutthroat philosophy and another is into negotiated settlements?
- To what degree are people encouraged to express their points of view? How willing are people to *sell* their points of view? To what degree does the current culture allow people to sell a point of view that differs from a mainstream position?
- How different are the philosophies and campaign tactics of subunits? What happens if there are sharks in marketing and doves in engineering, or vice versa?

BRINGING IT
ALL TOGETHER

12

MAKING THE HIDDEN
ORGANIZATION SERVE
THE BUSINESS

T HE TERM *ORGANIZATION* can mean many things, including
the entire company or institution, as in such statements as,
"She worked for four different organizations before settling down
here." In earlier chapters of this book, *organization* has included
both organizational structure and the human resource management
systems used in deploying people throughout the structure. This
chapter focuses mostly on organizational structure. Generally, *structure* refers to the ways in which a company or institution divides up
the work. The human resources department has *this* set of tasks and
responsibilities, while the engineering department has a different set.
Within the human resources department, this group is responsible
for compensation and benefits, while a different group takes care of
training. While structure is an innocent-sounding word, in practice
the elements of structure can be quite complex and open to both
company-enhancing and company-limiting shadow-side arrangements and activities. So let's take a brief look at the rational elements
of structure so that later we can review their covert or shadow side.

   • The organizational *geometry* of the company includes all
the organizational units and their relationships to one another. A
static picture of this is found on organizational charts. This tells us,
from a macro perspective, how the work is divided. For instance, the
apparel group constitutes one unit within a department store chain,

233

and there are subgroups within the apparel group such as women's, men's, and kids' apparel. Another group is responsible for furniture, for example.

- *Interunit coordinating mechanisms* such as strategy and cross-functional teams are needed to integrate the work of various units such as design, engineering, manufacturing, marketing, sales, and finance. In a department store, coordination among the merchandise, delivery, and customer service groups is essential.

- The *jobs, roles,* and *positions* of the organization define the work within each unit. These, from a micro perspective, tell us how the work is divided up. The kinds of jobs and the way they are designed should serve the work of the unit. For instance, in department stores the job of store manager is key. His or her leadership can spell the difference between mediocrity and excellence.

- *Intraunit coordinating mechanisms* such as meetings and task forces are needed to integrate work at the unit level. For instance, the apparel sales personnel in the department store meet to organize an upcoming three-day sale. The outcomes of the meeting should contribute to the success of the sale.

- Organizational *lines of authority* and *decision-making practices* define who has the authority to make what kinds of decisions both between and within organizational units. Delegation of authority is part of this package.

- *Communication processes* are needed to promote the information flow that is the lifeblood of the business. In a department store, immediate feedback of sales to the marketing and merchandise groups is essential. The store manager's communication of the spirit of both the company and the store strategy to sales personnel enables them to sell in a more committed and proactive way.

- *Mechanisms of control* such as policies, methods, guidelines, standards, rules, and regulations are needed to assure that the right things are being done at the right time. For instance, stores have policies and procedures governing the display of merchandise. In chains a master display plan often comes from the central merchandising and marketing group.

Ideally, these elements of structure serve the business by optimizing information sharing, decision making, and work flow. Needless to say, they do not always do so. A simple reading of the above list reveals that its shadow-side potential is enormous. For instance, in what institution do mechanisms of control not cast a shadow? Who is not aware of the shadow-side potential of communication processes? The shadow-side workings of these organizational elements constitute the *hidden organization*—what really happens in the organization as opposed to what is stated on paper. Shadow-side culture, personal styles, social systems, and internal politics permeate the items on this list. Therefore, while it is easy to say that the organization should serve the business, it is another thing to get it to do so.

This is not to say that everything that goes wrong is part of the shadow side. Clearly, companies can and do make mistakes in all of the dimensions of structure. The wrong organizational units are created. The way the work is divided among them does not serve the business. The overall structure is fine, but managers don't know how to work it. Interunit work is poorly coordinated. Information-sharing processes are flawed. Jobs are poorly designed. The person in a key job does not have enough authority to get her work done. Rules are too rigid and fail to give managers the flexibility they need. While the litany is endless, there is nothing particularly sinister about this. These are out-in-the-open mistakes, not shadow-side problems.

However, identifying organizational mistakes and then failing to deal with them *is* part of the shadow side. For instance, in one company it became clear that a person in a key but poorly designed marketing position was standing in the way of the company's new growth strategy. It was a question of the wrong person in the wrong job. Her boss knew it. The president knew it. Those who worked in marketing knew it. People talked about it informally. But it was never brought up in a decision-making forum. Those in authority simply did not have the courage to do something about it. As a consultant I tried more than once to bring up both issues, flawed job design and flawed incumbent, but the replies I got were of the order, "Yeah, I know. We've got to deal with that." But nothing was done. The issues remained in the shadows.

Contrast this with a situation in Britain. The new chief executive of one of Britain's largest banks said early in his tenure, "I think at the moment we are very inappropriately organized. The problem is that what people are supposed to be doing and what they are actually doing are not the same thing." That is, there were published job descriptions and shadow job descriptions. This was not a new problem for the bank. It had been going on for years, but no one before him had named it and done anything about it. By stating the problem publicly, he was committing himself to managing the shadow side.

The Hidden Organization in Action

Each of the structural elements mentioned above has a shadow side—a set of arrangements that evolve without official endorsement. This set of covert arrangements often contravenes or takes precedence over what appears on organizational charts or in manuals. For instance, in one company, Ed Smith was named leader of a task force, but Sally Jones, a middle manager in his department, ran it. Those in the know understood the arrangement. Ed was a senior manager without portfolio. In a downsizing drive, he had been relieved of his position and given the title of director of special projects until his retirement, which was about a year away. While he added no value to the work of the task force, neither did he get in the way. This temporary arrangement seemed to satisfy everyone. Organizational arrangements like this are legion. They are often economically significant—that is, they add cost, value, or a bit of both to the company, but because they are shadow-side phenomena their economics are seldom explored.

There are five major types of shadow-side arrangements that define the hidden organization: (1) arrangements arising from the covert culture, (2) arrangements linked with people and politics, (3) arrangements adopted to correct flawed organizational practices, (4) arrangements on the shadow side of organizational controls, and (5) arrangements used to fine-tune the system. Of course, in practice these five sets of shadow-side arrangements are jumbled together. In the following discussion, cases are used to illustrate each of these categories, and suggestions are provided for dealing with arrangements that limit the business. Most of the suggestions are based on the strategies discussed and illustrated in earlier chapters.

Arrangements Arising from the Covert Culture

A company's culture—its embedded system of beliefs, values, and norms and the patterns of behavior they drive—plays an important role in generating the shadow-side arrangements that make up the hidden organization. This is true for each element of organizational structure: geometry, coordinating mechanisms, jobs, lines of authority, communication processes, and mechanisms of control.

Let's start with organizational geometry. In a software firm, a nontraditional, that is, nonhierarchical structure was set up under the assumption that it would serve the business better—ensure more responsiveness to customers, better new-product development, and more speed to market. However, the old culture, favoring the traditional hierarchical geometry, generated a shadow-side hierarchy that undercut the espoused new framework. A rather savvy manager went over the official organizational chart with me. There, clearly spelled out, was the new flexible matrix culture. Then he said, "But, of course, that's not how it works." He then showed me a second chart, this one hand-drawn, that translated the matrix chart into a traditional hierarchical chart. "This is how it really works," he said. In a matrix organization, many workers have two bosses—for instance, a functional boss in the engineering department and a second boss in a time-limited project. "In our company," he explained, "these two bosses never really talk to each other. As a result, the one with the most power is the real boss. The matrix is misleading since it is nothing but a messy hierarchical structure." Covert hierarchical arrangements took precedence over what was on paper. In fact, the company was not culturally ready for a matrix structure. The mindset needed to make it work was not in place.

Let's take a look at a different structural element—lines of authority and decision-making practices. In one large company a new, more liberal delegation policy was announced. Delegation in that company was stated in terms of the amount of money managers could spend without asking for authority to do so. But this is how it really worked: The delegation document said, in a loud voice, as it were, "You may spend up to $1 million on your own authority." But then somewhere in the background the company culture whispered, "Don't do it." An arrangement arose in which managers kept trudging to the superiors to "get their counsel" on projects they could have easily decided on themselves. The new delegation policy had been stated, but it was not really in effect. The new system was supposed to cut down on cost and speed decisions. But now decision making was slower than ever and the lost-opportunity costs of failing to get new products to market quickly mounted. But once more these costs remained in the shadows.

If the culture spawns covert organizational arrangements that do not serve the business, then the remedy is to use the appropriate strategies from the culture-change group outlined in Chapter Six. For instance, in both the examples just cited, one way of challenging the shadow-side arrangement would be to challenge the covert cultural norms generating the arrangement. In the first case, someone needed the courage to say, "We're not ready for a matrix structure. It won't work because we still have a hierarchical mindset. What we need to do is to identify the cultural norms needed to make a matrix structure work, espouse them, and use them to drive out the old culture." In the second case, someone needed to say, "I feel we have a new delegation system on paper but not in practice. Here's what I mean. The old conservative culture is keeping us in check-with-your-boss mode." In both cases, however, it took a couple of years and some radical changes in the business environment to get the covert arrangements generated by the old culture out of the system.

Directly challenging norms that maintain an arrangement that does not serve the business is one strategy. But sometimes an indirect approach is preferable. One indirect way, as noted in earlier chapters, is to use a business-based strategy to challenge and change some dimension of a culture. The following example deals with work practices and control mechanisms.

In one small company it had become the practice for most people to leave the office by about 1 P.M. on Fridays. Over the years a norm had developed: "It's all right to leave early on Friday." The new general manager felt lonely the first Friday or two, because he and those with whom he had scheduled meetings were the only ones around. It dawned on him that one-tenth of his staff's weekly working hours had evaporated. But instead of causing a big stink and starting off, perhaps, on the wrong foot, he decided on a number of business-based strategies. His thinking went like this: "Since the business is not falling apart, I would like to reclaim these hours but do so in a way that adds value to the business. I don't want to make them stay at their desks simply doing tasks, or pretending to do tasks, for the sake of doing them."

The first couple of Fridays he stayed and worked more or less alone. Then he called a meeting of three of his top lieutenants for the next Friday afternoon. Instead of an ordinary meeting, he conducted a brainstorming session. "Let's just take a few hours," he said, "to do some blue-sky thinking about the business." They did, and they loved it. They told him that this was the first time that they had shared creative ideas about the business. To make a long story short, he expanded the group, got other managers to do different kinds of creative work with their staffs, and finally made Friday afternoons one of the most useful periods of the week. He not only reclaimed the 10 percent of business time that was being lost but did it in a way that added much more than 10 percent of value to the business. The work created for Friday afternoon was challenging, interesting, team-based, cross-functional, and value-adding.

Arrangements Linked with People and Politics

Personal styles, the vagaries of the social system, and institutional politics are all fertile sources of covert organizational arrangements. Consider the interaction between *personal style* and organizational communication processes. The chief of staff in a large health care center was a busybody who found it difficult to delegate authority. While he tried to disguise these traits as "keeping his finger on the pulse of the institution," those who knew his style were not deceived. Over time he developed a network of informants—interns, younger doctors, nurses, nurses' aides, administrative assistants, and secretaries willing to share whatever gossip they came across in the institution. Since he was charming, people talked freely with him. He ended up knowing more about the shadow side of the center than anyone else. When a new computer system was being installed, he kept second-guessing the information technology professionals. He wanted to make sure that the system would serve his needs. The changes he requested or demanded made the system both more costly and less effective. His antics even kicked off squabbles among other stakeholders.

The next case involves the interaction between the structure of jobs within an institution and *the politics of self-interest.* Politically minded managers protect both their turf and their political cronies. One manager in an international agricultural research center lobbied for a new matrix structure because it would give him, as director of special projects, greater power and influence. Another director voted against abolishing positions with the title "deputy" in them, as in "deputy director," because he used his deputy to carry out all the managerial tasks he hated to do and to cushion and even absorb the criticisms leveled at his department. He did not want to be a manager; he wanted to do research. Of course, he did not say this in his campaign. Rather he pointed out how important these deputy positions were to the center's succession planning. He said that deputies either were or should be people who were being groomed to move into higher positions. Everyone talked about his ego and his meddling, but nothing was ever said in any decision-making forum that could have handled the issue.

In this case, too, the principle, "Get good business practice to drive out institution-limiting shadow-side arrangements" was used to good effect. The head of research communicated the new job-structuring strategy to everyone and then discussed the kind of organization that was needed to support the strategy. He carefully pointed out the new role of department heads. They were not to be mere administrators. Nor was their job so much to *do* research as to make sure that good research took place. He pointed out the value-adding nature of the new role and how it would contribute to the development of local research talent. Deputy jobs disappeared. Then, over a two-year period, those department heads who had the skills and will to carry out the new role were affirmed, while those who could not were replaced. He did all this with tact and firmness, affirming both the importance of the contributions of those who were "returning to academia" and of the new global development climate that demanded substantial change in strategy.

Here is a case that involves interaction between geometry and *the social system.* In one sophisticated but doggedly hierarchical organization I discovered a unit in the human resources department called the "strategic planning unit." I wondered what it was doing there. I asked them to tell me what they did. They said that they did research and wrote reports related to the institution's strategy. That struck me as a bit odd since the institution didn't really have a strategy. "And what do you do with the reports?" I asked. "We send them to senior managers," they replied, meaning, I supposed, to the assistants of senior managers. "And what happens to them then?" I persisted. "We're not sure," came the shadow-side reply. This unit had been created when strategic planning was all the rage. In a me-too way, the institution said, "We should be doing this." But instead of taking strategic planning or, better, the formulation of strategy seriously, with the head of the institution taking a lead role, it was delegated to the HR department. I read some of the reports. They were thoroughly researched, but they added no value. The unit was run by decent people who had friends at higher levels. Once the strategic planning fad had passed, senior managers did not have the heart to eliminate the unit—and their friends with it—so they looked the other way, rationalizing that the research being done could be valuable. Of course, they did not discuss this in any meeting, or informally among themselves. They simply put the issue out of their minds. This arrangement, with roots in the social system, was to allow this cozy little unit to go merrily on its way. Its function and value were never discussed in any decision-making forum. Needless to say, when a new president of the institution was appointed to "clean the place up," this unit was one of the first to be eliminated.

Arrangements Adopted to Correct
Flawed Organizational Practices

Covert organizational arrangements often arise to quietly correct some organizational mistake or to get around some flawed organizational system or process. Take performance management and appraisal systems, which constitute one of the organization's track-and-control mechanisms. Since these systems are so often poorly designed and engineered—so much so that they often add cost rather than value to the company—all sorts of arrangements arise to get around them. The covert arrangement in one institution was to allow productive managers to delay their appraisals. In talking to one of their star managers, I discovered that he was over two years behind in his appraisals. It became clear that their performance management system in its current form was a huge mistake, adding psychological and financial cost rather than business value. The problem was that the covert arrangements that managers used to maneuver around the flawed system, such as deferring appraisal reports, were often costly in themselves. The baby was thrown out with the bath water—that is, managers avoided not only appraisal discussions but also value-adding forms of communication such as mentoring and collaborative problem solving.

When mistakes are made, the remedy is not a set of avoidance strategies but a plan of action to fix the structure, policy, system, or practice that is not working. The problem is that the mistake itself becomes part of the routine of the organization, part of its culture. From the viewpoint of emotional energy, it is easier to let it go than to confront it. The starting point should be a set of economics-focused questions: How much is this mistake costing us? What are the lost-opportunity costs? How extensive are the covert arrangements being used to work around the mistake? What is their dollar-and-cents cost? How disruptive will it be to remedy the mistake? What is the most reasonable cost-benefit decision?

Let's take a more extended look at the shadow-side arrangements associated with jobs. Jobs, roles, and positions are part of the organizational microstructure. In an ideal organizational world, each job has a description. It is the organization's way of spelling out each worker's responsibilities: "Here are your responsibilities, here are the interfaces you are to manage, here is the authority you need to carry out these responsibilities, and here is what we expect of you in terms of accomplishments." The prevention principles that follow from this are clear: See jobs as assets and deal with them as you would other assets. Review them, define them clearly, refocus them, clean them up, build needed flexibility into them, eliminate them when they no longer add value—and do this as a matter of course. Of course, things are seldom this rational. And so arrangements such as the following emerge.

First, there is the *let's-hire-and-see* phenomenon. Some companies don't establish a clear-cut contract at all. It is as if they say,

"You will learn what you need to do on the job; that's all we can tell you right now." Except that they don't say it, and the fact that they don't remains undiscussed. One company hired a marketing whiz even though they had no open position. He was called a "special marketing consultant." The thought behind the hiring was, ". . . let's get him while we can." This alienated some people in the marketing department, because they saw his hiring as a slap in the face: "How are we falling down?" The consultant was sensitive to this but tried nevertheless to carve out a place for himself. He met a great deal of resistance and, finally, as frustrated as the people he was trying to help, quit. But the damage had been done. In most cases the lack of clear direction will not be as high-profile as this. But undiscussed and therefore unmanaged job description vagueness is more common than we would like to believe. Failure to provide clear but flexible job descriptions is a mistake. When it is not identified and corrected, it becomes part of the shadow side.

Second, even when there is a clearly stated job description, there is often in the shadows a hidden job description. One form of this is the *bait-and-switch* approach: a person is hired or promoted to do one thing but finds himself or herself doing another. Ellen was hired to head the information technology unit of a retailer but found herself spending most of her time dealing with logistics problems. Only much later did she learn that it had always been the president's intention to make the logistics group a division of the information technology department. The HR director had known this but had said nothing to Ellen as she was being hired. New hires who are victims of this bait-and-switch scam are, understandably, slow to complain. Even when they do complain, it is usually in forums where nothing can be done about it.

Third, there is the *incremental responsibilities* phenomenon. Responsibilities are quietly added directly or indirectly. Often the position holder welcomes the added responsibilities, seeing them as a sign of the boss's or some other superior's trust. This is a shadow-side phenomenon because no one keeps tally of the position holder's responsibility load. Eventually the position holder begins to let things slip. Then he or she is blamed for not "keeping up with the job." Then people in authority begin to ask, "Do we need someone else in that position?"

Fourth, there is the *hidden responsibilities* phenomenon. For instance, no job description points out that one of the major sets of responsibilities centers on managing shadow-side issues. No one tells the position holder that his or her job is to create a unit culture that is both aligned with the preferred corporate culture and tailored to the unit's specific mandate and circumstances. It is even less likely that the position holder will be told that the unit culture must successfully fend off the downside of the covert corporate culture. No one points out that the position holder will be held accountable for results even in the face of fierce political infighting. No one makes allowances for the time the position holder spends managing the idiosyncrasies of team members. Officially these things don't exist, so they cannot be factored into the job.

Fifth, there is the *homeless responsibilities* phenomenon. There are tasks that need to be done, but no one seems to be assigned to do them. Therefore, an individual takes them on, because if they are not done, they will affect the quality of his or her work. Jim, a new supervisor in a small manufacturing firm, noticed that no one was in charge of updating safety manuals when new directives came from the Occupational Safety and Health Administration (OSHA). Jim updated his copies, since he knew that all hell would break loose if there was an accident in his area that could have been prevented by the communication and implementation of the directives. When other supervisors found out that he was doing it for his group, they wanted copies. The outcome? Jim was saddled with the OSHA task even though it had never been assigned to him.

In all these cases, the first step is to determine whether the job-related arrangements add value or add cost. If they add value, then a determination must be made whether to surface and formalize them or not. The OSHA task added value. But Jim thought that surfacing it might be taken as complaining. He took a different tack. He lobbied his fellow managers informally and got them to make an upbeat presentation to senior management. Their message: "Safety is becoming a more and more critical dimension of this industry. Let's review what we are doing and become the safety leader." If an arrangement adds cost, determine whether the total cost of challenging an arrangement outweighs the cost of ignoring it.

Arrangements on the Shadow Side
of Organizational Controls

As suggested earlier, organizational control mechanisms have a dis-
tinct shadow side. Therefore, they are given separate treatment here.
The word *control* itself is a giveaway, because it drips with suggestions of power, politics, and behind-the-scenes activity. Recently,
there has been a sharp increase in the number of cases of flawed
control reported in the business press. One gets the idea that there
are a lot of loose cannons in the insurance and securities industries.
In one classic case, a trader in a securities firm managed to create
some $350 of phantom profits for one firm in order to boost his
commissions (Carley, Siconolfi, and Naj, 1994). The trader is reported to have said to senior managers at a meeting in January 1994,
"You do anything to win. You make money at all costs" (Kidder-
Peabody, 1994, p. 75). Of course, one of the problems in this case
was that the trader was *not* making money, at least not for the
company, and nobody seemed to know. Industry observers, gifted
with great hindsight, have faulted the company for lack of proper
supervision, but the picture seems to be more complicated than that.
We may well ask, To what degree do cases like this reflect flawed
company policy or murky norms buried in the covert culture? Is
what is reported in the press just the tip of the iceberg?

Let us take a look at the shadow side of three mechanisms
for control: first, policy; second, rules and regulations; third, methods and procedures.

The Shadow Side of Policy. Policy casts a long shadow. It is sometimes shorthand for the norms of the covert culture. One manager,
in the job for less than a year, had introduced a bit of flex time into
her unit as a kind of experiment. She wanted to see whether people
wanted it or not and whether it helped or hindered productivity.
When her boss got a whiff of it, he told her to stop, saying that it
was against "company policy." She combed the manuals and could
find nothing that related even remotely to flex time. When she went
back to him with her findings or lack thereof, he said, "You're right,
but what I meant is that we have a policy of fairness and of organizational discipline. Flex time creates inequities and disturbs the

order of things." It is easy to create policy on the spot by invoking tradition, translating vague policy terms into specific caveats, and extending specific policies to cases they were not meant to cover. What he should have said is, "If there are new ideas around here, they will come from me. And I don't want my peace and quiet disturbed, and flex time would do just that."

Since policies should serve the business, and since the business and the environment in which it is operating are constantly changing, they need to be reviewed and updated just as technology needs to be reviewed and updated. Indeed, since policies are norm guidelines, updating them is one way of managing culture. The manager above took a risk by bringing up work policies at a general management meeting. She said something like this: "While we are on the cutting edge in terms of information technology, our work practices lag behind. My fear is that this technology loses its edge by our failing to factor in the needs of our work force. Perhaps there is something I don't know, but our policy manuals seem to be out of date." Since there was a groundswell of agreement, she knew that she was not in immediate jeopardy with her boss. She joined a line-management task force that was to work with HR to reengineer work policies. She also started to cultivate a network of contacts that included managers senior to her boss to protect herself from any kind of retaliation.

The Shadow Side of Rules and Regulations. Rules are drafted to provide the kind of order that serves the business. That's the theory. Yet in most organizations, rules are often bent, broken, or bypassed to get things done. The manager who does everything by the letter of the law can cause a great deal of damage. Often enough, when workers such as air traffic controllers want to express their displeasure to management, they "work to rule." Following the letter rather than the spirit of each rule and regulation soon brings the entire system to its knees. This tells us something about the rationality of the rules in the first place.

It is often impossible to move forward in a business without bending or breaking some rules. I once said in jest to the CEO of a retailing firm, "I've been taking your name in vain." "How?" he asked. I told him that I had asked groups of store managers to imagine one of their resource-poor stores. They did this quite easily. Then I asked them to pretend that the CEO, a very dynamic, results-oriented manager, had been put in charge of that store. "What would the store look like six months down the line?" They immediately knew the kinds of things he might do and the results he would achieve. This helped them to become more assertively creative in running their own stores. He sat there thoughtfully for a while, then said, "I know I'd get the results, but I was just thinking of the rules I'd have to break to get them." Of course, actual store managers were afraid to break the rules. The underlying culture said, "A rule is a rule; don't break any of them."

Consider your own college experience. The course catalogues are often very imposing tomes. People are impressed by the number of offerings. But they are often more impressed, and even scared, by descriptions that make the courses seem highly demanding. Prospective students might read the outline of a course and say to themselves, "I couldn't possibly fulfill all those requirements." And yet students just like them have taken and passed these very courses. The language of the catalogue, which reflects the set of arrangements publicly endorsed by the university, often enough gives way to the less rigid demands of the instructor. The actual accomplishments of the course do not always meet the published standards, which, in some cases, are beyond reach anyway. It is almost as if there were a principle that states: "Here is the ideal, but it is left to each instructor to translate this ideal as he or she sees best for both the students and the institution." This may even mean that the course as it is actually conducted bears little resemblance to the description in the catalogue. Given the fact that college teachers are quasi barons and baronesses in the realms of their classrooms, all of this can take place without a hitch.

Note that this arrangement cuts both ways. On the one hand, it can provide the kind of flexibility that enables teachers to contribute more effectively to their students' learning. Courses can be tailored to the needs of a group or even an individual. On the other hand, this arrangement might breed sloppiness and diminish both the standard of instruction and the learning of students. Once the purpose of a rule or a set of rules is understood, then some kind of institution-enhancing balance can be struck between rule enforcement and rule relaxation.

The very creation of rules can have a shadow side. Sometimes people in authority create rules to make up for mistakes—a form of shutting the barn door once the horse has escaped. In one U.S. military institution, some cadets were dismissed just prior to being commissioned. The officer defending them claimed that the dismissals were based on secret standards that had been created *post factum* to deal with this specific case: "It appears that the school created new, unpublished, and unquantified standards regarding commissionability and applied them retroactively to these three cadets, thereby second-guessing all prior assessments of their fitness for commissioned service." The shadow side in spades. It may well have been that these cadets should never have been accepted in the first place. And it could well be that the cadets did not live up to military standards. But it is also likely that they were not given clear messages about their shortcomings during the four years spent in the school. Remember the MUM Effect discussed earlier. Even military officers don't like giving bad news. But these officers had the power to enforce *post factum* rules.

There are a number of ways to deal with the shadow side of rules and regulations.

• *Analyze the rule.* What is its purpose? Is it there to promote some good or to protect the company from some evil? How does it add value? How is it linked to business goals? How is it linked to best practice? To what degree is it an artifact of the culture? To what degree has it outlived its usefulness? In what ways does it need to be changed? Should it be eliminated?

• *Determine the degree to which the rule is enforced.* It is possible to get a better understanding of the shadow side of rules by watching which ones are strictly enforced, which ones are sometimes enforced and sometimes not, and which ones are seldom enforced. It is also useful to review the reasons behind the degree of enforcement. In one company the enforcement of the dress code had more to do with the personal style of the office manager than the needs of the workplace. She would never allow a "casual" day, mainly because her style was very formal. Of course, this was never the reason offered. Rather she would say such things as, "Dress reflects attitudes toward the work itself."

• *Challenge rules that are enforced but do not add value.* If a rule cannot be challenged for shadow-side reasons (for instance, it is stupid, but it's the boss's favorite rule), evading it might be more acceptable. But determine the downside of evasion. One might ask, "Why not just drop it?" This is a rational answer to an issue filled with arationality. In human affairs it is infinitely easier to add rules than to drop them. Witness how our own legislative system works.

• *Understand the difference between rules and guidelines.* Rules must be followed, while guidelines are open to adaptation. If certain standards are essential, they should be presented clearly as such and expressed as *rules.* It would be madness for airline mechanics to ignore the procedures for attaching jet engines to the wings, saying, "Let's try it a new way and see what happens." The connotation of the term *guideline,* on the other hand, is quite different. People in the marketing department of the airline might quietly exceed a spending limit when it is clear to them that the business generated will more than compensate for the extra cost. The term *guideline* suggests common sense, flexibility, an understanding of desired business outcomes, equity, and the use of discretion.

In the end, rules and regulations will always have a dark side. They relate closely to politics and the idiosyncrasies of individuals. And individual interpretation of standards, rules, and guidelines is impossible to eliminate.

The Shadow Side of Organizational Methods and Procedures. The organizational methods and procedures that are on the books are not always the methods and procedures in use. I was talking to a vice president of human resources about some of the problems the company was facing. He told me that there was considerable dissatisfaction among younger managers over the way people were promoted to middle management positions. "Do you have a method?" I asked. "Of course," he said, and he pulled a two-page document from a file. "Here it is." After reading it, I remarked, "This makes sense. Do you follow this as it is written?" He hesitated and with a wry smile said, "Well, not exactly." It was clear that there was an espoused method and a method in use. When I asked him about the discrepancy, he put me off by saying, "You must know that most procedures like this have to be adapted to the situation in which they are used. That happens all the time, everywhere."

I handled this by asking him whether anyone besides myself had sniffed out the game. He hesitated for a while and then said that, although he had not thought of it in that way, a number of people must know what's going on. We went on to explore the downside of such an arrangement. It was evident that those who had caught on had discussed it with others. After my meeting I checked out my assumptions. Indeed, there was a great deal of cynicism about the promotion process. The bottom line was that the process had become highly politicized and did not serve the company's best interests. But now a great deal of tact had to be used to make the process as truly open as it appeared on paper. Senior management could not just announce, "Our espoused promotion procedures and our real ones are not one and the same. So we're going to make it what it should be." The promotion process ultimately became more congruent, but not entirely so, because there were a couple of senior managers who liked the shadow-side arrangement.

Every once in a while organizations should take a rolling zero-based approach to methods and procedures. That is, each year a subset should be reviewed. Those that no longer add value should be eliminated. Those that are outmoded should be reformulated. At this time it would also be useful to ask, "What is the shadow side of this method or procedure?" This should be a rolling process because, in many organizations, reviewing all methods and procedures every year would be impossible.

Arrangements Used to Fine-Tune the System

Finally, shadow-side arrangements and practices are used to complement and fine-tune the organization rather than merely make up for mistakes and flawed practices. More often than not, these add value. They give the system greater elasticity. Some of the common ones are:

- Skipping hierarchy levels in order to get the authorization to do something
- Ignoring formal communication channels both up and down
- Giving people value-adding assignments that move beyond official but anemic job descriptions
- Moving horizontally across organizational boxes—instead of up, over, down, back up, back over, and back down—to get needed information
- Creating speedy informal communication channels—what Krackhardt and Hanson (1993) call informal networks or the company behind the charts—to bypass slower formal ones
- Creating value-adding shadow reporting relationships, that is, working reporting relationships that never appear on the charts
- Violating policies and stretching rules selectively to get things done

This is just a partial list. Managers have a field day when asked to name some of the inventive strategies they use to complement processes in place and fine-tune the system. That is, they do more than just invent ways to get around a flawed system in order to get their work done.

Cary headed up the ten-person customer service group for a midsize retailer. As she developed a high-quality customer response system, it became clear to her that many of the complaints related to a lack of proper training of the sales associates in the stores. When the time was ripe, she invited Edna, the director of store training, to lunch and tactfully shared her findings with her. They established an informal feedback loop and customer service improvement "think tank." The number of customer complaints dropped significantly. Again, when the time was ripe, they contacted their respective bosses and, after some discussion, formalized and expanded their arrangement by establishing a customer service council that included Cary, Edna, and the regional field directors.

David Krackhardt and Jeffrey Hanson, mentioned above, see the formal structure as the skeleton of the company, while informal communication networks constitute the central nervous system. We can widen this and say that a range of informal organizational arrangements constitutes the central nervous system. Since there is no such thing as a perfect organization, arrangements like this are necessary to make it work.

Many of these fine-tuning arrangements are temporary. They meet an immediate need. Others, like the arrangement that led to the customer service council, are surfaced and formalized. Sometimes formalizing them is impossible. A department head in one institution reported to a vice president, at least according to the charts. For all practical purposes, however, he reported to the president. Since he and the vice president did not get along well at all, this arrangement worked in favor of the business. It goes without saying that the three of them did not get together and make a rational decision about this arrangement. Rather it evolved over time. In an ideal world, this situation would have been fixed in some way. In the real world of personalities and politics, this covert arrangement was the best solution.

Of course, arrangements like informal communication networks can be two-edged swords. While they can be used to cut across functions and divisions to get things done quickly, they can also be used to sabotage plans and oppose change. Savvy managers know how to tell the difference between arrangements that fine-tune the system and those that do not really add value to the business but serve other shadow-side agendas. They can also spot arrangements that were meant to add value by fine-tuning but are now running the danger of becoming problematic in themselves. Wise managers know that the formal processes and procedures of their organizations are usually complemented by informal arrangements. Arrangements that are system-enhancing and otherwise benign can be ignored, while arrangements that are system-limiting need to be addressed.

Why is it that people do not write down what really happens in a system and then make it part of operations, thus melding the informal system into the formal? This is similar to waiting to see where people walk after a new building is put up and then putting sidewalks where pathways have been carved. The answer seems to be that there are some advantages of maintaining both the formal and at least parts of the informal system. If a system has both formal and informal aspects, the total system has a degree of flexibility it would not otherwise have. For instance, the rules and regulations that are not enforced are still "on the books" and can be used as a backup if the informal system of rules and regulations fails.

The informal system at its best tempers the rigidities of the formal system, takes into consideration the idiosyncrasies of people, spreads both authority and responsibility more widely throughout the system, blends justice with equity, is sensitive to quality-of-work-life issues, manages roadblocks to productivity quietly and efficiently, and, generally, deals creatively with the kinds of tensions that are common in the struggle to balance productivity with the quality of work life. From a manager's point of view, the price of such advantages may be loss of formal control, but then there are trade-offs in every system.

The same happens in everyday life. Wise parents understand that their teenage children will find a variety of ways to distance themselves from the injunctions of their elders in their search for independence. Such parents may well ignore certain violations of rules and regulations provided that the security of both the family unit and of individual members is protected.

Making the Structure Work: The Role of Work Processes

While it is easy to divide up the work of the institution, it is often difficult to put it back together again in a way that optimizes information sharing, decision making, and work flow. Once work is fragmented, either among units or within a unit, shadow-side factors take over. Such things as ego, empire building, and turf protection give rise to the kind of "segmentalism" (Kanter, 1983) that stands in the way of clarity, speed, and efficiency. To counteract both structural flaws and the business-limiting shadow-side realities that structure often begets, many companies are stressing work processes through which a product or service is designed, fashioned, and delivered to the customer instead of individual organizational functions such as manufacturing and marketing.

How can we picture these processes? Assume, for instance, that you have just purchased a pair of jeans in a shop. How did they finally end up in your hands? There was a *process* or a series of step-by-step processes—from planning to purchase to transportation to marketing to display to sale, to name some of them—that led to your purchase. Companies are asking themselves a number of questions about these processes. How can we streamline them? How can we make them more cost-effective? How can we automate them and thus reduce human error? In order to answer such questions, companies engage in process *mapping*. For instance, the processes that ultimately put that pair of jeans in your hands are literally mapped out on a wall from beginning to end. Only after such process-focused questions are asked and answered does the company ask the structure question: What kind of structure will best support these processes? These maps are often very revealing. They show such things as unneeded work, reduplication of effort, diversions, disconnections between one group and the next, bottlenecks, and so forth. Behind these process flaws lurk not only structural flaws but also many of the shadow-side practices and arrangements outlined in this book. Process mapping in one large health care institution revealed that there were a number of activities that produced no value-added outcomes. For instance, the billing department, sticking rigorously to a methodology designed to protect the department from criticism, produced documents no one used. The intrahospital transportation unit, headed by a person who often behaved in a vain and insensitive way, was a continual source of bottlenecks. The failed relationship between the head of surgery and the head of diagnostic imaging was another source of bottlenecks.

Here are some questions, then, on the relationship between structure and process flow and the shadow-side realities that can damage this relationship:

- Do we have a clear idea of all the core and ancillary processes and steps needed to deliver our products and services to customers?
- To what degree are these processes clean, efficient, and effective?
- Do we have the right units with the right relationships doing the right things, that is, making the right contributions to the process? What shadow-side activities and arrangements prevent or interfere with this?
- What are we doing to make sure that these units work synergistically so that the process flows unimpeded? Do we have the kind of *interunit teamwork* that serves the process?

- Do we have the right set of jobs to move the core and ancillary processes and work flow of the company forward? Are these jobs value-added, clearly structured, and yet flexible? What kind of business-limiting shadow-side arrangements keep jobs disconnected from essential processes?

- Does the right information get to the right person at the right time so that decisions are informed and work processes are permeated with the right kind of intelligence? What are the sources of problems in this area?

- Is decision-making authority located where it best serves the interests of the business? Do people use the power they have in a timely fashion to add value to the business? Do decisions actually speed the flow of the process? In what shadow-side ways does authority fail to serve process flow?

- Do we have friendly controls that add value by channeling effort and preventing mistakes? Do our controls, at least in the longer term, actually speed up decision making and work flow? What shadow-side activities or arrangements corrupt the control process?

13

EPILOGUE:
MAKING CHAOS
YOUR FRIEND

H ERE'S WHAT A COMPANY looks like on paper, at least in some ideal world (Egan, 1993):

- A viable *strategy* provides clear-cut focus and direction for the entire enterprise and each of its units.
- A coordinated set of *operations*—work processes and programs—translates strategy into quality products and services that provide value for internal and external customers.
- A straightforward *organizational structure* serves the business by optimizing information sharing, decision making, and work flow.
- Flexible *jobs,* based on strategic and operational needs, are designed to channel value-adding work.
- Informed interunit and intraunit *teams,* with a solid understanding of both company and unit strategy, deliver value-adding outcomes.
- Well-designed *human resource management systems* are effectively used by managers and supervisors to get the right people, socialize them into both strategy and culture, equip them with the right competencies, and deploy them usefully throughout the structure—the right person with the right skills in the right job in the right unit.

- An effective *management system* is used to get and develop the right set of managers—that is, managers who are good at executing these master tasks and helping people give their best.
- There is a critical mass of *leaders* at all levels of the organization who play a vital role in fostering the kinds of institution-enhancing innovation and change that keep the company on the cutting edge.

The company in day-to-day operation often looks quite different from the company on paper. The master tasks outlined above are often tightly coupled in plans but quite loosely coupled and sloppily executed in practice. The fact that this chronic mismanagement is not identified, challenged, and dealt with in open forums puts it solidly in the shadow side. The idiosyncrasies of individuals, the vagaries of the social system, and organizational politics—all aided and abetted by the covert culture—conspire to create the company behind the company and the hidden costs that go with it.

Savvy managers are not deluded by what is written on paper or depicted on charts. They are vigilant. They continually ask themselves and others, "What's really going on?" Understanding the loosely coupled nature of their enterprises, they know when to move into maintenance and repair mode when things begin to fall apart just as well as they know when to move into innovation mode to create a future for the business.

On the other hand, savvy managers also know when to keep things loose. Sometimes when I look out at a bouncing wing during a turbulent period of a flight, my head tells me that without that flexibility both the wing and I would be in deep trouble, but the other less rational side still doesn't like it. "One more bounce and it will snap off!" is the conclusion of this part of my being. The loosely structured aspect of organizations is something like that. Many of us have been raised to overvalue order. Therefore, we tend to put things in order even when some forms of messiness would serve the enterprise better. We are uncomfortable with trying to balance stability with instability.

The value of messiness is not a new idea. Draper Kauffman (1980) put it well when he pointed out that "loose systems are often better. Diverse, decentralized systems often seem disorganized and wasteful, but they are almost always more stable, flexible, and efficient in the long run than 'neater' systems" (p. 40). Highly adaptable companies often look sloppy. Being buttoned down in a fast-changing world is the beginning of the end. Screwing everything down tight can add destructive stress to the system. The trick in all this is to know what kind of looseness helps in what kind of situation. There are two questions to be asked. First, to what degree are the undiscussed messiness and loosely coupled business and organizational practices signs of sloppy business practices? Second, to what degree do these phenomena represent the kinds of adaptiveness and flexibility that serve the business? The determination to put the cards on the table and answer these questions with absolute honesty may make all the difference.

Befriending Chaos

When researchers discovered that the average manager's day looked little like the orderly chapters in management books dealing with classic planning, organizing, staffing, leading, and controlling, they were just catching up with what most managers, at some level of their beings, already knew. Freedman (1992) points out that old scientific management was about control, while present-day management is about making sense out of chaos. Not all managers are good at this new role: "Managers are prisoners of the very systems they are supposed to manage. They understand neither the underlying dynamics of these systems nor how to influence those dynamics to achieve organizational goals" (p. 33). Companies and institutions have always been messy, but by all accounts they are getting even messier. Some writers are beginning to use the term *chaos,* especially now that there are some signs that chaos can be useful and that, to a degree, it can be leveraged, if not controlled.

The prevalence of messiness and chaos are suggested in the following facts about the current business environment:

- Management has never been a neat occupation.
- As Freedman points out, "the links between [managerial] actions and results are infinitely more complicated than most managers suspect" (p. 33).

- Most institutions are saddled with some sloppy management practices.
- Ineffective management practices make things even messier.
- The chaos in the environment is invading the workplace in increasingly insistent ways.
- Business uncertainty is increasing rather than decreasing.
- Shadow-side realities and arrangements permeate the business and add to the mess.
- New unpublished rules of employment are taking the place of old unpublished rules.
- Contemporary management trends blur the manager's role and contribute to the chaos.

While all of these are important indicators of messiness, a few words about the last two items on this list are in order.

The New Rules of Employment

The old, unpublished, and therefore shadow-side terms-of-employment charter was simple and clear: "If you put in a decent day's work and keep your nose clean, then you can expect to stay with us either until you want to leave or until you retire." Now, however, a new and more complicated—and for many, more ominous—charter is emerging. The reasons for the new charter are clear. Global competition and fast-changing global marketplaces have sent rigid, slow-responding players such as GM and IBM reeling. While some companies such as Johnson & Johnson still prefer a longer-term employment contract, others such as Apple Computer and General Electric seem to have moved toward contractor charters—some call these *social contracts*—with unpublished provisions like these:

- Since we now live in a global, highly competitive, fast moving, and uncertain environment, we must move from a longer-term employment contract to a *contractor contract.*
- We will contract for your services, and you will commit yourself to give your best for as long as that relationship is mutually beneficial.
- When the economy and competition and other forces outside the

control of the company get tough, then your job might be in jeopardy, because the business itself might ultimately be in jeopardy.

- While you are here, it is not enough to do what is required. You must keep finding ways to be of value to the business. To stay with us, you must be a contributor rather than a mere player.

- To remain a contributor you must grow and develop. You must become a "learning person" just as the company or institution becomes a "learning organization." While we will provide opportunities, you must be in charge of your own development.

- Your tenure with us will probably be longer if you keep developing competencies that relate to our sometimes changing core businesses.

- Keep an eye on how we are changing and what we are outsourcing. If we outsource a function, that means that we will probably outsource you.

- Promotions, which might have been assured in the past, will be very scarce. We are now by necessity a flatter organization. In fact, expect to see more flexible structures take the place of hierarchy around here. Also, expect to be paid for performance rather than for being "in place."

- Therefore, expect lateral moves into positions that at the time add value to the business and through which you can develop. *Lateral* no longer automatically means "dead-end." When it does, see the handwriting on the wall.

- Lifetime careers are no longer the norm. There might well come a time when you will want to leave us. It is also probable that there will come a time when we will want you to leave, most likely through no fault of your own. In either case, the "fit" will no longer be right.

- As different as this contract is from the "traditional" one, it can be a good deal for us and a good deal for you. It depends on how well we mutually execute it.

In many companies, some version of this contract is an emerging reality. And it applies as much to the executive suite as it does to the ranks of middle managers. It adds to the messiness because it adds uncertainty to the workplace.

Blurring of the Manager's Role

A number of workplace changes have contributed to the blurring of the manager's role. For instance, currently there is a blurring of the distinction between manager and managed. Since layers of management have been removed from many companies, the tasks for which many middle managers were responsible have been distributed to those whom they used to manage. Empowerment programs blur the distinction. The manager in some cases says, "Now that we all know the strategy and our roles in implementing it, I will be getting out of your way more and more. I'm here as coordinator, coach, and counselor. I will add value in any way I can." Self-managed teams by definition blur the distinction.

This blurring leaves some managers confused about their role. "I know what it means to be in charge. I'm not sure what it means to be a coordinator, facilitator, coach, consultant, and counselor." Since in many companies this blurring and these role changes are not discussed in any formal way, all of this lies in the shadows.

And so we end up with confused managers, managers without the skills for their new roles, managers who abdicate because they see their power slipping away, managers who resist change, and managers who try to sabotage the new order. All this adds psychological, social, and monetary costs to the system that are never accounted for.

Managing Shadow-Side Chaos

Some messiness and chaos, as we have seen, are nothing more than sloppy management and should be eliminated. A lack of strategy, sloppy work practices, overruns, waste, missed appointments, a chaotic reporting system, poor or poorly managed controls, the lack of coherent policy, decision reversals, or capricious management of people are not forms of creative chaos. They are self-induced and enterprise-limiting. A Chicago-based software firm went under because of sloppy management. The cash ran out. This company had prided itself on its free-form structure, its lack of formality, and its open culture. Employees had been allowed to work as many hours

as they wanted during the week. Extra hours were "banked" and
could be used at the discretion of the employee. One day Ted was
looking for Jane. She had critical contributions to make to a project
whose deadline had arrived. "Where is she?" Ted asked. "I think she
said she was going to Bali to use some of her banked hours," was
the reply. "When will she be back?" No one knew.

How is the manager to befriend messiness and chaos rather
than either futilely attacking it or merely becoming its victim? Two
things will help: a new mind-set regarding messiness and some
broad strategies for leveraging it. What follows is based, loosely, on
ideas generated by DeMott (1989), Stacey (1992), Weick (1969, 1979),
and my own experience.

Developing a Different Mind-Set

The mind-set needed to befriend messiness at the service of the
business does not come naturally to many managers, especially
those in functions such as engineering where rationality must hold
sway. The new mind-set means becoming comfortable with such
assumptions as the following:

- *Messiness and chaos are here to stay.* The more we move
toward globalization, the more hectic things will become. Many of
the changes taking place, such as the movement toward lean organizations, are structural rather than episodic. Waiting for them to
go away will ensure the demise of the institution.

- *The ability to accept and deal with disruption must become a common managerial skill.* Giving in to or fighting messiness must give way to living with and leveraging messiness. The
best managers are not put off by the destabilizing and erratic. They
see both as threats that need to be managed and opportunities to be
developed.

- *Messiness and chaos can enhance the fortunes of our enterprise* if addressed creatively. For instance, unbridled competition
almost always produces or reveals market niches that can be filled.
The messiness and chaos in the computer business opened windows
of opportunity for mail-order entrepreneurs.

- *There are often patterns in chaos,* even though they

might not be the usual ones. For instance, the retail industry has been in turmoil for a number of years now. Major bankruptcies have been the order of the day. The best retailers spot patterns and thus opportunities in this chaos. Some of these patterns are an emerging emphasis on value rather than price, the fact that people lead such complex lives that they no longer have as much time for shopping, and shopping as entertainment. The best companies realize that retailing is no longer something that you *do* according to pre-set rules but something that you continually *create*. Stores like the Gap and the Limited became successful in the 1980s by creating new forms of retailing. And they know that they must continually recreate themselves.

• *Winning companies and institutions will be those who deal proactively with chaos.* AT&T is both streamlining and complicating itself because the industry it is in, that of computers and telecommunications, is becoming more and more complicated and filled with uncertainty.

General Strategies for Leveraging Messiness and Chaos

Here are some of the strategies that managers are using for dealing with chaos. Admittedly, some have a fuzzy feeling to them. They need to permeate, not replace, the rational strategies that are more familiar to most managers.

• *Don't be surprised or thrown by disorder.* Learn to expect it. Learn to look for it. Let it act as an awakener.

• *If things are too orderly, investigate.* Something is going wrong. If the cauldron is not bubbling, that might be worse than if it seems to be boiling over. Be grateful when disorder comes to the surface (for instance, an out and out fight between the heads of two units), because it is a royal route to understanding the disorder below, in the shadows. Don't prevent disorder from manifesting itself.

• *Use contention and debate to stir the pot.* This is not a question of proposing contention for its own sake. Once issues have been openly debated, then it is time to make decisions. Top-quality negotiation skills are then needed to reconcile differences.

- *Float ideas in the organization and see where they lead.* Encourage others to do the same. Don't worry about the life span of these ideas. Useful ideas will live on and find their way into the business.

- *In making decisions, don't move too quickly to closure.* Let ideas stew. Let the marketplace rather than personal preference set limits to the length of stewing.

- *Relax the rules at the service of discovery.* For instance, suspend the performance management system and see what control mechanisms develop naturally to fill the void.

- *Have half-a-dozen pilot projects going at any given time.* Wal-Mart managers are expected to experiment. The CEO has estimated that department heads conduct some 250 experiments, most of them secret, in Wal-Mart stores on any given day.

Both pure-form rationality and pure-form messiness fall short of the mark. Combination strategies are needed to manage a messy business. Planning needs to be complemented by improvisation. Analysis by intuition. Waiting and sifting and ruminating by speed to market. A fix-it mentality by a break-it mentality. Fixed rules by extralegal processes such as so-called skunk works.

The 1994 Ford Mustang, a car many thought doomed, came into existence because of a skunk-works team. The team broke many of the rules that govern Ford's product development process. Rules were relaxed in what is ordinarily a rigidly disciplined corporation. At several points the project was almost dropped as the team struggled to reconcile differences between finance and feeling. As in this case, it is the right mix between pure-form rationality and unbounded arationality—"This car just has to exist!"—that makes the difference. There are some nontraditional approaches to strategy that have this mix. Strategy as hustle—ceaseless searching for new products for new markets and new competencies to make it happen. Strategic incrementalism—making strategy evolve step by step in order to take advantage of opportunities created by a changing business environment. Strategic opportunism—seizing opportunities as they present themselves even though they do not fit into the preordained plan. In a chaotic environment, these serve many companies well.

And so we come to the end. As stated in the Preface, this is not all that you need to know and do to manage the shadow side of the organization. It is a starter kit. But by this time, novices will have learned something new, and wise old salts will have gained some perspective on what they have been doing for years.

REFERENCES

Agor, W. H. (1988, March). Finding and developing intuitive managers. *Training and Development Journal,* pp. 68–70.

Anfuso, D. (1994, March). Novell idea: A map for mergers. *Personnel Journal,* pp. 48–55.

Argyris, C. (1976). Theories of action that inhibit individual learning. *American Psychologist, 31,* 638–654.

Argyris, C. (1982). *Reasoning, learning, and action: Individual and organizational.* San Francisco: Jossey-Bass.

Argyris, C. (1985). *Strategy, change, and defensive routines.* Boston: Pitman.

Argyris, C. (1986, September–October). Skilled incompetence. *Harvard Business Review,* pp. 74–79.

Baker, W. E. (1994). *Networking smart: How to build relationships for personal and organizational success.* New York: McGraw-Hill.

Bart, C. K. (1988, November). Budgeting gamesmanship. *Academy of Management Executive,* pp. 285–294.

Bartlett, C. A., & Ghoshal, S. (1990, July–August). Matrix management: Not a structure, a frame of mind. *Harvard Business Review,* pp. 138–145.

Block, P. (1987). *The empowered manager: Positive political skills at work.* San Francisco: Jossey-Bass.

Block, P. (1993). *Stewardship.* San Francisco: Berrett-Koehler.

Bloom, H., Calori, R., & de Woot, P. (1994). *Euro management.* London: Kogan Page.

Carley, W. M., Siconolfi, M., & Naj, A. K. (1994, May 3). How will Welch deal with Kidder scandal? Problems keep coming. *Wall Street Journal,* p. A1.

Cross, J. G., & Guyer, M. J. (1980). *Social traps.* Ann Arbor: University of Michigan Press.

Daniels, A. C. (1994). *Bringing out the best in people.* New York: McGraw-Hill.

DeMott, B. (1989, May–June). Reading fiction to the bottom line. *Harvard Business Review,* pp. 128–134.

The economics of crime. (1993, December 13). *Business Week,* pp. 72–85.

Egan, G. (1993). *Adding value: A systematic guide to business-driven management and leadership.* San Francisco: Jossey-Bass.

Egan, G. (1994). *The skilled helper: A problem-management approach to helping* (5th ed.). Pacific Grove, CA: Brooks/Cole.

Freedman, D. H. (1992, November–December). Is management still a science? *Harvard Business Review,* pp. 26–38.

Gilbert, T. (1978). *Human competence: Engineering worthy performance.* New York: McGraw-Hill.

Guyon, J. (1991, October 23). Inequality in granting child-care benefits makes workers seethe. *Wall Street Journal,* pp. A1, A7.

Hays, L. (1994a, April 28). IBM aide quit under pressure, executives say. *Wall Street Journal,* p. A3.

Hays, L. (1994b, May 13). Gerstner is struggling as he tries to change ingrained IBM culture. *Wall Street Journal,* pp. A1, A5.

Hyatt, J. C. (1994, March 7). GE chairman's annual letter notes strides by "stretch" of the imagination. *Wall Street Journal,* p. A7A.

Hymowitz, C. (1988, October 4). Spread the word: Gossip is good. *Wall Street Journal,* p. B1.

Kanter, R. M. (1983). *Change masters: Innovation for productivity in the American corporation.* New York: Simon & Schuster.

Kauffman, D. L., Jr. (1980). *Systems 1: An introduction to systems thinking.* St. Paul, MN: Future Systems/TLH Associates.

Kets de Vries, M.F.R., & Miller, D. (1984). *The neurotic organiza-*

tion: Diagnosing and changing counterproductive styles of management. San Francisco: Jossey-Bass.

Kidder-Peabody: Jett-lagged. (1994, April 23). *Economist,* p. 75.

Kilmann, R. H. (1985). Five steps for closing culture-gaps. In R. H. Kilmann, M. J. Saxton, R. Serpa, & Associates, *Gaining control of the corporate culture.* San Francisco: Jossey-Bass.

Kleiman, C. (1994, May 1). Making diversity work. *Chicago Tribune,* Section 8, p. 1.

Kohn, A. (1993). *Punished by rewards.* Boston: Houghton Mifflin.

Kotter, J. P., & Heskett, J. L. (1992). *Corporate culture and performance.* New York: Free Press.

Krackhardt, D., & Hanson, J. R. (1993, July–August). Informal networks: The company behind the charts. *Harvard Business Review,* pp. 104-111.

Landsburg, S. E. (1994). *The armchair economist.* New York: Free Press.

The law of the lunch. (1989, May–June). *Harvard Business Review,* p. 221.

Luthans, F., & Kreitner, R. (1975). *Organizational behavior modification.* Glenview, IL: Scott, Foresman.

Magnet, M. (1994, March 7). Let's go for growth. *Fortune,* pp. 60-72.

Marcom, J., Jr. (1986, April 7). Behind the monolith: A look at IBM. *Wall Street Journal,* p. 15.

Maxtone-Graham, M. (1991, June). Put a mentor in your manual. *Training,* pp. 12-13.

Michaels, D. (1993, October 11). Lot Polish Airlines takes on a new look but fight to reshape carrier continues. *Wall Street Journal,* p. A7A.

Miletich, L. N. (1988, April). A business bestiary. *Administrative Management,* pp. 11-13.

Miller, L. M. (1978). *Behavior management: The new science of managing people at work.* New York: Wiley.

Miller, M. W. (1993, October 27). As IBM losses mount, so do the complaints about company perks. *Wall Street Journal,* pp. A1, A14.

Murray, R. B. (1983, Fall). Working well. *Journal of Religion and Applied Behavioral Sciences,* pp. 8-12.

Neuhauser, P. C. (1988). *Tribal warfare in organizations.* New York: Ballinger.

O'Brien, T. L. (1993, December 20). Company wins workers' loyalty by opening its books. *Wall Street Journal,* pp. B1–B2.

Pfeffer, J. (1994). *Competitive advantage through people.* Boston: Harvard Business School Press.

Pinchot, G., III. (1985). Intrapreneuring. New York: HarperCollins.

Rethinking IBM. (1993, October 4). *Business Week,* pp. 86–97.

Rosen, S., & Tesser, A. (1970). On the reluctance to communicate undesirable information: The MUM Effect. *Sociometry, 33,* 253–263.

Sarason, S. B. (1972). *The creation of settings and the future societies.* San Francisco: Jossey-Bass.

Stacey, R. D. (1992). *Managing the unknowable: Strategic boundaries between order and chaos in organizations.* San Francisco: Jossey-Bass.

Tesser, A., Rosen, S., & Tesser, M. (1971). On the reluctance to communicate undesirable messages (the MUM Effect): A field study. *Psychological Reports, 29,* 651–654.

Torres, C. (1993, August 31). For technology winners, seek out the "cannibals." *Wall Street Journal,* pp. C1–C2.

Watson, D. L., & Tharp, R. G. (1993). *Self-directed behavior: Self-modification for personal adjustment.* Pacific Grove, CA: Brooks/Cole.

Weick, K. E. (1969). *The social psychology of organizing.* Reading, MA: Addison-Wesley.

Weick, K. E. (1979). *The social psychology of organizing* (2nd ed.). Reading, MA: Addison-Wesley.

White, J. B. (1993, January 13). GM's overhaul of corporate culture brings results but still faces hurdles. *Wall Street Journal,* pp. A3, A5.

Yates, D., Jr. (1985). *The politics of management: Exploring the inner workings of public and private organizations.* San Francisco: Jossey-Bass.

INDEX